the PATH of Life

Reflections on the Journey

DEACON PETER HODSDON

aventine press

Published by Aventine Press
55 East Emerson St.
Chula Vista CA 91911
www.aventinepress.com

ISBN: 978-1-59330-849-0

Library of Congress Control Number: 2014904460
Library of Congress Cataloging-in-Publication Data
The Path of Life/ Deacon Peter Hodsdon

Printed in the United States of America

Table of Contents

Acknowledgments

There are many in the cloud of witnesses who have influenced my journey of faith up to now. The foundation started with my parents, of course, and I am immeasurably grateful for the gift of faith they presented to me on my Baptismal day in 1954. As a child, the good Sisters of St. Joseph guided me and 35 squirming classmates through 8 years of parochial school. Thanks as well to the Jesuits, who challenged me to own my faith journey while attending Santa Clara University. But faith only grows with abundant doses of tender love, and for that I thank my wife and soul mate, Katie.

My vocational journey to the diaconate was ably guided by the San Diego Diocesan staff, in particular Sr. Carlotta DiLorenzo, CSJ, Jose Ernesto Gonzalez, and Bernadeane Carr. To the people of St. James Parish in Solana Beach, California, I offer my thanks for your wonderful support as I've shared these reflections over the years.

Chapter 1 - Waking Up

Our journey into spiritual awareness must start somewhere, somehow. To some of us, this recognition begins in childhood. To others, as they reach maturity. But for many – I would say most – waking up comes later in life, usually after the well-worn platitudes and answers we thought were accurate prove flimsy and weak.

God allows life to happen because it seems that sometimes we need to wake up. We have a hard time listening to God when things are going great. When things get tough, when we are no longer in control, God's invitation to us for a relationship takes on added clarity and power. And when things are darkest on our journey – if we allow it to happen – Christ breaks through! And resurrection happens.

Why Bethlehem?

Scripture Referenced: Lk 2:1-14

> *While they were there, the time came for her to have her child,
> and she gave birth to her firstborn son. She wrapped him in
> swaddling clothes and laid him in a manger, because there was
> no room for them in the inn.*

Why Bethlehem? We take this beautiful story quite for granted. But
have you ever really thought, "Why Bethlehem?"

One of my little fantasies is that Luke the evangelist spent some
quality time with Mary before he wrote his gospel. It's possible –
most historians would agree that Mary was probably young, no more
than 16, when Jesus was born. If Luke wrote his gospel in the 70's,
that would make Mary a pretty old lady, maybe early 80's, but still
conceivable. There are so many wonderful details in his narrative:
the trip to Bethlehem, the star, the angels, the shepherds, the manger.
I can just hear Luke asking Mary this question, "Why did you go to
Bethlehem? You're from Nazareth – why did you go to Bethlehem?"
Mary replies, "Oh, it was some government thing – Joseph said we had
to go." So Luke gives us this census idea, which sounds good, but there
is no *historical* evidence that it ever happened as Luke describes it.

But wait a minute. Wasn't there a prophecy? Yes, the book of
Micah, which says: "But you, Bethlehem, too small to be among the
clans of Judah, from you shall come forth for me one who is to be ruler
in Israel…" (Mi 5:1) So did Mary and Joseph go to Bethlehem to fulfill
the prophecy? Hmm, seems a bit implausible. You can hear Joseph,
"Mary, I was reading Micah. We're in the wrong place! We have to go
to Bethlehem!" Mary replies, "Are you nuts?" So whether a census, or
"some government thing," let's distill it down to a likely reality: they
went to Bethlehem because *they had to go.* Why else would a woman in
her eighth month of pregnancy travel? This is totally outside of Mary's
comfort zone – and she was already facing terrible uncertainty about
this child she was carrying. She is young, most certainly frightened for
her child's safety, and uncomfortable physically. Mary and Joseph are
not in control here.

So why would God do this to them? Ahh, it's not God doing this, it's life. Life has a knack of taking us out of our comfort zone, in small ways and big ways. Life is natural disasters. Life is slipping on a step and breaking an arm. Life is a lost job. Life is a serious illness. Life is the loss of a spouse. Life is a whole sequence of challenges and sufferings and questions. Life is having to go to Bethlehem when you're ready to give birth. Life is finding no place to stay, the 5-star Hilton filled up, the 1-star barn a welcome sight. Life can be tough.

But now, as we look just a little bit closer at Luke's gospel, the theology, the deeper meaning is made apparent. In the midst of this out-of-control experience, the Bethlehem valley in Mary's life, Christ breaks through! Literally, fundamentally, Christ breaks through! A healthy baby boy is born. Is there anything more joyful than holding an infant in the first moments of life? Christ breaks through.

Isn't that true for us too? God allows life to happen because it seems that sometimes we need to wake up. We have a hard time listening to God when things are going great. When things get tough, when we are no longer in control, God's invitation to us for a relationship takes on added clarity and power. And when things are darkest on our journey – if we allow it to happen – Christ breaks through! And resurrection happens.

We call this cycle of dying and rising *made holy* the Paschal Mystery. It seems that something needs to die in order for something new to be born. Life is an endless cycle of these moments of opportunity, these little deaths. Jesus demonstrates through his life how to face these deaths – with humility, prayer, patience, and forgiveness. He never seeks scapegoats or plays the victim. He accepts the death, trusts in the Father, and is resurrected.

Why Bethlehem? From the moment of *birth*, Jesus was engaged in the Paschal Mystery, foreshadowing his life of ministry. From the moment of birth, Luke shows us that the cycle was true for the Holy Family just as it is true for us. It all leads to the cross. There is no other way. The Good News is that Jesus will accompany us on the journey if we let him break through. With his help, we can deal with anything, because we know it ends in resurrection.

So don't fear Bethlehem. When our ultimate Bethlehem occurs on our death bed, and we let Jesus break through, you can bet angels will sing Hosanna for us too.

Two Moments of Awareness

Scripture Referenced: Lk 2:41-52

> *And he said to them, "Why were you looking for me? Did you not know that I must be in my Father's house?"*
>
> *But they did not understand what he said to them.*

Many of us are surrounded by family at Christmas time. Have you ever had any surprising news? Did someone challenge you to reconsider your belief about them? Have you yourself had any surprising God moments? How did you react? Did you embrace the challenge or fight it? Today we celebrate these "God moments" by considering a family much like yours and mine.

This gospel passage is sandwiched between the beautifully rendered infancy narrative of Luke and the start of Jesus' ministry. Luke takes this story almost verbatim from the apocryphal Gospel of Thomas. Why this story? What do we find here that is important to understand about not only Jesus, but about us as well? The story of Jesus lost and found is rather simple in its telling, very believable, rich in detail, human emotion, and low comedy. Every parent can relate to a lost child story, since we've all lost a child at some point or another - in the house, outside at a park, in a store, or some other alarming setting. And every one of us has had the experience of being lost as well, although most men I know would deny it!

The story of Jesus found in the Temple is a story of *awareness*. There are two people who are moved into deeper awareness by these events – one is Jesus, and the other is Mary. Poor Joseph, as usual, is given no lines – we can only guess at his thoughts. So let's start with the outline of the story. Luke first establishes that Mary and Joseph are pious, upstanding Jews, performing an annual pilgrimage to Jerusalem for the Passover feast. After the festival ends, as the caravan of families heads back home to Galilee, Mary and Joseph lose track of Jesus, both thinking he was with the other parent. In dismay, they rush back to Jerusalem, and after a frantic search for three days, they discover Jesus in the temple, impressing the teachers with his wisdom and understanding.

So what is happening here? Note that Jesus doesn't consider himself lost at all – he quite openly wonders what all the fuss is about. His remarkable confidence and sanguine attitude can be chalked up to the typical recklessness of any teenager, or we can go a little deeper, as Luke intends. Jesus has experienced an awakening, a recognition of his true identity as the Son of God. Think back on your own life. When did you realize that you were someone unique, someone special, that you had value? It comes at different ages, doesn't it? But it is usually associated with puberty, with a recognition that we are not mere children anymore. We don't know the precise mechanism, but Jesus has become aware that he is being held up by his Father in heaven, is being transformed and transfigured, and more is to come. Luke tells this story because it is the start, the dawning reality of Jesus. He is becoming aware of a unique calling, a unique identity that supersedes his earthly existence. What a frightening yet exhilarating awareness that must have been!

Now for Mary – what awareness is made available to her? Well, if there's one authentic ring of truth in this story, it's her reaction to finding Jesus. We're told she's astonished, and none too happy. In fact, she's upset that Jesus seems unmoved by their obvious distress. Despite what she already suspects about her remarkable child, he is still her baby, her son, and all of the ache of motherhood is contained in that simple question, "Son, why have you done this to us?" And just as Jesus will do frequently in his adult ministry, he answers her question with a question – "Did you not know that I must be in my Father's house?" There's the challenge, there's the awareness moment, and just like us when we are challenged, Mary doesn't get it at first -- we're told that they didn't understand what he said to them.

Two moments of awareness: Jesus seeing himself in a new way, Mary challenged to see him in this way too. Can we relate? Do any of these scenarios ring true? Mom, I'm in love. Mom and Dad, I want to get married. Dad, I want to join the Marines. Mom, I think I'm pregnant. Dad, I don't want to go to college anymore. Mom and Dad, I think I'm gay. Mom, can I move back in? Dad, can I borrow five thousand dollars? Have any of those questions or statements ever come at you? Or, more to the point, have *you* had such conversations with *your* parents?

Awareness moments are nearly always alarming and a bit scary for everyone. But awareness moments are *God* moments. You can tell an awareness moment because your first reaction is always, "Oh my God!" What do we do with these moments? Today's gospel tells us what to do. Jesus, awareness of his identity now clear, doesn't go off half-cocked, bragging about himself and making demands. He shows his parents respect and *obedience*, a word that is often misinterpreted. Obedience means to be open, to not assume that you have all of the answers. Jesus models awareness tempered with an understanding that he doesn't yet know what to do with this awareness, this challenging new identity. He remains open. And Mary, we're told, kept all these things in her heart. She clearly took this God moment and pondered its meaning for her, for her son. She also remains open, obedient.

When we're presented with a God moment, we are often tempted to scream NO – I like things better the way they were before. I don't want this new reality. I don't want this in my life right now. I'd rather stay a teenager forever, never taking responsibility or making a commitment to anything. I'd rather my child stayed childlike, under my thumb, doing what I command. Both of these paths lead to pain, confusion, emotional immaturity, all harbingers of future distress. You see, a God moment forces us to face change, whether we're ready or not. That's a bit of the cross, a bit of suffering – we realize that we are not in control. What God calls each of us to be is often different from what we expected. What God calls our children to be is often not our dream for them.

But if we ponder the grace of the God moment, we realize, just as Jesus did, that we are not lost at all, that we are always in the presence of our Father in heaven, and nothing can take that away. And as parents we can take a lesson from Mary, and ponder the grace of the God moments that our children present us, and realize that these moments are treasures for the heart, despite their frightening appearance at the outset. Because, as St. John tells us, we are all children of God, and he treasures us in His heart, whatever we choose to do or to be.

Many of us are surrounded by family at Christmas time. Have you had any God moments? How did you react? Did you embrace the challenge or fight it? Can you find the grace in this moment? That's where we're asked to go – into *awareness*.

Magi Moments

Scripture Referenced: Mt 2:1-12

> *When Jesus was born in Bethlehem of Judea, in the days of King Herod, behold, magi from the east arrived in Jerusalem, saying, "Where is the newborn king of the Jews? We saw his star at its rising and have come to do him homage."*
>
> *When King Herod heard this, he was greatly troubled, and all Jerusalem with him.*

Matthew, as is also true of Mark and Luke, is writing to a particular community of early Christian believers. Matthew had access to Mark's gospel when he undertook to write his own version, so he takes much of Mark's material and adapts it in certain subtle and not-so subtle ways. You see, Matthew was writing to an audience of Jewish converts who were being forcibly expelled from their Jewish communities. At this point in Christian history, many believers in Christ considered themselves good Jews and good Christians simultaneously. But the Jewish authorities, particularly the ultra-orthodox Pharisees rejected that point of view and forced them to make a choice – either conform exclusively to the law of Moses or be expelled. This was serious business. To be expelled from the temple meant the loss of community, business interests, and yes, often family as well.

So why would Matthew feature this story of the Magi in his Gospel? It does not appear in Mark's gospel – it is exclusively his account. Why would his Jewish audience find this story significant? There are several key points here. First, the Magi are foreigners. They are not of the Jewish community. The term "magi" itself is difficult to define – it connotes men of wisdom, but with a bit of magic as well, a bit of other-worldliness. These aren't refugees or ne'er-do-wells, these are men of some prestige. Second, note that they come from the East, from the dawn, from the source of the sun. In the great Jewish prophetic tradition, wisdom and truth come from the East. Third, they follow a star – a sign from God that is entirely outside their control, yet still points to the homeland of the Jews. God as usual, uses nature to show us his presence.

Perhaps the key point for Matthew's audience, however, is this: as represented by King Herod, the Jewish community *doesn't get it*, doesn't understand the truth and wisdom that have come calling at their door. They react with fear and suspicion, even though the coming of the Messiah is written in their scripture and even read aloud to the King by the scribes. The Magi bring gifts of great value and significance, following the signs of God, even telling the Jews what is under their very noses, and yet, they are dismissed and viewed with great suspicion. Is it any wonder that Matthew wrote this? His audience are those who shook off the shackles of engrained thinking, of one-way thinking, of petrified tradition, and heard the word of God spoken in their hearts.

So, what does this have to do with you and me? Our tendency is to identify ourselves with the Magi, isn't this true? Our life is a journey of faith, leading to Christ, leading to revelation and joy. That's all very nice and romantic, but let's be honest. Once we get settled in our tradition, in our way, in our thinking, is it perhaps a little bit true that we are not the Magi anymore, but maybe residents of Jerusalem, or if you're a deacon, a scribe in Herod's court? Ouch, that can't be true, can it?

The danger we all face is the danger of complacency and self-satisfaction. Once we feel we're on the right highway, we zone out. I do this on the freeway all the time! Don't you? Get in the number two lane, hit cruise control, and resent anyone who forces you to touch the brakes. On the spiritual path, this tendency is just as prevalent. God is always trying to get to us, to continue the dialogue, but we stop listening. We have the answers! Well, I've got news for you – we see the truth through a dirty glass, a cracked mirror, a shadow of reality. God wants to clear the glass, but we have to accept that this means change, change of heart, change of focus, change of direction, getting off the freeway.

A very wise person once told me that God is found in life's interruptions and surprises. Let's stop a moment and consider just one example. A co-worker of mine, that I only know superficially, gave me a Christmas gift (to my shock, quite frankly). It was one of those page-a-day calendars, you've seen those right? She didn't know that I was a Catholic deacon. This calendar was a page a day of the sayings of the Dalai Lama, who is a Tibetan Buddhist monk. As you can imagine, I was quite amused. So what should I do? Should I throw it away? Give her a page-a-day catechism in return?

Here's the Magi moment – a little voice inside me said, "read it". So I did. Our Catholic Church tells us that there is truth in other world religions, that God has revealed himself in many and diverse ways. Our Catholic Church contains the fullness of truth, however, and that is a wonderful gift. But to open ourselves to how God has touched others who do not know Christ is a wonderful experience too. It has led me to a deeper understanding of our own Christian tradition, and made me a more thoughtful, meditative believer. It was a gift.

Now before you all go running off to an ashram in Tibet, I want to emphasize that this was in some way a Magi moment for *me*. The invitation that you get may be very different. But the point is to be alert for these moments. Ask God to reveal a new truth to you, one that may shake you a little. Maybe it's a new prayer form, maybe it's a pilgrimage opportunity, maybe it's a service opportunity in a jail, hospice, or homeless shelter. Maybe it's an opportunity to see the world through another's eyes, through a different window. Look for it – you'll know when you get it because you'll be tempted to say no at first – but you just might be passing up some *gold*. Look for the Magi moment.

Speak, Lord, for Your Servant is Listening

Scripture Referenced: 1Sm 3:3-10,19; Jn 1:35-42

> *Then Eli understood that the LORD was calling the youth.*
>
> *So he said to Samuel, "Go to sleep, and if you are called, reply, 'Speak, LORD, for your servant is listening.'" When Samuel went to sleep in his place, the LORD came and revealed his presence, calling out as before, "Samuel, Samuel!" Samuel answered, "Speak, for your servant is listening."*

One of the really important outcomes of Vatican II was a decision to revise the Lectionary, the book that features our Sunday Bible readings. The Church scholars who were tasked with this effort consciously attempt to link a selected Gospel reading to an Old Testament passage that in some way prefigures the Gospel, linking the two with a common theme. Sometimes it's a challenge to figure out the common theme. Today it's pretty simple, I think. Did you see the link?

Our first reading features a young boy hearing the call of God. Samuel, who is in training for service to the Hebrew people, sleeps in the temple precincts where the priests of God dwell. Hearing his name called, Samuel mistakenly thinks his master Eli is calling him and responds promptly and obediently, as any good pupil would. Eli says no, it wasn't him calling, and Samuel goes back to bed. It happens a second time, then a third. Poor Samuel must be wondering if he's losing his mind. But Eli, the wise teacher, comes to understand what is happening and reassuringly gives Samuel the right response the next time he hears the call. *Speak, Lord, for your servant is listening.*

Notice the similarities in the gospel reading from John. Andrew and his unnamed companion are likewise in the care of a great teacher, namely John the Baptist. And just as Eli did, John the Baptist points out a new direction for his pupils: "Behold the Lamb of God." They follow Jesus, a bit uncertain as to how to approach him. Then Jesus turns to them and asks the question that strikes to the heart of every one of us seekers, "What are you looking for?" A simple question that John invites us to take deeper, to answer from inside.

A few years ago, I was working a retreat in Donovan State Prison and I remember one of the prisoners asking me, "why do you come here?" My first reaction was to smile and answer, "oh, I had nothing better to do today." But something stopped me. His deceptively simple question had a deeper layer of query. It was, "what motivates you to spend your Saturday with the likes of criminals like me?" That was the real question, and I owed him an answer.

Before I tell you what I answered, let me try these same questions on you. Here you sit today reading this passage. As Jesus asked, what are you looking for? As the prisoner asked, why do you come to Church? As Eli asked, is someone calling your name? Do you feel a pull in your inner self that seems to come from outside of you? Does it call you in the night, in the silence? Do you sometimes turn on the radio or the television in an effort to drown out that voice? Is it bugging you? Welcome to the *call*.

The word vocation comes from the Latin *vocare*, which means "to call". When I was a young man, my pastor asked me , do you have a vocation? Did you ever hear that question? When heard in a religious setting, it almost always means a calling to the ordained or consecrated life. In fact, the Church recognizes four different vocational states: the single life, married life, ordained life, and consecrated life. Although in ages past, many people viewed these as a hierarchy, with ordained life at the top, that position is neither taught nor encouraged by the Church today. What the Church does teach is that by the simple act of being baptized, we are each anointed priest, prophet, and king – all inspiring titles! I wonder how many of us consider ourselves so blessed?

The actuality is that many of us who have chosen a married or single life do not see our choice as a vocation, do not see the hand of God in our life. The reality is that within these four big "V"s – single, married, ordained, consecrated -- there are a tremendous number of choices, perhaps "sub-vocations" that are truly responses to the call, responses that invite us into holiness. Theologian Frederick Buechner defines call as "the place where your deep gladness meets the world's deep need." St. Catherine of Siena says that "if you are what you should be, you will set the world ablaze." Neither of them say that you have to be ordained or a nun or a married person or single.

If your deep gladness is raising children lovingly and prayerfully, you have found your vocation. If your deep gladness is teaching social studies to 7th graders, you are answering the call. If your deep gladness is planting flowers in the warm soil, well, there is a deep need for flowers in this world. You too are answering a call. If fact, it's quite possible to have several sub-vocations within our life choice, each leading us joyfully to the fulfillment of a world's need. The reason why we often associate vocation with consecrated life is because individuals who find deep gladness in serving God by leading his people in prayer and service are obviously filling a deep need in the world. We endorse their choice and pray that more step forward.

But the Spirit does not grant the same gifts to each of us. Doing something that goes against our gift and our deepest gladness is sad at best, a disaster at worst. There's nothing so distressing as to see someone who hates their job, their life, their choices.

So if you're feeling a little uneasy about where you are today, here's some simple pointers. First of all, realize that finding your true vocation is a journey of prayer and trust in God. It comes to us in God's time and God is not concerned about years, days, hours, and minutes. Secondly, don't hesitate to find a wise person to help you discern your vocation. Samuel did, as did Andrew. You should too. Third, ask yourself what brings you joy – note that I didn't say happiness. That's too simple. Happiness is fleeting, like a good meal or a win by the home team. Joy is what sings in your soul, the thing you do that is so right that time is meaningless, and the world is made better for it.

Remember that prisoner who asked me, why do you come here? I thought about that for a few moments and then said to him, "I'm here today because I want to share a gift that was given to me. I invited Jesus into my life and he has shown me a path of peace and joy that I never expected. I want to help you find the same path." His smile back filled me with joy. Two months later, at the age of 47, I entered discernment for the diaconate. You see, sometimes the call comes from a most unexpected source.

Speak, Lord, for your servant is *listening*.

That's All I Need to Know

Scripture Referenced: Zec 9:9-10; Rom 8:9-13; Mt 11:25-30

If the Spirit of the one who raised Jesus from the dead dwells in you, the one who raised Christ from the dead will give life to your mortal bodies also, through his Spirit that dwells in you.

Consequently, brothers, we are not debtors to the flesh, to live according to the flesh.

For if you live according to the flesh, you will die, but if by the spirit you put to death the deeds of the body, you will live.

The story goes of a Religion teacher who challenges her young class to memorize Psalm 23, one of the most beloved texts in the Bible. Little Michael practices and practices and is finally ready. On the day that the kids are to recite the Psalm to the whole school, Michael goes up to the microphone and proudly begins, "The Lord is my shepherd…" Then he goes blank. The pause lengthens and Michael is clearly getting upset as he struggles to remember. Finally, he smiles and turns back to the microphone. "The Lord is my shepherd, and … that's all I need to know." And with that, he walks off the stage.

So, did Michael get it right? Yes, he certainly did! Jesus makes this exact point in the Gospel reading today, doesn't he? "…although you have hidden these things from the wise and the learned, you have revealed them to the little ones." *Little ones* is often translated as *the childlike.* This is a very important point that all of us here on the spiritual journey need to pay attention to. Even though God's revelation is available to all people, it is somehow *uniquely* and powerfully absorbed by those on the bottom of the ladder, those who are poor, those who are powerless, those who aren't very intelligent or well-educated.

God's action in revelation history is very consistent. He is forever tapping people who are nobodies, who are the last people we'd think God would want to use. He is forever upsetting our notion of what is appropriate. Notice in the first reading from Zechariah the reference to the king who is meek, riding on a colt, proclaiming peace. We immediately associate this prophecy with Jesus riding into Jerusalem on Palm Sunday. But see for a moment how absurd this image is – kings don't act this way! It would be like our President riding into town on a bicycle. But apparently, this is exactly what God holds up as an ideal.

I was in jail last Thursday ministering to the poor. Let me explain. Unlike a prison, jails are used for two purposes – for those serving sentences for minor crimes (no more than a year) *and* for holding the accused who await trial. So yes, jail is uniquely a place for the poor. If you are accused of a crime and have money, you make bail and you wait for your trial date to arrive in the comfort of your home. If you're poor, you don't make bail and you wait behind bars. With today's reality of crowded courtroom schedules, the wait can be months. Months of uncertainty, months of worry about your family, months of no privacy, months of noise and occasional chaos. Jail is for the poor. And here's the irony - I learn more from them than from any book or classroom or theologian.

God works powerfully in jails. Why? The people there are forced to stop, forced to cease their life flailing activity and ponder what is going on. In a way, they are on forced retreat, with minimal freedom of movement, their basic needs met, relatively safe. They have time, lots of it, and long days to fill. They are obliged to hear the voice in their hearts. For perhaps the first time in their lives, many are open to learning something new, to seeing life in a different way. The soil has been churned up, the seeds can now be planted. So do we hand them a copy of the *Summa Theologica* of St. Thomas Aquinas? No, we follow Christ's lead and keep it simple, keep it honest, keep it very basic – God loves us, and our response to that love is to love others too.

One time, I asked a group of women inmates sitting in a circle what they were most thankful for. As we went around the room, the answers were somewhat predictable – most mentioned children, husbands, parents, and so on. One young woman shocked me, though. She said, "I am grateful that I was arrested and put in jail. If I wasn't in here, I'd be dead. God has given me an opportunity to find him and through him, find life again."

If there's one common denominator among those who are jailed it is drug abuse. St. Paul's letter to the Romans draws a striking contrast between spirit and flesh. By flesh, Paul does not mean bodies, he means the dark side of human nature, our base selves, our little egos. In jails, the word flesh is often equivalent to drugs. As Paul says, "if you live according to the flesh, you will die." He could just as easily say, "if you live according to drugs, you will die." Paul's solution? "Allow the Spirit of Christ to dwell in you, so that by the Spirit you put to death the deeds of the body. Then you will live."

Some of us here today have struggled with drugs – I know this is true. It is perhaps a source of shame, a dark place to avoid. For others, drugs are not the problem. But something else almost certainly is – we are sinners, after all. When Paul speaks of the flesh, he means whatever it is that pulls us away from God. It could be any one of a number of idols – money, career, material things, pornography, sports, violent video games, television – whatever gets emphasis beyond the necessities of life. What do you think about when you're alone? Where does your mind turn? Spend a moment documenting your thoughts at these times. If it's not of God, then it's what Paul means by flesh. Are you a debtor to the flesh, as he asks? Does something not of God *own* you? That way is death.

What is the solution? Jesus tells us very clearly, just as little Michael discovered. The best answer is often the simplest answer. We can go read a book on theology or we can go find God written in creation. We can hole up in a church and surround ourselves with religious icons, or we can seek people who need help, who would welcome a visit, a smile, a brightening of their day. We can attend a retreat given by a great spiritual master, or we can babysit a four year-old who sees the world as a place of wonderment. Believe me, there's nothing wrong with books, churches, and retreats. But if that's our only perceived pathway to God, we're missing a whole lot. If we're just as attentive in simple circumstances as we are in reading a book, or praying fervently, or listening to a great preacher, then we will see God in action. We will see truth, we will live.

Above all, as Jesus would tell us, keep it simple. The Lord is my shepherd, *that's all I need to know.*

Going to the Dogs

Scripture Referenced: Rom 11:13-15,29-32; Mt 15:21-28

> *She said, "Please, Lord, for even the dogs eat the scraps that fall from the table of their masters."*
>
> *Then Jesus said to her in reply, "O woman, great is your faith! Let it be done for you as you wish." And her daughter was healed from that hour.*

The Gospel of Luke makes the point that Jesus grew in wisdom and understanding. We tend to think that Luke is referring to Jesus in childhood. But as human beings, we know that learning most certainly does not stop when we become adults, although there are some notable exceptions! Reading the gospels, we typically see Jesus in charge, possessing incredible insight, perceiving the thoughts of his disciples and the crowd, basically a person in total control. But in this passage from Matthew, Jesus gets a surprise, gets thrown for a loop. I love it because it shows us that Jesus grew in wisdom and understanding *throughout his life*. This is a moment that Jesus learns something new and unexpected.

Note that he is not in Galilee – he is actually north of Galilee in so-called "pagan" country. It's a bit unclear why he is in this region – the reading says he "withdrew" here, which suggests that he needed to get away for a while, to clear his head, to escape the persistent crowds. But even here, he is confronted with yet another person seeking healing, and worse yet, a Canaanite woman, who is so far down the social totem pole as to be at the level of yes, a dog. In the eyes of the Jews, she is nothing, practically invisible. Unfortunately, this "invisible" person has a loud and obnoxious voice, and the disciples, fully aware of their superiority, encourage Jesus to get rid of her. Send her away!

What follows is a very interesting verbal exchange. She kneels in front of Jesus and confronts him, not in a bold way, but in a humble way saying "Lord help me." Usually, that's plenty enough for Jesus – but he doesn't react as expected. He casually dismisses her, most likely using a turn of phrase that the Jews would use in everyday conversation about foreigners. Why should he, Jesus, waste any time and energy on non-Jewish people, on dogs? His mission is clearly to the tribe of Israel. But the woman zings him right back – please Lord, even the dogs get a scrap now and then. This startling reply clearly surprises Jesus. It's as if he suddenly sees her as the person she is, not a label, not an outsider, but a person who loves, who is persistent, who is humble, and who believes that somehow Jesus is the answer to her prayer. The blinding realization for Jesus is that his ministry is much bigger, much much bigger than I think Jesus even recognized. The Father wants not only to save the tribe of Israel, but the *whole universe*. Jesus is enlightened – he is delighted, and he immediately cures the woman's daughter as requested.

Okay, let's fast forward to today's world. Who are the people who are the nobodies in this world, those who are like *dogs*? It's very easy to find them. I suspect sometime in the next week you'll meet one at the bottom of a freeway ramp. Or walking downtown. How do you typically react? I've been told that these people will spend your donations for drugs or alcohol. I've been told that they're actually rich, their fancy cars hidden in a nearby parking lot. I've been told that they are criminals, thieves, the lowest of the low. Have you heard these stories? It's a very common trap. If we give them a label, say *thieving beggar* or *drug addict*, we don't have to think, we can just ignore them. Sort of like *Canaanite woman*. And just like Jesus, sometimes we need to be enlightened.

A while ago, my wife was driving down a freeway ramp and there was a person holding a sign asking for money or food. As it happened, she had half a turkey sandwich left over from lunch on the seat next to her. She rolled down the window, the man came over, and she offered him the half turkey sandwich. He gave her an intense look, then asked, "Is it white meat?" She replied, "Does it matter?!" As funny as that encounter is, it revealed that this was a real person, with tastes and preferences and peculiarities, just like us. He ceased being a homeless beggar, and became a human being.

So what labels are you carrying around with you that need to be re-examined? What does your hierarchy of acceptance look like? It's pretty simple typically – those that are most similar to you are at the top, those that are least like you are at the bottom. So take inventory for a moment. For example, I'm a white male, well-educated, fairly religious, got some money, married, one kid, employed, middle aged (ouch). So my opposite would be who? Perhaps a young, African-American woman with an 8th grade education, poor, unmarried, with a bunch of kids, who doesn't believe in God. Have I ever found my opposite? Yes, I have met her a few times, mostly in my prison ministry. Guess what? She's just as human as you and me. She has a name, wants, vulnerabilities, tastes, prejudices, dreams, and ambitions.

It might be difficult to find an exact opposite of yourself. You don't need to go to an extreme. Think about those one or two characteristics that really stand out, that really define who you are. If you're a staunch Republican, your opposite may be a staunch Democrat. If you have considerable wealth, your opposite may be someone who's quite poor. If you're very religious, your opposite may be an atheist. You know that you're on the right track if the person who is opposite is someone who scares you a bit. That's the key. Because if you fear the other, you will almost certainly demonize them and demote them to the level of an animal, just like the Jews of Jesus' time did. The only way to break that fear, to break that misconception, is through encounter and conversation, just like it happened to Jesus.

We can be very thankful that one very important person in the past decided to minister to *his* opposites. That person is St. Paul, isn't it? He tried ministering to his own people, the Jews, and they practically killed him. In disgust he turned to the opposites, to the Gentiles, to people like *us*. Yes, we are descendants of the outcasts, we are descendants of the dogs, we are descendants of the Canaanite women. Jesus looks on us with just as much love as he looks on his Jewish community. He wants to save everyone. He needs us to help him. Can we look beyond the labels, the fear of the other, and really, truly, help him? Christ doesn't see "in" people and "out" people. Can we show our Christian roots by our love for the outcasts, the dogs of today? That's how Jesus will rank us on the last day. Think about it.

Present Moments

Scripture Referenced: Acts 1:1-11

When he had said this, as they were looking on, he was lifted up, and a cloud took him from their sight.

While they were looking intently at the sky as he was going, suddenly two men dressed in white garments stood beside them.

They said, "Men of Galilee, why are you standing there looking at the sky?"

Ascension is one of those feast days that may be puzzling to you. I've certainly struggled with it a bit. It's a difficult concept to grasp. Why would we celebrate a day that features Jesus leaving us? Isn't a feast supposed to be a good thing? Can you really blame the disciples for looking up to heaven after Jesus departs? Put yourself in this scene. Amidst the awe of the moment, wouldn't you also be feeling a bit down and depressed? What's going through your mind? What do we do now?

I remember several of the good-byes in my life. I remember going away to college and seeing my sisters and my Mom cry. I remember saying good-bye to my dying brother - we hugged in the bathroom of all places - but it was OK just the same. I remember saying good-bye to my son as he walked into the kindergarten classroom. I was very concerned that he would make a scene. At the sight of him walking away so bravely, I was the one who broke into tears.

If we're honest with ourselves and look at the good-byes in our lives, I think we'll see that every good-bye contains at least two dimensions. Something ends and at the same time, something new begins. Something dies, and something is born. The problem we always have is not recognizing the inherent opportunity that every good-bye offers. If we continue to live in the past, somehow stuck in the desire for things to be as they were, we're no different than the apostles staring into the sky.

Since every good-bye is a gateway between the past and the future, it is a God moment. Why? God is present in the *now*, not the past, nor the future. *Now.* This may sound a little like a word game, a semantic exercise, but there's great truth here. Our "now moments" are happening as we are, as we sit here. Each moment slides into the past, gone to history, gone to memory. We can anticipate the future, and we always do, but there is little lasting value in that exercise. The future is utterly unpredictable. God is unconstrained by time, living totally in the *present*, which uniquely carries both the past and the future simultaneously. What mystics from all of the great religions will insist upon is that we only truly experience the Divine when we are completely in the present moment. You don't get there by *thinking* - you get there by *experiencing*, by being *attentive*.

Let me give you an example - one that I bet you've experienced yourself. I was in the store parking lot the other day, settling in after picking up some groceries, and I was flicking through the radio stations. Ready to pull out, I happened upon a classical music station that was just launching into Beethoven's 6th Symphony. I hadn't heard it in a while and I was suddenly transported. I put the car in park and just listened, delighting in the soaring melody and instrumentation. I didn't care about the ice cream in the bag, the cost of gas, the next task on the to-do list. I was simply in the moment and I knew that in a very real way, I was touching the Divine or more accurately, I was receptive to the Divine touching me in that moment.

So how does this connect to the Ascension? The key point to this reading is not the physical ascension of Christ into the heavens. In many ways, focusing only on this does us a disservice. The key point is that Jesus has passed from the realm of our time-bound physical existence into a new plane of existence, one that is not bound by space or time. Jesus as a man in the physical world cannot be in two places at once, cannot affect more than the few people who are sharing that limited space and time with him. Once he is in the spiritual plane of existence, he can be present in the heart of every believer, at every place and time. This is why he needed to move on - to *be* the way, not just *show* the way.

Today, many children in our Parish celebrate their first communion. Last Sunday, I had the honor of assisting at Mass in northern California for my god-daughter's first communion. Before Mass began, one little girl in the lineup with hands folded, looking quite angelic, beckoned me over to her. I figured she wanted a special blessing or to raise some worry or concern, so I bent over to her and asked, "yes?" She smiled at me and said, "how do you like the dress?" It's always about the dress, even at age seven apparently! I told her that I liked her dress better than my dress.

What makes Eucharist special is the knowledge that we are truly receiving Jesus. In the Eucharist, we aren't saying good-bye, we're saying *hello*. We're saying hello to new life, to a new way of being, to living in the present. When I was receiving my first communion, I remember asking Sister how long Jesus would be with me when I ate the Eucharistic bread. Her words continue to resonate with me. She said, "as long as you'd like him to be." How about forever?

Chapter 2 – Listening

God doesn't speak loudly, he speaks in a whisper so as not to frighten us. We can't hear that whisper if we're enveloped in chaos and noise. Find the quiet, then listen. Just listen. "This is my beloved Son. *Listen to him.*" Listen to him. Stop talking, get off the cell phone, turn off the TV, shut off the radio, *listen.* Observe. Open yourself. Invite God in.

If you do this, I guarantee that you will have a God-experience. It may not be an eleven on the God experience scale, but don't discount the possibility. But whether it is a one or a ten, each God experience will move you beyond admiring Jesus to following him, and all that implies. It is a journey of great joy, great challenge, and yes, great suffering at times. It is the journey of the soul locked with Jesus, and there is no better place to be.

Are You on the Right Road?

Scripture Referenced: Is 40:1-5,9-11; 2Pt 3:8-14; Mk 1:1-8

A voice cries out: In the desert prepare the way of the LORD! Make straight in the wasteland a highway for our God!

Every valley shall be filled in, every mountain and hill shall be made low; The rugged land shall be made a plain, the rough country, a broad valley.

Whenever I hear our first reading from the prophet Isaiah, with its emphasis on preparing the way of the Lord, I always think of driving on Interstate 15 from Escondido to Temecula. The freeway slices through hills and over valleys, with only gradual rises and falls in elevation. The road is built for speed and ease of passage. At various points on the road, you catch glimpses of Rte 395, the old highway, which was built on a much smaller budget so doesn't have the advantage of valleys filled in or mountains laid low. Rte 395 is forced to deal with a rugged countryside by going around obstacles and winding up steep hills. It's a much slower, more difficult journey. Advent Season is good time for us to look at the road we're on and ask the question, "Am I on the right road?"

This passage from the prophet Isaiah was apparently written toward the end of the Hebrew exile in Babylon, when optimism for release was emerging. This consoling, hope filled reading is directly referenced by Mark as he begins his gospel account. The voice of the one crying out in the desert that Isaiah mentions is tied to John the Baptist, who is seen by the Church as the last of the Old Testament prophets. John is a sort of hinge between the old covenant and the new covenant represented by Christ. His clothing, his mannerisms, his desert origin, even the gross food he eats all stamp him as a prophet. Even the people of the time recognize John for what he is, pouring out of the cities and villages to hear him, much as we think of a big religious tent revival in American culture. John's message is eerily similar to what we still hear today – "Repent! Turn back to God! Get on the right road!"

In between these two powerful images, we have the rarely heard second letter of Peter, in which we are told that with the Lord, one day is like a thousand years. By that logic, it's been merely two days since Christ was resurrected! The point, of course, is not to take this literally, but to answer the question, "When? When is Christ coming back? When will the final judgment take place?" Peter is quick to tell us that in an effort to save everyone, the Lord is patient and gives us each the time we need to come to repentance, to come to understand what it means to be on the right road.

So, how do you know you're on the right road?

Does the right road mean no suffering? Does the right road mean you have money? Does the right road mean you have no money? Does the right road mean that everyone likes you? Does going to Church on Sunday mean you're on the right road? Does being ordained mean you're on the right road? Does being baptized with holy water mean you're on the right road? The answer to all of these questions are "no" and "yes" and "maybe" because they're the wrong questions to ask. These criteria are all outward signs, things you can see and measure and judge, things that don't really tell you much about what's truly inside a person.

John tells us exactly what it means to be on the right road. Remember what he says right at the end? I have baptized you with water, he (meaning Christ) will baptize you with the *Holy Spirit*. What does *that* mean? It means that you are on the right road if you have allowed the spirit of God to infuse your entire life. You are baptized with the Holy Spirit if you have been completely immersed in the Spirit to the point that you and the Spirit act together in harmony. You remain you, and the Spirit remains the Spirit, but together you are Christ-like. Now what does that look like?

It's a person who is very independent, and yet treasures relationships with others. It is a person who has a core of steel and a heart of gold. It is a person who cries to see the injustice of the world, and acts in their own unique way to battle and fight it. It's a person who owns material things, but is never themselves owned by anything or anyone. It is a person who exudes peace and that others seek for wisdom and counsel. It is a person who is bumped and bashed around by life, just like the rest of us, but never seems to be bruised or angry. This person is on the right road – it may look like old highway 395, but they move like they're on I-15.

How do we find the right road? Here's some Advent tips:

- Get to a quiet place and stop the noise. Try to do this daily. God doesn't speak loudly, he speaks in a whisper so as not to frighten us. We can't hear that whisper if we're enveloped in chaos and noise. Find the quiet, then listen. Just listen.
- Open yourself to the Spirit. This is an act of your will. You must ask for the Lord's spirit to enter you, to permeate you, to baptize you. This is harder than it sounds, because part of us fights this, that part that wants to be a little god or goddess, alone and independent, beholden to no one. We need to listen to that other part of us that wants the Spirit desperately. That's your soul calling for its Abba, its Daddy.
- As Christmas approaches, get beyond the sentimentality, the childlike focus, and ask some tough adult questions. Who do I want to be? What would it feel like to be truly at peace? What needs to be expunged from my life now? What needs to die so that something new can come alive? Hard questions. Answer them.

Advent is about waiting, about urgency, and God's patience. Heed the words of Peter's letter –

"The Lord does not delay his promise...but is patient with you, not wishing that any should perish but that all should come to repentance. But the day of the Lord will come like a thief, and then the heavens will pass away with a mighty roar..."

Brothers and sisters, we don't have all eternity to get on the right road. We have *now*.

Surprise!

Scripture Referenced: Lk 2:22-40

> *Now, Master, you may let your servant go in peace, according to your word, for my eyes have seen your salvation, which you prepared in sight of all the peoples, a light for revelation to the Gentiles, and glory for your people Israel.*

Did you get any surprises for Christmas? Something you really didn't expect to get? Even if you didn't this year, I'll bet you can think of a gift you received in the past that truly surprised you. When I was 13, my parents surprised me with a guitar for Christmas. I don't remember asking for one, and up to that point in time, I certainly hadn't shown a lick of musical talent. But they felt moved to get me a guitar. I was delighted. I immediately began "practicing", which meant jumping around and strumming madly like Elvis. I even took lessons, which continued up to the day my little brother accidentally stepped on my guitar and punched a hole through the back. My career as a rock star was over. I was secretly pleased – my fingers hurt.

Our readings today feature all sorts of surprises. In our first reading, Abram and Sarah are surprised by a pregnancy. Many couples are surprised by a pregnancy, of course, but what makes this pregnancy particularly amazing is that both were considered well past child-bearing age. In the letter to the Hebrews, we are told that Abram's faith in God allowed this to happen. Keep that in mind – there is an apparent link between faith and surprises.

In the gospel reading from Luke, we have three surprises. The first to be surprised is Simeon, who was told that he would see the Christ before he died. We're not told when the Spirit revealed this to him, but we do know that Simeon is a very old man when Mary and Joseph walk into the temple with the child Jesus in their arms. He immediately recognizes Jesus for who he is (which is pretty amazing in its own right, since all babies look pretty much the same), and proclaims a beautiful prayer of serene release, "Now, Master, you may let your servant go in peace…" Simeon's faith revealed Jesus, another link between faith and surprise.

The next surprise is for the prophetess Anna, whose story closely parallels Simeon's. She's eight-four years old, which is pretty old in today's world, but is practically record-breaking in the first century. We are told that she too is a person of deep faith and devotion to God, and like Simeon, recognizes the Holy Family instantly. But the ultimate surprise is for Mary and Joseph. Luke tells us that they were amazed at what was being said about Jesus. Here they are, two very poor peasants, making their obligatory trip to Jerusalem to offer a thanksgiving sacrifice to God, and these two strangers come up to them and begin telling them about the glorious redemption now at hand through the baby in their arms.

You might wonder about this a bit. If the gospel stories are true, we know that Mary had some inkling that this was a special child. And Joseph's dreams tell him likewise. Why were they surprised? Realize that up to now, the revelation each of them received was a *private* revelation, specific to each individually. This meeting with Simeon and Anna is not only confirmation that their private revelations are true, but that somehow God is letting other people know about this baby as well! It's not a secret!

So let's review the connections in our readings today. Apparently, faith in God will lead to a pleasant surprise. Abram, Sarah, Simeon, and Anna all demonstrate this reality. There's a second reality, however. The surprise does not come at once – it seems necessary to wait, to maintain vigil, to keep watching. All four of our faith-filled people are surprised in old age. You have to wait until the cake is baked before you can eat it. You have to wait for the tree to mature before it bears apples. You have to wait for a child to grow up before it can act like an adult. And at some point, you'll be surprised. Look, the cake is done. Look, the tree has tiny apples on it. Look, my son actually asked me for advice. Look, my daughter kissed me good night for the first time in five years. Surprise!

Have you been praying for something for a long time? Something that seems out of your hands, that perhaps only God can make happen? Maybe you're seeking a soul mate, or perhaps hoping for a new baby? Maybe you're praying for the conversion of a loved one, a child or a parent. Maybe you're praying for a cure to a lifelong illness. If you find yourself nodding, these readings are for you. Keep the faith, hang in there. It may take longer than you think. But the important thing is to keep listening, keep praying, because some day the Spirit will reveal your answer. It may be exactly what you want, it may not be – but it is apparently guaranteed to be a bit of a surprise.

Remember that anything that comes from God is good. It cannot be otherwise. It may not feel good in the short run, but it is always good in the long run. Trust in this truth, just as Abram did. Trust in this truth, as surely Mary and Joseph did as they live one surprise after another with the child Jesus. Trust in this truth as you live your own messy yet holy family life.

If you're currently praying for something significant in your life, or even if you're not, consider this. Is there someone praying for you? Is there a blindness, a dark place in your life that affects you today? Are you blocking or pushing something away, something that you know is good for you? God is oh so patient with us, isn't he? We enter relationship with Him, then we abandon Him. We try other paths to fulfillment, and we fall on our face. We seek substitutes for God and we're inevitably disappointed. God is patient. As we grow in faith, as we walk more closely with our God, we too will begin to notice that our world is clearer, more visibly imbued with the supernatural, the spiritual. And one day, *we* may see the need to change something in us, to try something we didn't really consider before.

Maybe you're the surprise someone else needs. Think about that. *Surprise*!

Recognizing God Moments

Scripture Referenced: Is 42:1-4,6-7; Lk 3:15-16, 21-22

After all the people had been baptized and Jesus also had been baptized and was praying, heaven was opened and the holy Spirit descended upon him in bodily form like a dove. And a voice came from heaven, "You are my beloved Son; with you I am well pleased."

When we celebrate the Feast of the Holy Family, we hear the story of Jesus lost and found in the Temple. It was a significant revelation for Jesus, as it most certainly represented his first "aha" moment, a realization that he was unique in the eyes of God, owning a relationship with God as a Son to a Father, with all of the inherent challenge and meaning wrapped in that bond. Given that Jesus is only 12 years old when this occurs, he isn't quite sure what to do with this knowledge, and wisely chooses to return with Mary and Joseph to Galilee and remain obedient to them. And for the next 18 years, he does exactly that, living the life of a typical Jewish man of the time. We are told nothing of these missing years in the Scripture, so we can only speculate that he continued to pray and ponder his call, and just like many of us, look for a sign from God as to his next step.

John the Baptizer was that sign. John's preaching of repentance and forgiveness was electrifying the countryside, drawing people from throughout the region. Jesus is drawn to John, clearly listens to him, and in a show of solidarity with the entire people of the region, allows himself to be baptized in the waters of the Jordan. But the key point of the story is not that Jesus was baptized, but that the sign he was seeking from his Father in heaven is confirmed. Wrapped in prayer, Jesus receives a message from God through the Holy Spirit, a message so powerful that it takes bodily form as a dove, and the message is direct and clear: "You are my beloved Son; with you I am well pleased." The words are from two Old Testament sources, the first phrase *You are my beloved Son* is from Psalm 2 and refers to a description of the Messianic king, and the second phrase *with you I am well pleased* comes directly from our first reading from Isaiah, chapter 42, describing the suffering servant. In essence then, God tells Jesus that he is the Messiah, and that his mission is to suffer for the people, that his road is to the cross. Jesus has the sign he needs, and his path is now clear.

I remember the first time someone talked about asking for a sign from God. I was working at a big company and this lady was discerning whether or not to change jobs. She was weighing the pros and cons and summed it up by saying that she was looking for a sign from God as to the best choice. I was a little shocked, since in my mind it seemed a bit presumptuous to think that God would waste time on such a thing, and besides, how did you know you were actually getting a sign from God? Did you have to wait for a dove to come land on your head?

As my spiritual walk has progressed over the last several years, I have come to know certain truths about how God speaks, about prayer, about signs, and about awareness. I'll share these with you, but I want to emphasize that my experience may not be the same as yours, that when it comes to the spiritual journey, one size does not fit all. However, there are enough consistencies in the way God speaks to us that I am confident that you can relate, and may have experienced similar revelations yourself. In the end, I can only take you as far as I have gone myself, and I am certain that many of you have gone much further.

The first truth is that you don't need to be *worthy* to hear God speak. You don't need to be morally perfect, ethically pure, or even the least bit religious. You don't need to be Catholic – you don't need to be baptized or in a state of grace. You simply need to be human. Our second reading from Acts depicts a shocked St. Peter realizing that the Holy Spirit has descended upon the house of Cornelius, who was a Gentile. Peter sums it up nicely by saying, "In truth, I see that God shows no partiality." I too have seen God's grace come down on the most unworthy people you can imagine – drug dealers, rapists, murderers, thieves, addicts, and the like. Worthiness has nothing to do with it.

Secondly, God is speaking to us all of the time, in every circumstance, and does indeed care about every decision we make, from the most mundane to the most significant. The problem is that we are not listening all of the time, and we tend to switch on our God radar only when we decide something is important enough to be brought to prayer. We shortchange ourselves constantly, missing the chance to be in conversation with our God whose line is always open. St. Paul tells us to pray always. What he means is to be in awareness always, to be open to God's voice in our heart always – this is how God wants to be with us – we pray in the Mass that it is through Him, with Him, in Him that we walk in Christ. Yes! That's so right. People who "get this" will tell you that there are no such thing as coincidences, that God is in the interruptions, that every moment is a God moment. A deacon friend of mine loves to travel on airplanes, because he sees in every person who sits next to him an opportunity to get to know God a little better – not necessarily by talking to them, but by listening.

Thirdly, over time we begin to recognize the voice of God, as distinguished from the voice of the world. How do you know that an experience is a message from God and not, as Ebenezer Scrooge called his first ghost, "a bad bit of uncooked potato"? What characterizes such moments? First, God's voice comes to us in a way that is uniquely suited to us as individuals. Many people hear God in nature, many in music, still others in the Word. Some need to hear it, some need to see it. What is it for you? Secondly, God's message, His recommendation, is always good for us: objectively good – good in a way that may be challenging to us, but will leave us a better person for taking the path. Thirdly, God's message always calls us to His mission in some interesting way – the voice of God is not simply for our own little selves. We must use it to reach others.

If you're still not sure if God has spoken to you at all, *ever*, try this. The only way you begin to recognize the voice of God is by looking at your past. Look at the good things that have happened to you, the times when you were truly rescued, steered in a better direction, taken down a new path – examine those times, and backtrack to the cause. How did you come to that new point, that better you? Was it a person? A moment of clarity? A cry for help answered?

Once you begin to understand how God speaks to you, the next step is to simply put yourself into these situations often. For me for example, I *hear* God – it is very much a matter of physical listening – to music, voice, good preaching, conversation. For others I know, it is visual – art, nature, activity. For others it is silence and darkness, a complete absence of stimuli. What is it for you? Put yourself consciously into these awareness generators, these moments of openness, and you will get signs from God. It's a relationship, and it's *worth it!*

Suffering, Transformation

Scripture Referenced: 2Cor 12:7-10

Therefore, that I might not become too elated, a thorn in the flesh was given to me, an angel of Satan, to beat me, to keep me from being too elated.

Three times I begged the Lord about this, that it might leave me, but he said to me, "My grace is sufficient for you, for power is made perfect in weakness."

For seven Sundays in Ordinary Time, we read from the 2nd letter of Paul to the Corinthians. You can be excused for not noticing this – we start reading this letter of Paul in mid-February. Lent and Easter interrupt the flow of Ordinary Time as it does every year, and only since Pentecost do we return. But today is the last time we'll read from 2nd Corinthians this year. It's kind of a shame – this is one of Paul's most personal letters, filled with emotion, both positive and negative. It's real life, and the section we read today is very typical of the whole letter.

Here is Paul, describing how he is suffering from some unknown malady that clearly distresses him. He calls it "a thorn in the flesh", which sounds bad enough, but then he goes on to call it "an angel of Satan" that beats him. What could this be? Much ink has been spilled speculating on this thorn. Some scholars think Paul had epilepsy, some think he had an addiction, others that Paul was talking about a person who really knew how to push his buttons. Maybe it was the apostle Peter? Maybe it was a teenager…?

Whatever it was, Paul doesn't tell us. But he clearly wanted it to stop. Not once, not twice, but three times he begs the Lord that it might leave him. And what does the Lord say to him? "My grace is sufficient for you, for power is made perfect in weakness." Isn't that an extraordinary statement? That doesn't sound like the answer to a prayer. How could power be made perfect in weakness? Doesn't power come from strength?

Many years ago, when I was in graduate school, I took a class in the psychology department from a professor whose area of expertise was the study of personal relationships. He was discussing the topic of power and he said something that has always stuck with me. "The person who has the most power in any situation is the person who has the least to lose." Think about it. What made Mahatma Gandhi so effective in leading India to freedom? He and the Indian people had no army, no strength in any objective way. By a series of non-violent marches against the British rule, his campaign called "right against might" won the day. Tiananmen Square in 1989 – what was the compelling image that you remember from that time? I have one. A single, unarmed man walking up to a line of tanks and stopping them cold. He had nothing to lose, and it was very clear who had the power at that moment.

There's an important corollary that I invite you to consider in light of the scriptures. *The person who has the least to lose is the most free.*

The great monastic traditions – built by the likes of St. Benedict and the followers of St. Francis – usually, if not universally require vows of poverty, chastity, and obedience. Ever wondered why? Are they all masochists? No, they understand the truth of what Paul hears from the Lord. As they shed their attachment to material things, to family, and to their own autonomy, they by definition take on lives of simplicity. In this simplicity, they clearly have nothing to lose. With nothing to lose, they ironically have freedom, peace, and yes, power. How power? Power in the sense that they are beholden to no one but the Lord Jesus. When a person like this speaks from the heart, how can we not listen? They have no agenda -- the person cannot be bought, cannot be coerced, cannot be seduced. They are free to speak the truth.

The vast majority of us are not monks, of course, so how do we use this guidance from Paul's life? Do we toss out our material goods? The question is not about what we own, but about what owns us. I suspect that the answer changes over our lifetimes. When we are young, starting out in life, we are driven by ambition and the need to show the world that we can make it. This is normal – we need some successes to build a healthy ego. But after the age of 30 or so, success is no longer a good teacher. Sure, it feels good, but it doesn't teach us anything about the important things in life. And if we're not careful, the job, the car payment, the mortgage, the media, -- they begin to direct our lives, to literally "own us". And when failure begins to enter our lives, whether our fault or not, new owners can appear – alcohol, drugs, and chronic illness.

So let's return to St. Paul. He is suffering – apparently from some chronic pain. Notice the first part of the statement the Lord makes to Paul. "My grace is sufficient for you." There's something about suffering that opens a door to the Divine. God does not want us to suffer any more than a parent wants his child to suffer. But like any good parent, sometimes we have to allow our child to make a mistake, to suffer a little, to wake them up to a truth about life, about relationship, about what is important. God does the same with us. The world is a painful place at times, but if we are open, God brings his grace to the moment, and we can be transformed.

Remember the woman with the hemorrhage from Mark's gospel? She had nothing to lose and in that utter weakness, she found the strength to touch Christ's cloak and realize the power of healing.

We all have thorns in our lives. And like Paul, we dearly wish that they would go away, be healed, leave us forever. God's answer – seek my grace. God's desire – transform us. If we do not learn to transform our pain, brothers and sisters, we are doomed to transmit it to others. I am convinced that this is the pattern of the world. So what is the model we seek to follow? Jesus Christ – who bore a *crown* of thorns, and never once complained, fought back, or called down fire from heaven. In that apparent *weakness* as he was led to a horrific death came the *power* to save the entire world forever. So, when we are feeling that thorn, ask Christ to walk the road with us. He's been there.

"God" Experiences

Scripture Referenced: Mk 9:2-10

> *After six days Jesus took Peter, James, and John and led them up a high mountain apart by themselves. And he was transfigured before them, and his clothes became dazzling white, such as no fuller on earth could bleach them.*
>
> *Then Elijah appeared to them along with Moses, and they were conversing with Jesus.*

Let's talk about "God experiences". What does that mean? Basically, a God experience is an unmistakable encounter with the divine. It will come when least expected, and will often leave you a different person for the experience. Several years ago, I was on a retreat in the mountains and I had a "God experience". No, I didn't have a vision of angels or moving mountains or anything like that. In a moment of silent listening, in the peace of the afternoon, I was moved to realize that it was impossible for me to earn God's love. God loved me completely and fully already – there was nothing I could do to receive more or less of that love. And in that simple revelation, I was moved to tears. God was with me, deeply and profoundly, felt in the core of my heart. That moment changed my life.

How many of you have had a God experience in your life? How many of you have had an experience that you are convinced was directly linked to God? Don't be concerned if you haven't yet. Let's explore this concept in a bit more detail. Let's consider a most amazing God experience in the lives of Jesus and his three favorite disciples, namely the Transfiguration.

First, a little bit of context is necessary. Just prior to this point in Mark's gospel, Peter has made an inspired answer to Jesus' question, "who do you say that I am?" Peter answers in reply, "you are the Messiah." Yet even though Jesus praises Peter for this act of faith, it is clear that Peter and the apostles had no real idea of what that *really* meant. They were picturing Jesus as the glorious King of Israel, and yet Jesus keeps speaking of His suffering and death. It is incomprehensible to them, and Peter goes so far as to rebuke Jesus, telling him to stop this talk about suffering and death. Jesus reacts angrily, calling Peter "Satan" and telling him that he thinks as men do, not as God does. Peter and the apostles might be baffled, hurt, and maybe a bit resentful.

So a few days later, Jesus leads Peter, James, and John up the mountain and they all have a "God" experience. In the pantheon of God experiences, this isn't just a ten, this is an eleven! Four elements stand out:

- First, Jesus himself is transfigured before their wondering eyes, his clothes dazzling white. If they had any doubt as to the divine nature of Jesus, this display was clearly meant to remove those doubts.
- Second, Elijah and Moses make an appearance, and even though these two men had died hundreds of years before Jesus, the disciples instantly recognize who they are. Elijah, the first and greatest prophet of Israel. Moses, the leader of the Exodus, the greatest God-event in Israel's history, and giver of the Law.
- Third, in an utterly human reaction that endears Peter to us all, he follows his typical modus operandi, "don't just stand there, say something!!" So he makes an expansive gesture, suggesting that they camp out with Moses and Elijah and hang around a while.
- Fourth, perhaps saving Peter from more "foot in mouth" statements, a cloud overcomes them and the voice of God speaks, "This is my beloved Son. Listen to Him."

Shortly thereafter, the vision ends and the four of them leave the mountain, each the same yet each different too, the memory of the experience searing their lives forever. The apostles, particularly Peter, no longer attempt to steer Jesus toward their version of Messiah-hood. There is no doubt that Jesus is someone very special and although they don't know what to make of him, they are with him now for the long haul. Jesus, in turn, uses the Transfiguration experience as the trigger event for his journey to Jerusalem and the inevitable suffering and death that follows. It's as if Jesus needed that last confirmation – "Am I on the right track? Is this what you ask of me, Father?" The resounding *yes* is all that he needs.

So what do we take from this Gospel? How do we connect to it?

Laced throughout this short episode is the story of faith and how God nudges it along.

Note that God always acts first. He draws us to Himself by showing us who He is – never violating our free will, always inviting us through the very nature of His being. It is usually seen by each of us in creation, in the beauty of nature in our world. The power of a thunderstorm, the crash of the sea, a spectacular sunset, all of these are invitations to see God in their origin, to appreciate that power and beauty. This is typically our first "God experience". For some people, alas, who refuse to go further in exploration, it is their only God experience.

But for many people, a decision is made to investigate who this Creator God may be. The wisdom of the world's organized religions attempts to answer those questions, and we who sit in the Catholic Church are especially fortunate since we are closest to the fullness of that truth. Over time, we come to accept the teachings of the Church, responding to the stirring of faith, seeking to fill the hole in our hearts. But eventually we come to the big question, "who is this Jesus?" Peter illustrates both sides of the equation for us. Prior to the Transfiguration, I think that Peter greatly admired Jesus, seeing him as a great teacher and healer, definitely "king material". After the Transfiguration, Peter goes beyond admiration to the next commitment level, that of *following* Jesus. This is what Jesus asks of us. Note that Jesus never says, "worship me" or "bow down before me" or "applaud me". Jesus says simply, "follow me".

Note how Peter makes the transition, however. You might say that he was "stuck" before the Transfiguration. We get stuck too, locked in a sort of admiration of Jesus, somewhat content to avoid the tough challenge inherent in "follow me". How do we get "unstuck?" What does the voice in the cloud say? "This is my beloved Son. **Listen to him**." Listen to him. Stop talking, get off the cell phone, turn off the TV, shut off the radio, *listen*. Observe. Open yourself. Invite God in.

If you do this, I guarantee that you, like Peter, will have a God-experience. It may not be an eleven on the God experience scale, but don't discount the possibility. I know for a fact that there are people in this assembly who have had profound and incredibly moving experiences of God in their lives. You know who you are. But whether it is a one or a ten, each God experience will move you beyond admiring Jesus to following him, and all that implies. It is a journey of great joy, great challenge, and yes, great suffering at times. It is the journey of the soul locked with Jesus, and there is no better place to be.

Listen to Jesus. Open yourself to God's action in your lives. See how God takes care of you, loves you, asks for your involvement in the world. From love comes justice, and from justice, peace. If God's love is not challenging you to transform, you're not listening. If you think everyone else needs changing except for you, you're not listening. But if you <u>are</u> listening, and you <u>do</u> say yes, don't fear the change. Don't worry, God will not turn you into something you don't want to be. No, you will become more fully human, more fully alive, more fully the person you already are in God, the one deepest within you that God loves the best. Ask for this revelation, this change – you won't be disappointed.

Chapter 3 – Yes to God

The path to God is fascinating. He draws us in, usually through the influence of another person, whether it is a relative, or a friend, or maybe a coworker. We are usually invited *to* something, to take a step, to take a little risk. Maybe it's to do some service, to teach at School of Religion, to become a lector, to help a family at Christmas. Each little yes we give takes us further down the road to Christ.

In the end, we all play hide and seek with God. In fact, I'll bet that some of you out there are hiding from God right now. It may be a game to us, but God is deadly earnest in his pursuit. He may seem like an angry parent at times; he may seem like a worried lover at other times. If you're hiding, ask why. Are you afraid of what he'll ask of you? Are you afraid to commit? He offers gifts of healing if we simply accept the relationship. He wants to find us as desperately as we want to find our lost children.

Light

Scripture Referenced: Is 8:23-9:3; Mt 4:12-23

"The people who walked in darkness have seen a great light..."

Have you ever noticed how often the word light is associated with God? Or with Christ? It is practically a synonym for God. We've all heard that God is love. Have you also heard that Christ is our light? The deacon sings the phrase, "Christ our light" three times at Easter Vigil as he carries the newly lit Paschal candle, singing once outside the church, once at the entrance, and once more in the sanctuary. The message, obviously, is that the light of God shines in his Son, Jesus Christ. So why this association of light and God?

Consider what light means to us human beings. It allows us to see clearly, to avoid danger, to recognize our surroundings, to discern good from evil. Light is clearly linked to the sun, to the greatest source of our light. All of the great religions tie at least some of their ceremonies around dawn and sunset. The Jews begin their celebration of Sabbath at sunset on Friday evening and continue it until sunset on Saturday evening. We Catholics follow this same lead by celebrating what is essentially a Sunday Mass on Saturday evening. This is technically the vigil of *Sunday*, the day of the sun, the day of light. During the Muslim feast of Ramadan, one must fast each day from dawn until sunset. If you've had a hungry day, you'd want to know when it was officially sunset, wouldn't you? The Muslims define the sun as having officially set when you can no longer tell the difference between a white thread and a black thread. It actually makes sense, you can try it sometime.

I remember once being on retreat in the mountains. It was April and late in the evening when I took a walk. It had to be close to freezing – luckily I was dressed warmly, but even so, I could feel the cold poking at me, from my toes to my nose. In the utter darkness of the mountains, I felt completely alone, completely in the dark, and I shivered. This, I thought, is what hell is. It's not flames and heat, it's cold and dark and alone.

At some fundamental, visceral level, God understands this. Light, after all, is the first thing that God creates. "Let there be light!" The word *light* appears in 46 of the 73 books of the bible. It is most often associated with change, with something new arriving on the scene. Our gospel writer Matthew directly quotes from Isaiah, our first reading, signaling to us that Jesus himself is the new light, the new sun, the one who is to come. And what does Jesus do? He calls Simon, Andrew, James, and John, two sets of brothers, launching his ministry by selecting these very ordinary men, these fishermen of Galilee.

Over 90 years ago, three children of Fatima, Portugal had a vision of the Blessed Virgin Mary. One of them, Lúcia, described seeing the lady as "brighter than the sun, shedding rays of light clearer and stronger than a crystal glass filled with the most sparkling water and pierced by the burning rays of the sun." These children would never be the same again. Nor would the many who have made pilgrimage to Fatima and been blessed with unexplained healings.

You've certainly heard it said when someone has made a big change, usually for the better that he has "seen the light". But what does it mean to see the light? Let's consider the fishermen Jesus called for a moment. Why would they drop everything, their livelihood, their friends, their daily lives, to follow an itinerant preacher? Note that Jesus asks them – they don't ask Him. This is important to recognize. The light comes to us unbidden, without our asking or even necessarily seeking it. Second, Jesus challenges them and intrigues them – "come be fishers of men" he says. What an odd statement! What does he mean? You can imagine Simon and Andrew looking at each other with amazement. But it makes sense. Fishermen need to know where to fish, what bait to use, and a lot of patience to succeed. Jesus wants these men to use the same qualities – smarts, perception, and patience – to capture the hearts of people. The lesson for us? The light doesn't come to change us into something we're not. No, the light challenges us to use the talents we already have! It's not a big deal at all.

Is the light inviting you to something? Do you have an intriguing, perhaps amazing invitation in hand? Is Jesus calling you by name? It's real if it brings you out of darkness. It's real if it brings you warmth, clarity, and community. It's real if it uses who and what you already are to make the world a better place. It's real if the gifts of the Holy Spirit (wisdom, understanding, counsel, knowledge, piety, fear of the Lord, courage) begin to permeate your life. This is the light.

How God Calls Us

Scripture Referenced: Lk 5:1-11

After he had finished speaking, he said to Simon, "Put out into deep water and lower your nets for a catch."

Simon said in reply, "Master, we have worked hard all night and have caught nothing, but at your command I will lower the nets."

When they had done this, they caught a great number of fish and their nets were tearing.

They signaled to their partners in the other boat to come to help them. They came and filled both boats so that they were in danger of sinking.

When Simon Peter saw this, he fell at the knees of Jesus and said, "Depart from me, Lord, for I am a sinful man."

Brothers and sisters, I think is safe to say that everyone in this church today has heard and responded to the call of Jesus. Do you remember when you first heard Jesus calling you? What was it like? Were you frightened? Excited? Confused? Inspired? Today's Gospel illustrates how Jesus called my favorite apostle, Simon Peter. What do we learn from this story? How does it help us guide others who may be hearing the call, too?

Jesus is teaching by the seashore, his fame already apparent by the crowds pressing in on him. He sees Simon's boat on the shore and asks Simon if he can enter his boat and have Simon pull out a bit into the lake so that Jesus can be better seen and heard by the crowd. Why did he choose Simon's boat? We know from earlier in Luke's gospel that Jesus had recently cured Simon's mother-in-law. So clearly, Jesus knows Simon. Simon, in turn, must be intrigued by this itinerant preacher, and therefore he agrees to do what Jesus asks. Now isn't that just like God? He *fascinates* us at first, getting our attention.

After teaching a while, Jesus asks Simon to do something decidedly odd: "Put out into deep water and lower your nets for a catch." Now one thing Simon knows is fishing, and this request must seem like the most frivolous, silly thing in the whole world. He knows that fish feed at night

– he's been doing it this way for years! How can this preacher (rumored to be a carpenter's son) have any knowledge of fishing? Who does this guy think he is? So, first aspect – God fascinates us. Second aspect – God challenges us. And Simon reacts to the challenge like we do – an appeal to reason, (we've worked hard all night)! But even though Simon is pessimistic and not very enthusiastic, he obeys! This is actually the key point in the story – for without Simon's obedience, nothing more would happen!

Well, surprise, surprise! He doesn't catch a few fish, he catches more than he can handle. Two boats full! So full, the boats are almost sinking! The other fishermen, James, and John, all are astounded. Jesus reveals the abundant nature of God, showering gifts on his children. Note that the gifts are beyond Simon's expectation or understanding! And how does Simon Peter react? This time he gets it right. He responds with honesty, truth, and humility, seeing the Lordship of Jesus and leaving everything to follow him.

Brothers and sisters, this pattern of fascination, challenge, obedience, and abundant reward is played over and over in our lives. It doesn't happen just once! In 1991, I was invited to join our parish's Christian Initiation team. I was fascinated and challenged, but agreed to give it a try. I quickly saw firsthand how God's grace enters the lives of people who are seeking him and changes their entire perspective on life. Some years later, God nudged me into deeper water. Go serve in prison ministry. I was fascinated, challenged by fear and uncertainty, yet ultimately agreed to give it a try. Once again, I was a witness to the power of God's grace. I saw the scariest looking guys in the world break down in tears when they realized that God would forgive them for their sins. Most recently, God has nudged me into the deepest water yet. I am responding to the call, fascinated yet challenged, to live the vocation of a deacon. I can tell you that the water is often over my head, but I am truly amazed and astonished at God's abundant gifts.

God calls everyone. He gets our attention, challenges us, asks for our obedience, and if we cooperate, showers our amazed senses with his gifts. As we in this church enter into the world, we will be asked to help others see the signs of God's call in their lives. In some cases, we'll be the very instruments of that call in their lives. But as *we* learn to say "yes", our witness will help others to say yes, too. So, do not be afraid. Put out into deep water. Our Savior awaits.

Abram's Decision

Scripture Referenced: Gen 12:1-4a; Mt 17:1-9

The Lord said to Abram: "Go forth from the land of your kinsfolk and from your father's house to a land that I will show you.

"I will make of you a great nation, and I will bless you; I will make your name great, so that you will be a blessing.

I will bless those who bless you and curse those who curse you. All the communities of the earth shall find blessing in you."

Abram went as the Lord directed him.

The Transfiguration story is one of our most beloved Gospel readings. It is filled with awesome wonder and power, with Jesus displaying the divine side of his nature to three astonished, overwhelmed fishermen. We know the story so well – the appearance of Moses and Elijah, Peter's somewhat strange offer to put up some tents, and ultimately, the voice from the cloud that knocks the apostles flat on their face in fear.

But how does this relate to Lent? Why this reading?

To answer that question, we need to turn to the first reading from Genesis. At first hearing, there doesn't seem to be much happening. The Lord is promising Abram all sorts of good things if Abram leaves town and goes to another land. What's going on here? One clue is the book – Genesis. Genesis means *beginning*. The first eleven chapters of Genesis contain all of the epic stories that attempt to answer the big questions that everyone has. How was the world created? How did evil enter the world? What causes great natural disasters? Why do we all speak different languages? Genesis gives us the Garden of Eden, Adam and Eve, Noah's Ark, the tower of Babel. These are mythic tales told around many Hebrew campfires over many many years. But inevitably, the question would arise, how did Yahweh come to choose the Hebrew people as particularly his own?

The answer to this question, the very *first* record of this unique relationship, occurs in the first four verses of Genesis, Chapter 12. We read, "The Lord said to Abram: 'Go forth from the land of your kinsfolk and from your father's house to a land that I will show you.'" What an astonishing, even strange request! We aren't told how Abram *heard* this request, whether he heard it in a dream, or from a cloud, or was bonked in the head by a camel. But he heard it, and that's not all. The Lord goes on to tell Abram that he will bless Abram, and make his name great. The Lord will bless those who bless Abram, and curse those who curse Abram. What a deal! It sounds like something out of a Godfather movie. Abram has a champion, a big brother, a silent partner, a rich uncle. If it stopped there, we would say that Abram was delusional, maybe a little nuts. But Yahweh says one other thing that is critically important. He tells Abram that "all the communities of the earth shall find *blessing* in you." Apparently, Abram is more than just the lucky winner of the God lottery. Apparently, Yahweh has something in mind for Abram that affects the entire world, that goes way beyond the surface of this remarkable calling. It is intriguing enough, fascinating enough, that Abram makes a decision – he leaves hearth and home, gathers up his belongings, and as verse four states, "went as the Lord directed him." Abram takes a risk, and in that decision, the Hebrew people, his descendants, become the chosen people, down to this day, over six thousand years later.

Brothers and sisters, Lent is a call to change. But it is first a call to *listen*, it is a call to hear the voice of God in our most ordinary circumstances. Abram's encounter with God was so ordinary that the details weren't even recorded. It just happened. This is true of us too. Do you ever read those stories in the newspaper about how couples meet each other? Most of the time, it's a really simple, often comical encounter. I met my future wife Katie while I was pursuing the girl across the hall from her room in the dormitory. When Katie found out I was a math major, she asked for some tutoring. Hmmmm.

The path to God is similar. He draws us in, usually through the influence of another person, whether it is a relative, or a friend, or maybe a coworker. We are usually invited *to* something, to take a step, to take a little risk. Maybe it's to do some service, to teach at School of Religion, to become a lector, to help a family at Christmas. Each little yes we give takes us further down the road to Christ. Each no we give keeps us on the sidelines, missing the point.

And what happens as we keep saying yes, keep walking the road, keep seeing the face of God in the road we take? Ask Peter, James, and

John. They see things that no one else has ever seen. They see power, awesome glory, and hear the voice of God the Father. More than that, they see the promised blessing foretold to Abram in our first reading – they see Jesus the Christ for what He is. Can we expect the same thing to happen to us? Maybe. It's not guaranteed, but I will tell you without hesitation that if you walk the path, you will see some amazing displays of God's glory and majesty. The key is to keep saying yes, to keep your eyes open, to keep your ears clear, to walk the path when it is convenient *and* inconvenient.

If this sounds a little dangerous, a little scary, listen to the words of Jesus. He sees his friends face down in the dirt, shivering with fear, and he says, "Rise, and do not be afraid." The encounter with God can be truly awe-inspiring, perhaps frightening. But Jesus knows exactly what it means to be a human being, exactly what it means to be afraid. He's been there, he's experienced it, he loves us too much to let it get to us. Jesus always shows us how to walk the long journey, how to keep saying yes.

So the question is: what invitation is sitting in your mailbox, your in-box, your cell phone, your voice mail, or just sitting in your brain gnawing at you? Can you listen to that invitation? Is it pulling you into a tighter relationship with God? Is it pulling you to a place that feels a little dangerous? Use this time of Lent to discern your answer – don't snap judge either way. But remember, sometimes the most ordinary things are doorways to a glimpse of the glory of God. Do not be afraid.

The Elder Son

Scripture Referenced: Lk 15:11-32

He said to him, 'My son, you are here with me always; everything I have is yours.

But now we must celebrate and rejoice, because your brother was dead and has come to life again; he was lost and has been found.'

This most beloved parable is featured on nearly every retreat master's short list, especially for men's retreats. Why is it so popular? In short, it is the story of all of us who take the spiritual journey seriously, who seek a relationship with God. The father in the story represents God, of course, and the irony is present from the very beginning. The two sons already live in God's house and although we are not told why, the younger son rebels and decides to make a clean break. We are invited to see our young, rebellious selves here and nod in understanding. Note carefully that the father does not try to stop the son, or warn him, or in any way impede his desire to leave. The father loves the son even though the son treats him rudely and selfishly.

When did you first rebel on your faith walk? It's not a question of "if", but when. A mature faith is not an inherited faith, but an owned faith, a faith that is grasped consciously and fully. When it comes to the faith journey, we apparently need to reject the gift at some point in order to grasp it later, to really make it our own. For me, this came when I went away to college. Even though I was attending a Jesuit university, I was overjoyed at my freedom and decided that Mass was not for me. Interestingly enough, I still went to Mass when I came home for the holidays, partly because I didn't want to confront my parents, and partly because something compelled me to continue the faith journey.

The younger son in the story goes off and lives a life of dissipation, as we're told. The story dramatically details the appalling crash in the young man's fortunes as he sinks to the lowest gutter of life for a Jew, feeding the pigs. The message for the spiritual journey is the same. Rejecting God's house inevitably leads to a life of emptiness and degradation, because the world cannot fill the hole in our hearts. It is incapable of doing so, even when we achieve wealth, fame, and fortune. For me at Santa Clara, it expressed itself as a loneliness, especially on Sunday evenings when the "Church kids" would go to 10 PM Mass at the Mission. I used to walk by the Church on the way to my dorm after the library closed and hear the music playing inside. Like the son in the story, I was hungry and eventually I came to my senses. When I went to Mass again after my long journey away, I was struck at how my vision had changed. What was once a boring liturgy was suddenly a celebration of thanksgiving, of Eucharist. Experiencing all of this with my new girlfriend Katie was an added bonus, and as my wife, she continues to walk the path with me to this day.

So is that it? We're in the house, we rebel, we experience the loss of God, and we come to our senses and return? Is that it? No – there's another lost son in this parable, the elder son. He represents the other extreme, the one who is already in the house of God but has grown blind to the beauty of the faith he professes. More than anyone else, we need to face the elder son in the story and check out the similarities we have with him. For the elder son has lost the joy of being with God, has fallen into a different, more subtle trap, the trap of treating the faith journey as simply another reward and punishment system, just like work and school and government and sports and politics. The elder son works in the fields and has convinced himself that his father really doesn't care about him as an individual, that his work is unappreciated, taken for granted. The faith journey to one such as this is a death march, and the reward will only come when he ultimately dies and gets to heaven, or so he thinks. This character truly believes that the road is narrow and difficult, and only a very few (himself included of course) will get there intact. His resentment at his father's treatment of his wayward brother tells us all we need to know about him -- and the fact remains that we understand his point of view perfectly.

So many of us have this elder son view of the faith journey don't we? We treat religion just like any other human endeavor, with rewards and punishments handed out in accordance with our effort and striving, or lack thereof. Not sure about that? Let's test it. You read about a convicted killer on death row who claims he's found Jesus. Your reaction? Joy? Or cynical suspicion? A shabbily dressed person of a different skin color comes into Church and sits in your pew. Your reaction? Joy at meeting an unexpected member of the body of Christ? Or fear and disgust? You hear on the news that a mosque has caught fire and burned to the ground. Your reaction? Delight that something bad has happened to one of *them*? Or sadness that misfortune has struck a fellow seeker of God?

So how does the father treat the elder son? He attempts to break through the resentment, to dismiss the reward and punishment mentality, to show the son that it is not about achievement, but about relationship. Oddly enough, the only thing that seems to matter to the Father is a reconciled son. Note what the father says, "We *had to* celebrate and rejoice…" There's no other response possible!

So what happens next? What does the elder son do? Does he go into the party? Does the father's pleading have any effect? We don't know. The story ends here because Jesus ended his story looking directly at the Pharisees, the good Church people of the day. He's doing the same thing with us now. Here's one way to connect the dots as we look at this remarkable story:

First of all, and perhaps most difficult for parents, recognize that our children need to rebel against the faith in order to test its applicability to their lives. They need to walk the younger son's journey, and we, like the patient father, must wait in readiness for their reawakening. It can take time – don't lose hope, keep watching the road. Second, if you find yourself uncomfortably relating to the older son, take a step back from the doing, judging, testing mode that permeates our world and focus on your relationship to God. If you see God as a grim, judgmental taskmaster, can you be anything but resentful at the prospect of God's immense mercy towards others who are not good, practicing Catholics? Seek God first, and in knowing him, know why this God is so loving, and join in rejoicing when anyone lost is found. God wants everyone in heaven – everyone! And finally, if you have family and friends that each represent lost younger sons and resentful older brothers, can you act the part of the Prodigal, loving father and offer reconciliation to both parties? Can you be a bridge builder rather than a side taker? Stretch out your arms to both – just like Jesus did – and realize that it can hurt. But also believe in the power of resurrection – and rejoice in the prospect…

Missionary Call

Scripture Referenced: Lk 10:1-12, 17-20

> *After this the Lord appointed seventy-two others whom he sent ahead of him in pairs to every town and place he intended to visit.*
>
> *He said to them, "The harvest is abundant but the laborers are few; so ask the master of the harvest to send out laborers for his harvest.*
>
> *Go on your way; behold, I am sending you like lambs among wolves."*

When I was in 4th grade at Sacred Heart School in Auburn, NY, I decided that I would become a missionary when I grew up. The reasons were mostly very romanticized notions of heroic sacrifice – a kind of Catholic Superman. I even went so far as to fill out a little reply card to the Maryknoll Missions. There was a hidden agenda as well – I wanted to generate some mail. As one of seven children, to have a letter come in the mail to you personally was a major event in the household. However, just like the 72 we hear about in the Gospel today, my meager attempt at missionary work generated a surprise for me too.

It's rare in the Gospels for Jesus to speak so directly and clearly. His word today is not a parable with a hidden message. This is not a challenge to the Pharisees. This is not a highly theological commentary to the Jews. These are *instructions* to the 72 going out into the world, two by two. They weren't the 12 apostles – they were everyday people. It is a useful exercise to put ourselves into their shoes. After all, we are called by our baptism to likewise go out into the world. What does Jesus tell them?

- Go out in a spirit of gentleness, peace, and humility. You will stand out as a lamb among wolves. Yes, you're in danger of being attacked, but that should not bother you. In seeming weakness lies great strength and power.
- Live simply. Money means nothing, material things mean nothing. In today's language, we speak of *detachment*, that

ability to own things with an open hand, rather than with a clenched fist.

- Share your peace freely and openly, and expect nothing in return. Notice the emphasis on peace. A peaceful person exudes peace without even trying. It's wonderful just to be in their presence.
- Accept gifts graciously. I am convinced that there is a human need to give, part of our soul-wiring. When we give people a reason to give, a goal that is laudable, people give freely of their treasure. Jesus says to tap that generosity and expect it to happen.
- Cure the sick. Jesus isn't necessarily speaking of physical healing, even though that is our first thought. Sickness takes many forms and some of the most distressing illnesses are those of the spirit. Many physically robust people are mired in resentment, jealousy, anger, greed, lust, and other ills. If you are a person of peace, you will draw people who wonder what you have and how you found it. Your witness can be a cure.
- Finally, if you are rejected, move on. Don't measure success in human terms. Sometimes our witness speaks more loudly when we leave a situation, when our absence leaves a hole. Sometimes, we need to practice the tough love inherent in the phrase, "shake off the dust from that town".

When the 72 return, they are rejoicing. To their amazement, even the demons are subject to their commands in the name of Jesus. Remember that *demons* are a catch-all explanation for any distressing sickness or condition in that era, especially a condition that seemed to steal the heart or soul of an individual. The demons are still with us today, don't kid yourself. They have different names like methamphetamine, heroin, cocaine, alcohol. Hearts and souls are seemingly stolen in other ways as well – dementia, Alzheimer's, schizophrenia. Do we truly believe that Jesus has the power to heal these conditions as well? Ask one of our healing ministers in the Church today.

Remember that Maryknoll card I sent in as a 4th grader? About six weeks later, I arrived home from school and my mother greeted me at the door. "Peter, there's someone here to meet you," she said. To my astonishment, there in the living room was a Maryknoll priest! Now understand that I grew up in the boondocks, way out in the country.

This guy came from a long way. I'm not sure what motivated him to come, but in about 15 minutes, it was pretty clear that I wasn't ready to enter the seminary anytime soon. So after another cup of coffee from my doting mother, he said good-bye and drove off.

So, was his trip wasted? No. He was planting seeds. He was watering a young shoot of faith. He was tilling soil. His name, long forgotten by me, is certainly not forgotten by Christ. It is written in heaven along with the other 72 names from today's gospel, along with the millions of people who have done likewise over the ages. Is your name written in heaven? When you do the simple things, when you witness with your peace, your simplicity, your faith, then your name is written in heaven. When you share your time with a child, pointing out God's wonders; when you share your time with an old person who doesn't seem even aware of your presence; when you give your peace to a co-worker or friend who is struggling with life; yes, your name is written in heaven. Our tendency is to downplay our potential, the possibilities open to us. We're not qualified, we're not holy enough, we're not inspired. Keep in mind that Jesus specializes in ordinary people. He does best with rejected stones. Try being a missionary this week – I'll bet you'll get a surprise or two.

Hide and Seek

Scripture Referenced: Ex 32:7-11,13-14; Lk 15:1-10

"Or what woman having ten coins and losing one would not light a lamp and sweep the house, searching carefully until she finds it?

And when she does find it, she calls together her friends and neighbors and says to them, 'Rejoice with me because I have found the coin that I lost.'

In just the same way, I tell you, there will be rejoicing among the angels of God over one sinner who repents."

Many years ago when our son was about 3 years old, he really connected with the game "hide and seek". Of course, a 3 year-old doesn't always make a very informed decision about when the game of hide and seek is appropriate. One day, he decided to play the game while we were shopping at Sears. He climbed into the middle of a circular rack of clothes and very shrewdly hopped up onto the lower rung of the rack so that we wouldn't see his feet. Of course, we were unaware that the game had started. It's amazing how fast a kid can disappear. We called for him, looked around frantically, and struggled to keep our composure. When he finally let out a whoop and appeared from the clothes rack, we were torn between immense relief and a desire to wring his little neck. Do you think that God ever feels that way about us?

The Gospel depicts stories of a shepherd and a woman who each lose something important. In this day and age, we may not think much of a sheep or a coin. We'd probably say to ourselves, "oh well, that's the way it is, easy come, easy go", but they don't. Each one goes to rather extravagant lengths to seek and recover their valuable asset. And they don't stop there! When they find what was lost, they rejoice and draw in their neighbors and friends to share their happiness. It all seems a little exaggerated and over the top, doesn't it?

It's interesting to contrast the Gospel with the first reading from Exodus. God is clearly fed up with the Israelites. After all he's done for them, they worship a golden calf?! God says to Moses, "Stand aside and let my wrath blaze up against them to consume them." Basically, he wants to ring their little necks! But Moses acts as a mediator and talks God out of it, reminding God of the promises made to Abraham, Isaac, and Jacob. This isn't the only time Moses acts as a mediator in Exodus. In fact, you often get the impression that Moses is the only thing that stands between the Israelites and sure destruction at the hands of a very impatient God.

So which God is the real God? Is God impatient and ready to strike, as Exodus indicates, or is he aching at our transgressions and prepared to track us down to the ends of the earth to bring us back to himself, as the Gospel suggests? Is God nice one minute and harsh the next? Is it possible that he is both?

So let's clear up a few things. First of all, God is always the same. He is the same God that spoke to Abraham, that spoke to Moses, that spoke to the prophets, that speaks throughout the ages. Jesus, by nature of his sonship, uniquely reveals God, not only showing us the nature of God, but showing us on a personal level how to access and yes, trust God. The God Jesus reveals is a God of tender love, mercy, and forgiveness.

So why the portrayal of a seemingly angry God in Exodus? Understand that the Israelite people were living in primitive times, among other cultures with very primitive understandings of nature and their environment. Most of their neighbors believed in many gods, in particular gods of war, fertility, sun, and moon. Given the primitive, almost childlike understanding of the world, God in turn needed to be parental, in charge, perhaps even a bit domineering to get Israel's attention. Over time, much as an adolescent grows up and begins to ignore his parents, so too did Israel drift away from God. The prophets attempted to bring Israel back to Yahweh, but due to the hard hearts of the people, their missions typically failed, with the truth each spoke only becoming clear after some foretold calamity hit. One of the characteristics of Jesus is the truly adult way He related to people. He wasn't domineering or angry (although he had his moments), but in truth he focused on grown up themes – peace, suffering, power, mercy, forgiveness, and the law. He brought a new covenant, not written on stone tablets, but written on hearts. Is it any wonder that Jesus is often called the "new Moses"?

We are made in the image of God. But the question to ask is which image? What stance do we take when we are asked to image God to others? Are we judgmental, touchy, quick to find fault? Is our mission to be parent to the world? Sometimes we need to act in that capacity, particularly if we are relating to children, or, to adults who act like children. But that's a very limiting approach in the long run. Most people we encounter are not children, and quite frankly, resent being treated as such. Do we have the ability to image a God for adults, to image a God of forgiveness, peace, and love? That's not easy to do, but that's also why it's so critical for us to get to know that God. If we remain stuck with God the parent, we'll miss God the friend and lover. How do we find this God? Follow Jesus. He is both the image of the loving God and the pathway to Him. Ask him to enter your heart.

In the end, we all play hide and seek with God. In fact, I'll bet that some of you out there are hiding from God right now. It may be a game to us, but God is deadly earnest in his pursuit. He may seem like an angry parent at times; he may seem like a worried lover at other times. If you're hiding, ask why. Are you afraid of what he'll ask of you? Are you afraid to commit? He offers gifts of healing if we simply accept the relationship. He wants to find us as desperately as we want to find our lost children.

If we're not hiding from him, that's a good thing. But he's asking a favor of us – can we help him in the search for the lost? Can we be his eyes and ears, looking for clues and listening for the rustle of hidden hearts? Do you know the best part about helping God find the lost? We get to be part of the big banquet when he celebrates who's been found. I think they call that *heaven*. Come to the banquet.

Sons Three and Four

Scripture Referenced: Mt 21:28-32

"What is your opinion? A man had two sons. He came to the first and said, 'Son, go out and work in the vineyard today.'

He said in reply, 'I will not,' but afterwards he changed his mind and went.

The man came to the other son and gave the same order. He said in reply, 'Yes, sir,' but did not go.

Which of the two did his father's will?" They answered, "The first."

Coming as I do from a large family, I can relate to Jesus' story today about the two brothers. One of them says he'll do his Father's will, but reneges and does something else. The other says he won't do his Father's will, but thinks better of it, and does it eventually. Jesus forces his listeners to pick which one of the brothers is the better, and sure enough, they pick the one who starts out saying no, but ends up working in the vineyard after all. But, did you know that there's a third brother in the story that Jesus doesn't mention?

One fine summer morning, as my father headed off to work, he asked my older brother and I to wash the family station wagon. My brother was 11, I was 9, and we had anticipated a day playing baseball and goofing off, which of course, is the purpose of summer vacation. But we knew enough to say yes, we would, and so off to work my Dad went. We spent the day playing baseball, swimming at the lake, and goofing off, until it was suddenly 5 PM and my brother remembered our promise to wash the car. At my panicked look, he said calmly, "We'll just hose it down – he won't know the difference." So we quickly unreeled the hose, sprayed water over the car, sprayed water at each other (of course), and then went in the house to watch cartoons.

My Dad arrived home a short while later, strode into the house, walked into the family room, and with a flourish, turned off the TV. He turned to look at us and I knew that we were in big trouble. Not only did we have to wash the car, we had to vacuum it out and wash all of the windows inside and out with Windex. Dinner was late for us that evening. Throughout it all, my brother kept muttering, "who told on us?" It never occurred to either of us that it was possible to tell the difference between a wet car and a clean car.

So the story Jesus tells has a 3rd brother that didn't make it into the Bible. This brother says he'll do his Father's will and *does* it – but with such a sour disposition, and a lousy attitude, and so poorly, that it is worse than not doing the work at all. This is the indifferent brother, the apathetic brother, the lazy brother. This, dear people, is how so many of *us* respond to the Father's request to work in the vineyard.

The problem with this kind of apathetic yes to the Father is that the job just doesn't get done, does it? And we're not kidding anyone. Eventually, the Father will stop asking us, stop looking to us for help, and when we meet Him face to face on our last day, he'll ask a very chilling question, "Do I know you?"

So, enough with the guilt trip. Let's probe into what it means to work in the Father's vineyard. What did Jesus mean by this? Obviously, it's a metaphor – the vineyard is often used as a stand-in for the world. The master of the vineyard is God, who has planted the vines and expects a harvest. We, who dare to call ourselves his children, are to work the vineyard, maximizing its yield. Our job is to weed, water, prune, pick off dead leaves, nurture baby plants, pick the ripened fruit, and bring it in for the feast. Likewise, our job on this earth is to help each other, provide support, bind our wounds, drive off evil, raise healthy children, give of our time, our talent, and our gifts to maximize the number of people to join in the feast.

So, what is your ministry? Quick definition: a ministry is some task, work, or activity you do purely for the sake of God, for the sake of the vineyard, so to speak. It could be acting as a lector, or as a Eucharistic minister, or visiting the sick, the homebound, the prisoner – these are classic ministries. But it could be something else. Parents are spending a huge amount of time raising young children – this is just as much a ministry if you see it as giving glory to God. Whatever you do that is primarily motivated by the desire to please God is a ministry.

Now the reality is that ministries can grow stale and unappealing over time. We age, our lives change, our circumstances are different. Rather than becoming a 3rd brother and continuing to act in a ministry without any joy or sense of purpose, maybe the time has come to consider a new ministry. God is saying "Hey, thanks for weeding the vineyard for so long. How about planting some new vines? Or picking some grapes?" My first ministry was teaching 7th grade school of religion – many years ago. I turned into a 3rd brother pretty quickly – fortunately, I was able to find other ministries to replace it, ministries that fit me much better.

There is a fourth brother in the Gospel, of course. The "say one thing, do another" first brother, the "say no, but repent" second brother, and the apathetic third brother are each less than ideal in the eyes of any father, let alone God the Father. What about the fourth brother? He hears God's request to work in the vineyard, says yes, and goes out with alacrity, skill, and enthusiasm. That brother is best exemplified by Jesus himself, right? He's the one any father would love the most.

My apologies for using nothing but "brother" language throughout this homily, but the analogy Jesus uses carries through so nicely. I certainly don't mean to slight our sisters in Christ. Your ministries, your challenges, your contributions are equally important in God's eyes.

To summarize then:

- If you don't have a ministry, you're not listening to God's command to work the vineyard. Listen, assess your talents, and start doing something purely for the sake of God.
- If you have a ministry and you love it, you love how you are when you are in the midst of it, then you're definitely on the right track. Well done!
- If you do have a ministry and it's grown stale, take a look at other ministries and try something new! As C.S. Lewis says, you may be surprised by joy.
- Above all, keep listening to God's requests, to his nudging. Depending on your circumstances, you might be asked to do more than one ministry. Yikes.

Listen, search, love, act – you won't regret any of it.

Chapter 4 – Who is Jesus?

We want Jesus to follow our agenda, our recipe for making the world better. Jesus is all about healing, forgiveness and inclusiveness. Jesus cares so much for you that he will seek you out, even as you are walking away. He will address your deepest longing, your deepest fear, and shed light on your darkest places. When you ask him to stay with you because you are thirsty and hungering for more, he will stay with you. Once you recognize Jesus, you never need to be alone again. He's right here.

The Real Thing

Scripture Referenced: Is 35:1-6,10; Mt 11:2-11

Say to those whose hearts are frightened: Be strong, fear not! Here is your God, he comes with vindication; With divine recompense he comes to save you.

Then will the eyes of the blind be opened, the ears of the deaf be cleared;

Then will the lame leap like a stag, then the tongue of the dumb will sing.

A number of years ago, Coca-Cola came out with an ad campaign featuring the slogan "Coke, the real thing!" Do you remember that? If so, you're probably over 40 – that ad came out in 1969. Ouch. But what was Coke trying to say with that ad campaign? In short, Coke was concerned about all of those impostor colas out there, the Shastas, RC Colas, Pepsi-Colas, and the like who were stealing market share from Coca-Cola. Basically, if you weren't drinking Coca-Cola, you were imbibing an imposter!

John the Baptist, after a long run as a famous prophet, is decaying in jail, with an uncertain, but probably bad future ahead. Following the long tradition of Jewish prophets, John has challenged the people to repent, to start anew, or face the wrath of God. We're not entirely clear on the relationship between John and Jesus – the gospels are vague. We infer that they are second cousins, but we have no idea how much time they spent together, if any, up to the time Jesus is baptized by John. Once John is imprisoned, Jesus launches his ministry in earnest, and it is apparent that John's followers are wondering if Jesus is the heir apparent, the next prophet to emerge and carry the flag of repentance and warning.

The problem? Jesus isn't following the script. He's preaching forgiveness, the kingdom of God, the Beatitudes. This doesn't sound like good ol' prophecy in the line of Elijah, Jeremiah, and Ezekiel. John the Baptist, a *saint*, a *prophet*, is confused. So, John's followers go to Jesus and ask the Coca-Cola question, "are you the real thing?" It sounds a bit insulting, doesn't it? If Jesus says *yes*, he seems to be self-serving; if he says *no*, then he's claiming to be an impostor. So Jesus simply presents the evidence, much as a good lawyer would. Look – the blind see, the deaf hear, the lame walk, lepers are cleansed, the dead are raised! Come to your own conclusion. But why is this compelling evidence? John's followers were quite familiar with our first reading from Isaiah today. Do you recall what was said?

"Here is your God, he comes with vindication; with divine recompense he comes to save you. Then will the eyes of the blind be opened, the ears of the deaf be cleared; then will the lame leap like a stag, then the tongue of the mute will sing."

Believe me, they got the picture!

So here's the question for you. Who do you expect to show up on Christmas? What kind of a Messiah are *you* expecting? Bear with me a moment. Let's say that I was to tell you that Jesus Christ was going to walk through that door in five minutes. What would you expect him to look like? In this time? In this place? Think about it. What would you expect? What if Jesus said to you personally, "Friend, what do you want me to do for you right now?" Some of you might say, "heal my mother". Some might say, "stop the war in Iraq." Some might say, "let the Chargers win today". Some might say, "take me to heaven right now". Some might say, "send this person or that person to hell where they belong". What would *you* ask of Jesus?

Are you ready for his answer? Here it is. Jesus says, "I have come to give sight to the blind, cleanse the lepers, make the outcast presentable, make the lame to walk, open the ears of the deaf, and raise the dead." Does your request qualify? Are you in synch with my mission? If so, your wish is granted. Otherwise, I'm sorry, no.

If Jesus' answer is disappointing to you, you are not alone. John's disciples were probably disappointed too. We want Jesus to follow our agenda, our recipe for making the world better. Jesus is all about healing, forgiveness and inclusiveness. You see, Jesus not only heals, but he makes things whole, he brings nature back into harmony, he calms the storm. Jesus gives us a taste of heaven – there's no doubt that everyone in heaven will be truly whole, physically, spiritually, and emotionally. This is why Jesus says that the least in the kingdom of heaven is greater than John. They are whole. We celebrate the hope of that destiny today.

Jesus wants everyone to be in heaven, everyone to be whole, everyone to be happy that everyone else is there. If your idea of heaven is everyone *except*....then you've got some soul work to do. We have nine days to go. Jesus is open to your pain, your brokenness. Ask him to heal you, and oh by the way, heal everyone else too. Heaven is big enough for everyone. Can you handle that? Ask Jesus to come into your heart today, he's the real thing.

Innocence and Forgiveness

Scripture Referenced: Lk 22:14-23:56

> *But Peter said, "My friend, I do not know what you are talking about." Just as he was saying this, the cock crowed, and the Lord turned and looked at Peter; and Peter remembered the word of the Lord, how he had said to him, "Before the cock crows today, you will deny me three times."*
>
> *He went out and began to weep bitterly.*

Each year we hear the Passion proclaimed and each year we react with a sort of stunned silence. The sheer drama of the reading pulls us in – we know the story, but since it's a little different among the four gospel authors, we're not exactly certain what's coming next, what little detail will be uniquely offered. This year we hear Luke's account, and there are several distinctive aspects to his version of events. A couple of scenes stand out. In the other three accounts of the Passion, Pilate is the main judge, but Luke tells us that since Jesus is from Galilee, Pilate dictates that Jesus be brought before Herod, the governor of Galilee who was in Jerusalem for the Passover. So once again, as it was 33 years before, Jesus finds himself subject to the whims of a governor named Herod. Herod is especially delighted to meet Jesus, because he "hoped to see Jesus perform some kind of sign", that is, perform a miracle. For those of you familiar with the rock musical, *Jesus Christ Superstar*, there's a marvelous line in Herod's song to Jesus.

> *"So, you are the Christ. You're the great Jesus Christ.*
> *Prove to me that you're no fool; walk across my swimming pool.*
> *If you do that for me, then I'll let you go free. Come on, King of the Jews.."*

And then, at the end of the song, as Jesus remains stoically silent, Herod sums up his view of things quite well:

> *"Take him away. He's got nothing to say!*
> *Get out you King of the Jews!*
> *Get out of my life!"*

At least we know where Herod stands. But of all the unique qualities of Luke's version of the Passion (and there are many more), perhaps the one that stands out the most is how Luke handles Peter's denial of Jesus. During the last supper, Peter claims that he is prepared to go to prison and die with Jesus, a typically boastful statement. You can almost see Jesus shaking his head as he tells Peter, "before the cock crows this day, you will deny three times that you know me."

And of course, soon afterward, in the very courtyard of the house of the high priest, in the very courtyard of the house where Jesus is being held, Peter is challenged and three times denies he knows the Lord. The cock crows. And here is Luke with a particularly striking detail. *The Lord turned and looked at Peter.* Is it possible that Jesus actually overheard the whole exchange? That he was witness to the cowardly act by his number one friend and first lieutenant? That he heard the first Pope claim to the world, "I do not know him"?

We tend to focus on the physical suffering of Jesus at Calvary. It's not surprising that we do. After all, the gruesome torture that is crucifixion has fascinated and repulsed us for centuries. Mel Gibson's movie *The Passion of the Christ* seemed to delight in showing every agonizing detail. But it is interesting to note that none of the Gospel writers spend much time describing the crucifixion. They are very matter of fact about it. Luke says simply, "they crucified him and the criminals there, one on his right, the other on his left." No grisly details describing the cross, the nails, the blood, the groans. Ever wonder why not?

Have you ever been wrongly accused of something? Maybe something small, maybe something big? I remember one time when I was about 10 years old. Some friends of mine and I were making mud balls and throwing them at each other. Hey, it's a guy thing. Anyway, a couple of my friends came up with a brilliant idea – let's throw them at a car driving by. So they did – splattering the car pretty good. I just stood off to the side and watched. To our amazement, the car turned in the driveway of my house. The driver got out of the car, walked up to the front door, and calmly rang the doorbell. My Mom answered and the driver pointed us out as the culprits. Despite my loud claims of innocence and appeals to my friends for validation, I was held accountable and was forced to apologize to the man and clean his car. I was furious for weeks at the injustice of it all.

Now take that amusing little story and make it life and death. Knowing your complete innocence, you are subjected to a mock trial, beaten up, and sentenced to death. Not only that, but all of your friends run for the hills as soon as you are arrested. There is nothing you can do about it, nothing at all. What makes the crucifixion of Jesus a shocking event is not the physical pain – after all, many in that day and age were crucified – but the fact that an utterly innocent person was the victim. Not only is Jesus innocent, but he must suffer with the knowledge that he is forsaken by virtually everyone he knows, by virtually everyone he has gathered as his followers – there is no one who will speak up on his behalf. Where are all the people he cured, where are his hand-picked disciples, where is the Roman centurion whose daughter he brought back from death? Where is Lazarus?

In the midst of this utter failure of everything he fought for, abandoned and alone, Jesus shows us why he is the Christ. He ties himself to the Father of the Prodigal Son. He ties himself to the woman caught in adultery. He stares at the worst that the powers of darkness can throw at him – the physical pain and the even more horrible psychological pain of abandonment, and he says, "Father, forgive them, they know not what they do." He models what the world needs to see and understand, now more than ever. When we are hurt, when we are unjustly treated, we have a choice. We can take the easy road and play the victim, loudly proclaiming our innocence and passing the pain to as many people as we can find. Or, we can forgive and stop the chain of violence, stop the angry reprisals, stop the war. To maintain peace, to truly change the world for the better, sometimes we have to give up the right to be right. Sometimes we have to accept no payment for our suffering. Sometimes we have to let God be the judge. Pray about this as we walk our Holy Week. Please.

On the Road

Scripture Referenced: Lk 24:13-35

> *Now that very day two of them were going to a village seven miles from Jerusalem called Emmaus, and they were conversing about all the things that had occurred.*
>
> *And it happened that while they were conversing and debating, Jesus himself drew near and walked with them, but their eyes were prevented from recognizing him.*

The road to Emmaus, a story of revelation that is one of the most beloved in the gospels, is especially relevant because it is a journey we all take, and not just once, in our walk of faith. Let's take a closer look.

Our two main characters are named Cleopas and... hmm, no name at all. Who is this second disciple? We don't even know if it's a man or a woman. So, just as we did at Easter with the *beloved disciple*, put yourself in this person's sandals and be in the story. Let the other disciple be *you*. You two are leaving Jerusalem, heading for a place called Emmaus. To this day, no one knows where Emmaus is or was – it's simply a place seven miles from Jerusalem. What is important is that Emmaus is *not Jerusalem*, it is a different place. Symbolically and actually, you two are leaving town, getting out, washing your hands of this whole affair, heading back to the farm. You are discouraged, disappointed, had-it-up-to-here.

Then Jesus shows up and joins you. Luke says that "their eyes were prevented from recognizing him." What a strange statement! Does this makes sense? Why wouldn't you recognize Jesus? There are some very good reasons why you wouldn't. First of all, you definitely don't expect him to be there. He's dead, remember? But more importantly, you're wrapped up in yourself, in your sorrow, you're completely self-absorbed at this moment. I know that when I'm like this, I wouldn't recognize my best friend.

Worse than this, this stranger seems clueless as to what has happened recently. He asks the seemingly innocent question, "what sort of things have happened?" So you and Cleopas lay it all out – how Jesus was your great hope, the one to redeem Israel, how the chief priests and scribes handed him over to be crucified. And even more amazing, how the rumor is rampant that Jesus is actually alive, although no one has seen him. It's all just a bit too much, isn't it?

Then the stranger speaks. He seems a little exasperated, calls you foolish, and begins to explain how it really is. How the Scripture should be interpreted, how the Christ had to suffer and die, how it was all foretold. As you walk with him, you begin to understand more and more, and your spirit begins to lift. You look at him more closely and a part of you deep inside is breaking open, beginning to see something new. Time flies and suddenly, you've reached the outskirts of Emmaus. You stop outside the inn where you intend to stay. He gives the impression that he has farther to travel, but you insist that he join you for dinner – "stay with us, for it is nearly evening and the day is almost over." A part of you that has nothing to do with physical hunger wants more.

So the stranger joins you for dinner. What comes next is no surprise in Luke's gospel – Jesus is always having dinner with people, and sure enough, when he blesses the bread and breaks it, and passes it to you and Cleopas, the surge of joy that has been building up in you erupts and you suddenly see Jesus in this stranger. As soon as you do, Jesus vanishes. Not in a scary spooky way, but in a simple gentle way – he has moved on. You and Cleopas are so excited, you can barely sit still. You simply must rejoin the community and tell them what has happened, so off you go in the dark, retracing those seven miles back to Jerusalem. Quite a story!

A number of years ago, I attended a religious education conference and had a taste of that experience. My wife and I attended a talk given by Fr. Richard Rohr, a Franciscan priest. I was at a time in my life when I was searching for ways to better know and understand God's will in my life. Fr. Rohr's topic was men's spirituality, and for an hour and a half, I was mesmerized. I felt that God was speaking directly to me amidst the 400 people in the room. It's not that Fr. Rohr was God – he simply has a gift of teaching that clarifies and focuses the gospel. At the end of the presentation, we drove home and Katie and I talked the entire way. My heart was burning within me, and thoughts were flying through my head. It's amazing we weren't in a car accident, but the Lord watched over us. Over the years since then, I've had other similar experiences when God's spirit has taken hold of my soul. Has that ever happened to you?

The road to Emmaus story tells us how it can happen to you. Some key points to note:

- Whenever you feel lost and confused, Jesus is likely to show up.
- Unfortunately, he may be hard to recognize. That's not His fault!
- He'll come to you as a stranger, or as an invitation, or as an odd encounter, an interruption. In my case, the only reason that I went to Rohr's talk that day is because a friend of a friend told me that I might enjoy listening to him. I went because the room he was speaking at was close to the parking lot.
- During the encounter, something deep inside you will recognize that this is important, but you won't be able to say why.
- The aftermath is characterized by incredible energy, a need to talk it out, and a compelling need to share the story with others.
- You'll want to take it to the next step. You'll want to replicate the experience, to seek out more depth. This is understandable and just what God has in mind.

The road to Emmaus is actually a love story, isn't it? Jesus cares so much for you that he will seek you out, even as you are walking away. He will address your deepest longing, your deepest fear, and shed light on your darkest places. When you ask him to stay with you because you are thirsty and hungering for more, he will stay with you. He's present in the breaking of the bread, which to us Catholics is very obviously a reference to the Eucharist. Once you recognize Jesus, you never need to be alone again. He's right here.

Are you on the road to Emmaus right now? Don't be afraid. Jesus is about to join you.

Stephen

Scripture Referenced: Acts 6:1-7; Jn 14:1-12

> *Thomas said to him, "Master, we do not know where you are going; how can we know the way?"*
>
> *Jesus said to him, "I am the way and the truth and the life. No one comes to the Father except through me.*
>
> *If you know me, then you will also know my Father."*

I would be remiss as a deacon if I didn't mention our first reading from Acts. This passage is the biblical basis for the ministry and ordination of deacons, and I am indeed honored to continue in this tradition. Note that the reason the apostles appointed deacons was because the people were complaining. So, if you want more deacons around here, you know what to do! One of the seven men ordained that day was named Stephen, a man filled with faith and the Holy Spirit. I'd like to tell you about another Stephen today.

My brother Stephen was first diagnosed with colon cancer in 1994, at the age of 38. He was operated upon, and although the doctors claimed that they had "got it all", there was always the nagging doubt that maybe they hadn't. Six years later, in late 2000, evidence of a massive tumor in his abdomen confirmed that the cancer had returned with a vengeance, and this time, there was no cure. Stephen's health declined slowly over the period of about one year – a long time to die. As the news spread through our family, we were all faced with questions, questions that perfectly mirror the questions of the apostles today. What do you mean you're going? Where are you going? How do we go with you? We don't understand. Just show us the Father and we'll be fine. For Stephen, the questions were similar. How could the cancer return? How much time do I have? Will death be painful? Should we pray for a miracle? Where is God in all of this?

Jesus speaks words of incredible tenderness and hope to the apostles. Do not let your hearts be troubled. I am preparing a place for you. I am the way, the truth, and the life. If you see me, you see the Father. These words are comforting in the abstract, but do they hold water when the reality of death, our own death or someone we love, is staring us in the face? Can we hang our fate on these words? Are they believable in our every day pain and loss? Are they credible?

When Stephen was diagnosed with Stage 4 cancer, the ending was inevitable, even if the path of the disease was unclear. During this time, more than once, we prayed that God would take him quickly, would spare him a long decline, a painful end. The irony was that the days leading to his death were not simply necessary, they were precious. He needed those days, we the family (Mom, Dad, brothers and sisters) needed those days, and although the decline was gradual, God needed those days to polish my brother's rough edges and prepare him for the room that Jesus was making ready for him. You see, my brother was addicted to drugs, and this demon inside of him was not going to let him go without a fight.

As the last year of his life proceeded, Stephen grew in prayer and openness to God's working in him. He had the benefit of many people praying for him, and the support and care of a loving family around him. But the battle was still fierce, and we often felt that we were losing. But God is infinitely patient and gentle, and if there is ever an argument against euthanasia, it is this – never interrupt God's work in progress. Euthanasia is a form of abortion, isn't it? It just takes place at the other end of the racetrack we call life. My brother needed every day of his long fall. He needed to see God in himself and in those around him. He needed to see the demon of addiction and kick it out of his life. As my niece so aptly put it, "no one should meet their Maker stoned". Fighting addiction is messy business, painful to witness and painful to sustain. Stephen's journey to sobriety took us all for a ride, marked by prayer, tears, disharmony, and conflict. One day, close to the end, Stephen finally came to the light and told my sister that he didn't want or need drugs anymore. He died shortly before Christmas on December 23rd, 2001.

Jesus is the way, the truth and the life. We are His arms, his legs, his eyes, and his hands on this earth. That makes us his instruments – that makes us the road builders for the way, the truth, and the life. How? One of the strongest mandates of our faith is to comfort the dying. What this means, among other things, is to give people a chance to see how much God loves them. A deacon friend of mine, Herb, is active in hospice ministry. Herb was visiting a dying man named Bill one afternoon. Herb asked Bill if he would like to make a confession to a priest. Bill told Herb his story, ending with the statement, "It's too late for me. I've rejected God and He knows it." Herb watched as Bill caressed and stroked his pet dog. Inspired, Herb said to Bill, "is there anything that this dog could do that would make you love him any less?" The man's eyes widened. Herb went on, "Aren't you more precious in God's eyes than even this dog?" Bill paused for a moment and said, "call the priest." Herb simply showed the man the way to Jesus.

In Celtic spirituality, there is the notion of a "thin place". This simply refers to those times when the veil between this physical life and the life of the spirit is so thin as to be transparent. When we're in the presence of a dying person, we're on holy ground. If we are in prayerful watchfulness, prayerful awareness, we often see through the veil. The dying person is shifting between these planes of existence, and that is a privileged place to be. Don't fear it – it is a rare gift to share.

After my brother Stephen died, my mother was visited by a friend, a woman who is a mystic. In her prayer life, this woman often has visions of people that are quite remarkable. My mother, knowing this, asked Margaret if her son, my brother was OK, was in heaven. Margaret smiled and said to my Mom, "Stephen is very busy up there. He's preparing a room for you."

I am the way, the truth and the life. Can *you* hang your fate on these words of Jesus? This is our Easter hope. The theme of Pope Benedict's U.S. visit is "Christ our Hope". These are simply nice sounding words until you really need it. My family needed it. Perhaps you've been there too.

Can you can hang your fate on these words of Jesus? Yes, you can!!

Two Saints, Two Journeys

Scripture Referenced: Acts 12:1-11; Mt 16:13-19

He said to them, "But who do you say that I am?"

Simon Peter said in reply, "You are the Messiah, the Son of the living God."

Jesus said to him in reply, "Blessed are you, Simon son of Jonah. For flesh and blood has not revealed this to you, but my heavenly Father."

Today is a bit unusual. Rather than celebrate a typical Sunday of Ordinary Time, we are celebrating the feast day of St. Peter and St. Paul. Their feast is always on June 29th, and considering the importance of this feast in the life of our Church, we allow the feast to take center stage if it happens to fall on a Sunday, as it does this year. As a child, since I was named for St. Peter, it always bothered me that I had to share a feast day with St. Paul! Why couldn't I have my own? From earliest Church memory, these two have shared a feast day. Do you remember how feast days for saints are created? A saint's feast day is the day that they die, the date that they enter heaven, a date of death and new life simultaneously. Does this mean that two of our Church's greatest saints died on the same day? Were martyred on the same day? It is entirely possible. Historians are fairly certain that they both died in the same year, 64 AD, at the hands of the emperor Nero in Rome. What a disaster that must have seemed for the small Christian church of the time! What a tribute to the Holy Spirit that even that calamity could not stop the spread of Jesus Christ to the world!

Peter and Paul came to knowledge of Christ in very different ways, didn't they? It is instructive to consider their stories and ask the question, which one reflects my journey? What does it say about God? About our relationship with Christ? What does this awareness call us to do?

Peter's understanding of who Jesus Christ is comes about gradually. Peter himself is a bit impetuous, and he has a habit of leaping first and looking at what he had done after the fact. He acts, and then thinks about it. Acts, thinks. The pattern is revealed again and again. Peter leaps out of the boat to walk on the water to Jesus, and then once out on the churning sea, thinks about what he is doing! As today's Gospel tells us, Peter proclaims Jesus to be the Christ, but then thinks about it, and less than 4 verses later, tells Jesus he should reconsider this journey to Jerusalem to die on the cross. In the courtyard of Caiaphas, Peter denies Jesus three times. At the cock's crow, he suddenly realizes what he has done, and weeps bitterly at his cowardice. In our first reading from Acts, Peter is freed miraculously from prison, but thinks it is all a dream. Then Peter "recovers his senses" and realizes what has happened. It seems that Peter is forever recovering his senses after something important happens.

Are you like Peter? Is your faith life a continual motion of action, occurrence, and contemplation? Do you mostly get it after the fact? Do you need to look in the rear view mirror and see the signposts, the evidence of God working in your life, to suddenly realize that he's been walking and talking with you all along? Is this your faith life?

Or are you like Paul? Paul is not the least bit uncertain about anything. He is convinced that he has the answer, the right way to do things. Yes, our friend Paul has an ego the size of Mt Tabor. He is well educated, a scholar of the Jewish law, a Pharisee, a Roman citizen, a king of his world. He is going to single-handedly rid the world of these Jews for Jesus, these violators of the Law with a capital L. But Jesus has a different idea. He shocks Paul, knocks him down, stunning him completely. It's as if Jesus takes Paul back to the point of birth. Paul is left helpless, blind, barely able to walk. Paul's been reset - <Ctrl> <Alt> <Del> !!

Unlike Peter, Paul is not the least bit impetuous. Paul gets zapped by the Lord, stops everything, and thinks it over very carefully and deeply. After his conversion experience, Paul goes out into modern day Turkey and disappears for 14 years. He ponders the meaning of his life, his focus on Jewish law, and the significance of this powerful encounter with the risen Lord Jesus. When he is ready, he acts. And he acts with power, authority, certainty, heading straight into the lion's den, the Jewish community of the time. When his overtures there are stymied, he turns to the Gentiles and takes the message of Christ to the world. Thank God for Paul!

So are you like Peter, or are you like Paul? Despite my namesake, I'm probably more like Paul. I needed some surprises, some aha moments to get me going. Whichever person you resemble, however, it's not a question of one being better than the other. Whether you act first, and think about it later, or think first, and then act – the key point here is that Jesus takes them just as they are. Jesus doesn't ask either of them to become someone they aren't. He simply inspires them to use the gifts they already have, to become the best men that they can be. To become *like* Christ while still being Peter and Paul *individually*.

This is exactly what Jesus wants to do with us, with me and you. When I was considering the diaconate, I was concerned that Jesus wanted me to become a different person. I was afraid that I would lose something even though gaining a closer relationship with Him. It would be zero-sum game – something comes in, something else must go. But it's not like that at all. What Jesus does is take the best parts of us and make them better – he makes our dim little light shine brighter. I've still got all of that other stuff in me, stuff that I like and don't like. I'm still a work in progress. I suspect that you are too.

Today our Church launches the jubilee year of St. Paul – Paul was born 2000 years ago. Many of us are ambivalent about Paul – his letters seem dense at times, hard to understand. He can seem arrogant and his certainty about things is off-putting. But he also has written some of the most beautiful prose in history. Do yourself a favor in the coming year. Buy a good book on Paul – a good commentary. Or see a movie about Paul. Read his letters to the Romans or the Corinthians. Read them straight through. Get into his head a bit; see how his mind works. Despite the denseness of his prose, the love he has for his small Christian communities is really quite touching. Share what you learn with others.

So, whether your faith walk is more like Peter or more like Paul, in the end they both gave their all to Christ. Can you do the same? Do you know all *about* Jesus or, do you *know* Jesus? Is he a model to be copied or a life to be lived? Who do *you* say that he is?

The Nature of Truth

Scripture Referenced: Dn 7:13-14; Rev 1:5-8; Jn 18:33-37

As the visions during the night continued, I saw One like a son of man coming, on the clouds of heaven; When he reached the Ancient One and was presented before him, He received dominion, glory, and kingship; nations and peoples of every language serve him. His dominion is an everlasting dominion that shall not be taken away, his kingship shall not be destroyed.

Today we celebrate the feast of Christ the King. As a Church feast, it's been around only since 1925, which means the feast is as old as my mother – a connection she might not truly appreciate. But let me ask you - does the feast of Christ the KING make you feel a little uneasy? Is it a little jarring? Didn't Christ actively avoid the very suggestion of becoming a king? Then why do we celebrate the feast of *Christ the King*? What is this feast supposed to teach us?

First of all, this word "king" is very problematic, especially for us Americans. The original 13 colonies rebelled against a tyrant king, and vigorously rejected a monarchy as our form of government. Today, kings seem mildly anachronistic, old-fashioned, and at best kind of quaint. Think about how we use the word king in our language. There are millions of references to the word king in our world – think of King Kong, the LA Kings, and of course, Burger King. At worst, the word king embodies everything we fear – having to subject ourselves to the rule of a single, autocratic human being with all of his foibles. *King* has a lot of baggage.

So what do the readings tell us? The first reading from Daniel has the prophet telling us of his vision of the end times, when "one like a son of man" (which is simply an ancient phrase meaning a human being) is presented before God and given dominion over all the universe. His kingship will not be destroyed. Elements of the book of Daniel read very much like the book of Revelation, and sure enough, our second reading from that most mystifying of books has Jesus coming down amid the clouds in everlasting glory. These visions of Christ are quite grand, and we are left a bit awestruck by the language. And, I would venture to say, it is a bit hard to relate to such a grandiose person. Are we supposed to grovel in the dust? Or run for the hills? Is that what Jesus wants?

Notice the gospel reading now. The Church Fathers chose this reading very carefully. In stark contrast to the readings from Daniel and Revelation, we are thrust into the middle of John's depiction of the Passion. Here is Jesus, scourged, beaten up, crowned with thorns, being questioned by the Roman procurator Pilate, who seems to hold all the cards. Pilate is clearly interested in this Jesus person, who dares to speak back to him man to man. Pilate presses Jesus to incriminate himself, to have Jesus claim to be a king, thereby allowing Pilate to crucify him for treason. But Jesus does not fall for it – he carefully defines his kingdom as one that "does not belong to this world". So you are a king! Pilate claims. Jesus again refuses to claim the title, but goes on to define who his subjects are – *anyone committed to the truth*. The reading ends there, but if you go home and read the next verse, we hear Pilate asking cynically, "and what is truth?"

Here is the crux of the reading. Pilate sees truth as "relative", something that is defined by those in power to intimidate and control those who are subject to it. Truth is whatever the political power says it is. However, truth to Jesus is not relative – it is absolute! There is no deception in God. God's truth is so clear, so right, so loving that it shines like a beacon of light to those who seek it. If we allow ourselves to become a child of the light, as St. Paul encourages, we begin to see the world as God sees it. Sometimes the light shows us great suffering and sin, sometimes the light shows us greatness in action, but whatever it shines on, the truth is shown in all of its stark simplicity. This is why Jesus is called the light of the world. He is the ultimate in truth, the king of truth if you will.

But, if we are to accept Jesus as King of Truth, we need to do a little soul searching. Like many of you, I have some trouble with authority. (You may wonder why I became a deacon in the Catholic Church! Another day, another homily.) As children, we are kings of our universe – with wonderful, loving servants called parents who feed us, clothe us, and hug us. Not bad. But as we approach adulthood, we demand our independence and stride off to conquer the world as rugged individuals.

This is especially true for men. Acknowledging anyone as better than we are is downright painful. So accepting Jesus as king of truth is a matter of humility as much as a matter of understanding. This is a good reason to have a feast – to remind ourselves that we are not gods.

To be committed to truth is also a big responsibility. There are many people who are more than happy to tell you what the truth is. The media engine continually defines the world in ways that allow us to dispense with a thoughtful response, to simply shut up and accept. Just two weeks ago, the Catholic bishops gathered in Maryland and re-emphasized certain church teachings, particularly the Church's prohibition on artificial means of birth control. The press immediately noted that American Catholics don't agree with this teaching. I was struck by the response of Bishop Braxton of Illinois, "The Catholic Church articulates what we believe to be true, and we don't stop believing what's true because it's statistically unpopular." You may have difficulty with any number of Church teachings, and that doesn't mean that you are in sin. God desires us to use our intellect and to seek the truth, as uncomfortable as that may be. The key question is -- are we humble enough to allow a truth to enter our lives when we don't like it very much? This is what it means to be a subject in Christ's kingdom of truth.

So what else is it like to be in Christ's kingdom, to be his subject? I'll leave you with two observations. First of all, if you truly turn your life over to Christ and let him lead you by His truth, your life will be very exciting, very interesting, and very surprising. We are told that God writes straight with crooked lines. Expect a wild, exhilarating ride. Second observation – life with Christ will also lead you to places of great pain, sometimes your own pain, but often the sharing in the suffering of others who need you to bring Christ there.

Brothers and sisters, we ultimately celebrate the feast of Christ the King because of the invitation veiled in the title. Who is Christ? Why is he a king? Why should he be my king? Shall I seek the truth? If I seek the truth, I will find the ultimate good king, the King of Truth. And the truth, as we have been told, will set you free. Seek Him.

Integrity

Scripture Referenced: Col 1:12-20; Lk 23:35-43

He is the image of the invisible God, the firstborn of all creation.

For in him were created all things in heaven and on earth, the visible and the invisible, whether thrones or dominions or principalities or powers; all things were created through him and for him.

He is before all things, and in him all things hold together.

Picture yourself in the doctor's office. The doctor sits down and says to you, "I'm sorry, friend, but you have a disease that will kill you in 7 days. There's nothing you can do about it. I suggest you put your affairs in order." So there you sit. Do you have the picture? What do you do? The Good Thief on the cross next to Jesus had mere hours to live. The bad thief likewise had just hours to live. They react differently to the inevitable, to the death sentence.

Christ the King is a feast day marked by readings of incredible irony and contradiction. Our second reading, Paul's letter to the Colossians, which actually predates the Gospel, extols Jesus as the firstborn of all creation, one who is before all things, and in whom all things are held together. All things are reconciled through Jesus, both in earth and in heaven. You can't get much more royal and kingly than this. But the Gospel, an episode from Luke's Passion narrative, shows us a very different picture. Here the title "King" is meant to be mocking and sarcastic – the soldiers are attempting to humiliate Jesus with a crown of thorns and a sign that labels Jesus as a joke, a fake, someone to be sneered at. How do we reconcile these two views?

Our tendency is to focus on one or the other of these accounts and ignore or downplay the other. We either want our Jesus to be an exalted king of the universe, or we want Jesus to be down in the pain and muck of a cruel world with us. There's nothing new about this – the Church has been swinging between these extremes for centuries. The former view, with the divinity and grandeur of Jesus emphasized, is usually labeled Christology *from above*. The gospel of John is a good example of Christology from above. Jesus is in control, all-knowing, and a master of his fate. His connection with God the Father is clear and solid, with no hint of human doubt or despair. This view dominated much of the Church in the middle ages – the very cathedrals in Europe are designed to instill awe and wonder as gaze up at the high ceilings, the murals and stained glass windows.

Contrast that view with the Christ in the synoptic gospels, particularly Mark, a view we label Christology *from below*. Jesus is very human, often frustrated with his disciples. He is racked with doubt in the garden of Gethsemane, sweating blood in his anguish. He is tempted by the devil, both before his ministry begins and most strikingly here in his final hours. Note in today's gospel that Jesus is challenged three times (that magic number) to "save yourself, save yourself, save yourself". It must have been maddening for Jesus to hear that and know that He could indeed save himself with a simple act of will. But he doesn't. He absorbs the beatings, the blows, the unjust pain, and willingly dies with words of forgiveness on his lips. The absurdity of it is amazing. In the eyes of the Roman legion, this is a naked, bleeding loser.

We are invited to ponder this paradox today, to take this very last Sunday of the Church year and ask the question, "who is this person Jesus anyway?" Is he the very human Jesus of the gospel, dying in agony? Or is he the awesome wonder-God who holds the world in his saving hands? Or is he somehow both at the same time? I invite you to consider that Jesus is the ultimate in *integrity*. He is most assuredly *both* God and man, fully and completely both, and you'll notice that he never acts in such a way as to betray his humanity or his divinity. His miracles are as much about compassion and caring as they are about power. He takes forgiveness to levels never before heard of. On the cross, in his divinity, he knows that the unwitting soldiers and Jewish leaders are playing right into God's hands, fulfilling the words of the prophets with one action after another, thinking they are crucifying a loser, but in actuality they are instruments in the salvation of the world. In Jesus' humanity, he suffers every excruciating blow, in complete solidarity with the rest of suffering humanity, from ages past to ages future. He holds it together, arms outstretched, between heaven and earth, the picture of paradox and integrity. Is it any wonder we worship before the cross?

So where's the lesson for us? It's a simple question really – do you lead a life of integrity? Are you authentic and true to the inner self that is the real you? Have you integrated the spiritual and the physical dimensions of your life? Are you two different people depending on your environment? Are you blown in many directions by the winds of our times? Do you live in fear? Or do you live in calmness and patience? Are you running from the devil? Or can you laugh in his face, secure in your sonship and daughtership in Christ? These are hard questions.

Here's a way to think about integrity in your life. Let's go back to the doctor's office. You've been told that you have 7 days to live. What do you do? I'm sure that for most of us, after the initial shock wears off, a mental to-do list begins to form, probably tinged with some regret that we can't do it all. We begin to see all of the things we should have done. We begin to think about people who we are estranged from, who need our forgiveness. We consider if we're worthy of heaven, if we've lived a good life. So here's the test – to the extent that we do *anything* differently from what we were doing before we entered the doctor's office, to the extent that we decide to act in some *new way* for our remaining days, that difference is a measure of our integrity gap. If we already lead lives of total integrity, if our inner true selves and our outer physical selves are completely in synch, we act *no differently* on leaving that doctor's office. But, if we feel the need to turn our world upside down, we are not leading lives as integrated people. How big is your gap?

Someone out there has only 7 days to live – not necessarily in this Church building, but somewhere out there. Some have 2 days to live. Some have 5 years, 20 years, 90 years. One thing you can be certain about - there's a number next to your name. The bad thief on the cross next to Jesus had mere hours to live. He mocks Jesus. The Good Thief on the cross next to Jesus had mere hours to live. He asks for forgiveness and finds Paradise. Membership in the kingdom of God is about opening your heart to that part of yourself that is the best of you, the part that God is most proud of. Let that heart speak to you, let that heart guide you, and you will live a life of total integrity. Live your life as if your days were short and you will discover integrity. And Christ, the king of integrity, will walk the path of life with you now and after death. It's the same path.

Chapter 5 – Relationship

God wants a *relationship* with us. As simple and profound as that is, a relationship. This is the one thing we can give God, because it is a matter of choice. Our choice. God made us with free will, an astounding gamble really, and God simply wants to enter into relationship with us.

You can have a relationship with God – yes you can. All you need is to say – I'm sorry, God, I'd like to try something new, please. Then God says, "you're forgiven". Always. Every time. Then God'll say to you, "Can you help me – can we work together in making this world better?" Because we certainly can't work together with God if there's no relationship there, can we?

Repentance and Forgiveness

Scripture Referenced: Lk 3:1-6

> *In the fifteenth year of the reign of Tiberius Caesar, when Pontius Pilate was governor of Judea, and Herod was tetrarch of Galilee, and his brother Philip tetrarch of the region of Ituraea and Trachonitis, and Lysanias was tetrarch of Abilene, during the high priesthood of Annas and Caiaphas, the word of God came to John the son of Zechariah in the desert.*

How many of you have seen Our Lady of Angels Cathedral in Los Angeles? To be honest, it's not much to look at from the outside, but the inside is striking in many, many ways. One of the more interesting features is a long series of tapestries that run down the entire length of the Church, on both sides. At first, you notice that the tapestries feature saints down through the ages, from the earliest apostles to the present day. It's fun to try to figure out who is who – but then if you look more closely you notice something else. Amid the saintly lineup there are everyday people, people just like you and me, men in business suits, kids on skateboards, women with shopping bags, all races and colors. The truth slowly sinks in – saints continue to walk among us, and more than that, sainthood isn't reserved for the folks with halos. It's for all of us.

Our Catholic faith tells us that God is not bound by time. Eternity doesn't mean that time goes on and on. Eternity means that time is irrelevant – that's why the tapestries make perfect sense. The saints may not be alive in a bodily sense, but that doesn't mean that they aren't with us, just as much a part of the body of Christ as you and I are. Eternity also means that we are able to celebrate the same event over and over, reliving it in a very real way, remembered and actually happening at the same time. This is paradoxical in one sense, but exciting in another. We can live Christmas as a real event again and again, learning something new each time, something that resonates with us differently because we are different.

We have a tendency to put Advent and Christmas into a place and time 2,000 years ago, but our Church challenges us to break that habit.

Advent is both then and now. Because God is just as assuredly present now as he was then. What we need to do is hear it a new way. So let's update the first reading from Baruch. Rather than Jerusalem, let's get local. "Solana Beach, Del Mar, Encinitas, take off your robe of mourning and misery; put on the splendor of glory from God forever. Up Solana Beach! Stand upon the heights; look to the east and see your children gathered at the word of the Holy One, rejoicing that you are remembered by God." Do you hear that call a bit differently now? The message is the same -- God loves you!

Now how about the Gospel? Luke carefully sets us in a time and place, defined by political boundaries and royal titles, both secular and religious. He is making the careful point that what he is describing really happened – it is an historical reality. Luke is saying in essence – go look it up! It happened. But it is also happening again. Listen. In the second year of the reign of Barack Obama, when Arnold Schwarzenegger was governor of California, and Jerry Sanders was mayor of San Diego, during the high priesthood of Bishop Robert Brom, the word of God has come to the people of St. James parish.

And just as was true 2,000 years ago, the question hangs in the air – will anyone hear the word of God? Luke accomplishes two purposes through his carefully crafted opening of Chapter 3. First of all, he anchors us in reality. The second, more subtle point is also made. God could have come to Caesar or Pilate or Herod or Caiaphas, but as is always true in salvation history, God chose from the bottom of society, coming to a man in the desert named John. And God's Word comes to us today. Who will hear the Word? Luke tells us that John heard the Word.

What was the Word John heard? Luke actually gives us two words – repentance and forgiveness. Why those two words? We know these words – we hear them so often that they have lost meaning. Why repentance, why forgiveness? We associate repentance with sin, don't we? Does God want us to repent because we're really bad? Is God mad at all of us? This is often how many of us think of God, isn't it? He's a big accountant, watching our every move, noting every little fault and sin, and woe to us on judgment day! When John was proclaiming a baptism of repentance on the banks of the Jordan river and people came out to him, what were those people like? I'll bet that they were just like us, everyday people who knew that they weren't always faithful to the law. I'm sure that there was a huge span of sinfulness there, from murderers to poor widows who had a single unkind thought. Note what John *doesn't* say to them – he doesn't say *behave*! He says *repent*! What's the difference?

John is like a farmer who takes a plow and breaks up the earth so that seeds can be planted. Repentance is a decision to try something new, to go down a new path, to consciously open yourself to a new way of life. It is an act of will. If we say, "I'm sorry" and then turn around and smack our little sister again, there's no repentance there. It's simply an empty promise. God doesn't want empty promises – he wants us to turn toward him. And what does he offer in return? Forgiveness. The second word of God, which is just as critical, just as important as repentance. Why? It's the response to our act of will, to our repentance, our turning. God is basically saying, "turn to me and I'll forgive everything – every valley of sin will be filled, every mountain of pain will be made low, the twisting road of evil shall be made straight, and the rough paths of broken relationships will be made smooth. God promises salvation, but we need to say yes, I want that. I want to try this new path. I want this gift.

You see, what repentance and forgiveness represent is an opening of the door, an opening of a relationship, the beginning of a dialog. The only way any broken relationship is repaired is through an act of repentance and an offer of forgiveness. It's a two-way street and that's what John is preaching to the people. You can have a relationship with God – yes you can. All you need is to say – I'm sorry, God, I'd like to try something new, please. Then God says, "you're forgiven". Always. Every time. Then God'll say to you, "Can you help me – can we work together in making this world better?" Because we certainly can't work together with God if there's no relationship there, can we?

Advent didn't just happen 2,000 years ago, it's happening now! Jesus is waiting to be born – but this time, not in a manger, but in a heart, yours. So Solana Beach, Encinitas, Del Mar, San Diego -- *repent*!

A Life Changing Word

Scripture Referenced: Jn 1:1-18

> *In the beginning was the Word, and the Word was with God, and the Word was God.*
>
> *He was in the beginning with God.*
>
> *All things came to be through him, and without him nothing came to be. What came to be through him was life, and this life was the light of the human race; the light shines in the darkness, and the darkness has not overcome it.*

In the beginning... Where else do we hear those opening words, "In the beginning..."? Yes, that's right, we hear them at the very start of the Bible in the book of Genesis. In the beginning, God created the heavens and the earth... John the Evangelist very deliberately echoes these words as he begins his gospel account of Jesus Christ. As you know, John's gospel is completely different from the Matthew, Mark, and Luke accounts. John emphasizes the divinity of Jesus, and he sets the tone right from the start, putting Christ at the point of creation, co-equal with God Himself. However, you'll notice that the name Jesus is never heard in the reading. Instead, we have this somewhat baffling term, the *Word*. In the beginning was the Word, and the Word was with God, and the Word was God. How do you get from the *Word* to Jesus?

John's gospel was written nearly a hundred years after Jesus left this earth. It was written to a very sophisticated community in Asia Minor, a community that had the benefit of at least two generations of thoughtful prayer and dialog about who this Jesus was all about. This community very likely had access to the other gospel accounts, and Paul's letters. John clearly saw no need to rehash anything from the other gospels – his purpose was theological, symbolic, and poetic. You won't find shepherds and angels and choirs of heavenly hosts in John's gospel. He has a different purpose, a higher purpose, a need to place Jesus in the entire divine plan.

The Greek term that we translate as the Word is *Logos*. Logos does not mean a word on a page – no, Logos denotes a spoken word. More than that, Logos implies a word of power, a word that causes change. Let's take an example. Have you ever said something to someone else that visibly affected that person? Perhaps the first time you said to your spouse, "I love you." Perhaps a word of encouragement to a co-worker or a struggling friend? Perhaps *you've* been changed by a spoken word? I remember distinctly the first day my baby son called me "dada". That's a life-changing word, isn't it? I'm not even sure that "dada" is a word! Words can cause damage just as easily, can't they? Taunts, insults, and put-downs are devastating to us. That old saying "sticks and stones can break my bones but names can never hurt me" is far from true.

Now take that concept of a spoken word of power and place that word in the mouth of God. Can any word of power be any more powerful than what comes from the mouth of God? When God created the universe, he *spoke* it into being, he breathed life from nothingness, from the void. God spoke the Word, and this Word had so much power that it was indistinguishable from God Himself. This Word, this Logos, was the means by which God created the universe. That's an amazingly powerful word, isn't it?

But here's the key point, the Christmas Day point, if you will. God's Word, the Logos, did not stop on creation day. It continues to maintain the universe in existence, and on a special day some two thousand years ago, the Word became flesh and dwelt among us. The Word of God took on flesh, was born of a woman, and became man, full of grace and truth. We call this amazing event the *Incarnation*, God taking on human form and living among us.

But the question remains, why did God incarnate in the person of Jesus? God doesn't need us. There's nothing we can give God that God doesn't already have. So why? What is God looking for from us? Apparently, God wants a *relationship* with us. As simple and profound as that is, a relationship. This is the one thing we can give God, because it is a matter of choice. Our choice. God made us with free will, an astounding gamble really, and God simply wants to enter into relationship with us. We can say yes, or we can say no. God will not force it, ever.

What we need to get our head around, what we need to *absorb* is that God emptied Himself, taking on our flesh and blood, to show us *through Jesus* what a perfect relationship with God looks like, to show us that through the model of Jesus we can find true happiness and peace. As St. Athanasius said so well, "God became human so that we could become divine." That's a very grown-up concept, not at all childlike and sentimental, a potentially life-changing realization, the Word, the Logos, in action.

And the really amazing thing is that God will accept a relationship that is anything but perfect. God will listen to us whine, cry, rage, or laugh. He will dance with us, and limp with us. He will accept our thanks, and accept our sneering reply. God loves us no matter what our response to his invitation. So what's in it for us?

When we're in relationship with someone, a little of the other person rubs off on us, doesn't it? The same holds true with God. He accepts any kind of a relationship, good or bad, because in the end, we become better. We can't help it. If we're in relationship with someone all powerful, all loving, and all good, some of that goodness rubs off on us.

Sometimes, amidst the shopping and carols and parties and food, we miss the point of Christmas, the amazing point of Christmas. Many of us try to recapture that magical childlike excitement that we all felt a long time ago, and feel vaguely depressed when Christmas present doesn't quite measure up to Christmas past. Manger scenes are cute, but they don't change lives. Shepherds are vaguely interesting, but they don't change lives. Angels are awe-inspiring, but they don't change lives either.

A relationship with God will change your life. Jesus modeled it for us two thousand years ago. As the Word, He continues to speak to us with forgiveness and encouragement, using words with power to change lives. All we need to do is say yes. And that's good news! Enjoy that good news. It's worth a smile, a thank you, and a toast to our Lord and King on this, His birthday.

Your Holy Family

Scriptures Referenced: 1 Sam 1:20-28; Lk 2:41-52

When his parents saw him, they were astonished, and his mother said to him, "Son, why have you done this to us? Your father and I have been looking for you with great anxiety."

And he said to them, "Why were you looking for me? Did you not know that I must be in my Father's house?"

But they did not understand what he said to them.

This Sunday is a feast within a feast. We're still technically in the so-called "Octave of Christmas", the eight days succeeding Christmas Day where we are to continue to celebrate the Incarnation, God's radical decision to become a human being. But today we take a moment, logically it seems, to consider the family we call "holy", the family of Jesus, Mary, and Joseph. We peek at the crèche behind me here and there they are, looking so serene and peaceful. They sure look holy – but after all, it's two saints and the Son of God! Of course they're holy! How do we relate? Last time I checked my family, there's no one applying for sainthood.

But for just a moment, let's really look at the Scripture readings, especially the Gospel. Is the Holy Family really so different from yours and mine? The first reading from the book of Samuel is a set-up for the Gospel. Hannah, who was thought to be barren, prays and prays for a child. God grants her wish and her son, Samuel, is born. As a mark of gratitude, Hannah presents Samuel to the temple to be raised as a priest, dedicated to the Lord. The reading ends with the terse statement, "Hannah left Samuel there." If you have the picture in your head of a little 3 year old being dropped off in the temple, fear not. Samuel was dropped off to start his training much like we drop our kids off for kindergarten, and he certainly saw his parents routinely over the years to come.

Now let's look at the gospel. The reading is significant and remarkable for a variety of reasons. Jesus is a budding teenager, aged

12, and in accordance with the Law, must take on the duties of a man and make pilgrimage to Jerusalem for the Passover. Such pilgrimages were done in a segregated way – the men would travel in a separate pack from the women and children. Many twelve year old boys, traveling with the men for the first time, would find the going a bit rough and sneak over to see Mom once in a while during the journey. All of us men can relate to that awkward in-between stage – not boy, and not man. It is no wonder at all that Mary and Joseph lost track of Jesus. They each thought that he was with the other group, and wouldn't realize the mistake until that night when the groups would come together for food and safety.

In a panic, Mary and Joseph race back to Jerusalem and search for him for *three* days. Can you imagine losing your child for three days? The tears, the frustration, the despair, the fear, the inability to sleep or eat. Jesus, meanwhile, has had a remarkable revelation for himself. He has found his true identity – we're not told exactly how he figures it out, but he is certain of it. Like Samuel, Jesus' true home is God's house. Unlike Samuel, he wasn't dropped off there, he went there on his own accord.

When Mary and Joseph finally find Jesus, they are astonished. Why? Well, Jesus himself is clearly not the least bit upset, or anxious, or fearful in being separated from them. He seems quite at home with all of the teachers and scribes. That had to be a bit exasperating after all they've been through. So Mary addresses Jesus in what may be the greatest understatement in the New Testament, "Son, why have you done this to us? Your father and I have been looking for you with great anxiety." And Jesus responds as only a teenager can who is completely wrapped up in his own world. "Why were you looking for me? Did you not know that I must be in my Father's house?" I don't know about you, but I think I might have said, "OK, fine – good luck. Don't forget to write."

You see, it's real life. It's the way it is in all of our families. The Holy Family didn't think of themselves as the "Holy Family". They were simply a family. It's not perfection, it's diapers, illness, A's, B's, and F's. It's not peaceful, it's tiffs, misunderstandings, impatience, and forgiving. It's not a little cocoon, it's relatives, cousins, tiresome aunts and uncles, and societal expectations. It's not all heaven, it's a lost child, tears, panic, and ultimate relief at finding him. The Scripture tells us that Jesus, Mary, and Joseph were a family, just like we are.

But let's finish the Gospel reading. There's a couple of more points to be made here. After Jesus speaks, something in him must have seen the red eyes, the exhaustion, the lines of worry and pain in his earthly parents, and even as a teenager, he must have thought, "Oops. I may be uniquely tied to my Father in heaven, but I am still a son to these wonderful people." He went back with them to Nazareth and was obedient to them. Jesus had more wisdom to gain – he was human as much as he was God – and he recognized that Mary and Joseph, in equal measure to both the Hebrew Scriptures and the teachers of the law, were a source of ongoing wisdom.

So what do we take from this feast as family members, for we are all members of a family?

- It's OK to struggle, to make mistakes, to try.
- Misfortunes will come to families – we're all part of the same human chain
- There will be moments of great joy, peace, and happiness
- There will be moments of great question, uncertainty, and anxiety

Through it all, remember that there is nothing we experience that God, in the person of Jesus, has not seen, lived, and yes, blessed. Fathers, don't lose faith in your children – even when they are teenagers and you'd like to drop them off at the Temple permanently. Mothers, as you watch your children grow, follow Mary's lead and keep all these things in your heart. Why there? Because a mother's heart is the storehouse of the family, where all of the good memories are held. Every child needs to tap that storehouse time and again, even when Mom is 80 years old and you are in your 50's.

So be thankful to mothers and fathers, or whoever has played that role for you, forming you in wisdom and grace.

Healing and Re-Entry

Scripture Referenced: Mk 1:21-28

> *Then they came to Capernaum, and on the Sabbath he entered the synagogue and taught. The people were astonished at his teaching, for he taught them as one having authority and not as the scribes.*

When I was writing my Master's thesis a long time ago, I was told that I had to carefully footnote every statement that I made. If some scholar somewhere had written anything relevant to my thesis topic, I had to either quote that person carefully or enter his book into my bibliography. It made for very awkward writing, and pretty boring reading! About 10 years ago, I went to the University of Washington library and found my thesis in the library book stacks. In over twenty years, no one had ever checked it out. So I did, and returned it the same day! It was still boring.

At the time of Mark's gospel, the scribes were like graduate students. When they spoke in the synagogues or public places, their answers were always carefully qualified. "As Rabbi So-and-so said, or as Rabbi Suchandsuch states", - this is the way they addressed any issue brought before them. Mark tells us that Jesus taught with authority, and not as the scribes. And then, immediately, he gives us an example. A man with an unclean spirit appears in their midst! Understand how horrible this is to the Jews. Remember that *unclean* does not necessarily mean dirty as in soiled. Unclean is a state of impurity, a state of being unsuitable in God's eyes. Touching a dead body made you unclean. Leprosy made you unclean. Bleeding in any way made you unclean. To be in such a state, even temporarily, meant that you were to be avoided. Because if you even touch someone who is unclean, then you are unclean also! It's like a diabolical game of tag. So imagine discovering an unclean person in this crowded little synagogue – you can picture the shock, the revulsion.

So, if you were a scribe in this situation, what would you say to the people? Right! Run for your lives! Get away! Does Jesus run away?

No. Jesus speaks with the authority of God and commands the spirit to be quiet and leave the man. It's the unclean spirit who does the running away now. Thank goodness Jesus was there. And quite frankly, most of us stop right there and move on. There goes Jesus, healing another person miraculously. Since I can't do that, there's not much for me to relate to here. Or is there?

What's really interesting about Jesus' healing miracles is that they usually achieve *two* distinct outcomes. First and foremost, he physically heals the person. But secondly, and just as important, though we often miss it, Jesus allows that person to re-enter community, to once more take up residence with family, friends, and co-workers. He makes them whole, physically and emotionally, and allows them to become *pure* again. In a way, he *re-creates* them.

With the benefit of science and a truly wonderful healthcare system, what would have been a miraculous cure in the past is fairly routine today. We can find help for all sorts of physical problems, whether temporary or chronic. We're no longer in an age when a sneeze meant death was calling you. (Unless you're a Mom with three little kids!) We no longer fear a broken bone or a stomach ache or a tooth ache – yes, they're annoying, but we are certain that a good doctor will bring us relief.

But what about the second goal of Jesus' healing ministry? The re-entry goal? Perhaps our call is not about miracle cures, but about re-creating people who are lost, who are unclean. Who's unclean in our Church today? Not dirty hands unclean, but ritually impure? Who might we consider *unsuitable*? Perhaps a person addicted to cocaine, or an alcoholic. Perhaps a person who has AIDS, or is just out of jail. Perhaps someone who has been married and divorced three times. Perhaps a person that battles pedophilia or works in a business we'd rather not visit. Perhaps a person who is dying, or homebound, facing four blank walls and an unknown future. The fearful little scribe in our brain says avoid them, stay away. But this Jesus who we worship says to us, "don't you dare avoid that person!"

We're not being asked to heal them physically. But we are being asked to follow the Master. Jesus has us step forward when everything in our being wants to step back. This is how we are called to follow Jesus, to reach out and help make these people whole again. How?

You've all heard of Alcoholics Anonymous. And Overeaters Anonymous, and Gamblers Anonymous. What makes these programs work? What makes recovery possible? Yes, the twelve steps are brilliant in concept. But the secret sauce, if you will, is the power of *relationship*. It's all about the power of community, a community of people who give a darn about you. If you know that you are loved, that you are watched over, that people are rooting for you, it's amazing what cures are possible. It's amazing the demons that get driven out.

Our calling, pure and simple, is to enter relationship with these people. God is Spirit, which means God is hard to see, to touch, to experience at a sensory level. We come to know God by other people primarily – certainly at first. At some point in time, God steps over the boundary of our sense perception and says hello, but that rarely happens at first. We rely on the witness of others to ignite our flame, to get us thinking in a different way. The model of God's love is what attracts us, and no one models that better than a person of faith. As the letter to the Hebrews states, faith is the realization of what is hoped for and evidence of things not seen.

People who are on the edges of our community, who feel like they don't belong with us, are the people that Jesus asks us to seek and find. By giving them the new life that they *hope* for, we plant a seed of faith. By mirroring the actions of Christ, we give them *evidence of things not seen*. Christ touches us, we touch them, Christ touches them, and healing occurs. It's a marvelous mystery, and the exact way to bring people to new life, to a sense of re-creation.

Look around you this week. Who in your circle of co-workers, neighbors, and acquaintances is in need of healing? If physical healing, reach out to them in prayer. If it's not a physical issue, but more of a sense of loneliness and alienation from the world, then reach out with an invitation. Not necessarily to take them to Church, but to be Christ to them, to be a friend. Speak to them as a "holy one of God". That's true authority!

153 Fish

Scripture Referenced: Jn 21:1-19

> *Jesus said to them, "Children, have you caught anything to eat?" They answered him, "No."*
>
> *So he said to them, "Cast the net over the right side of the boat and you will find something." So they cast it, and were not able to pull it in because of the number of fish.*
>
> *So the disciple whom Jesus loved said to Peter, "It is the Lord." When Simon Peter heard that it was the Lord, he tucked in his garment, for he was lightly clad, and jumped into the sea.*

This remarkable Gospel reading is taken from the very end of John's gospel. It is clearly an add-on, an epilogue, that was tacked on for a specific purpose. You may be thinking, "Where have I heard this account before? Didn't we hear Jesus help the apostles catch fish just a while ago?" And you'd be correct. This particular event shows up very early in *Luke's* gospel, preceding the call of Peter, James and John. Jesus tells the seemingly inept apostles where to cast their nets after a fruitless night of fishing and surprise, the nets are filled to the breaking point. This astonishing catch moves Peter and the rest of the apostles to follow Jesus. So why is it here in John as a *post-resurrection* event? Did it happen twice? Maybe, but more likely, what we have here is an excellent example of how two different Biblical authors take the same event and tailor it to suit a purpose, to highlight a particular point about Jesus to their audience. Luke uses this event to trigger the commitment of the apostles to Jesus. John uses the event to trigger the reconciliation of Peter to Jesus.

When John's gospel last mentions Peter, he and John are at the tomb. John sees the empty tomb and we are told that he *believed*. By implication, Peter was perhaps not sure, perhaps hopeful, but we're not told. Peter was certainly present at the appearance in the upper room that we heard about last week when Thomas was able to see and believe. But as far as the Gospel is concerned, Jesus has yet to directly confront Peter about his three denials. Do you know the feeling of having let someone down who you really love? That's where Peter is. So he does what every man does who is feeling down. He goes into task mode. He goes back to work; he goes fishing. His buddies come along because that's how guys help other guys out – they work on a task together. No, ladies, they didn't discuss any of this among themselves. They just went fishing and probably didn't say two words to each other all night.

Then Jesus shows up at dawn. Now you might wonder why the apostles didn't recognize him right away. But understand that it is probably still pretty dark, and it is typical for someone on shore to guide a fishing boat to where the fish may be by looking at the shadows in the water. So the apostles comply with Jesus' suggestion and strike the jackpot. At this point, Jesus is recognized and Peter answers the hope in his heart -- he compulsively leaps into the sea to get to the shore that much faster. The other apostles are struggling ashore with all of these fish and Peter helps them bring the catch in. Now it's Jesus' turn. Note the significance – he feeds them. He feeds them loaves and fish – does that ring a bell?

And now, the moment of truth arrives. Jesus addresses Peter directly and asks him three times if he loves Jesus. Peter's heart must be breaking at these questions. At one level, he must surely recognize that Jesus has every right to ask such personal, probing questions. At another level, he is "distressed". At each insistent *yes* that Peter makes, Jesus gives him a simple command, "tend my sheep". For each of the three sinful denials that Peter committed just days before, Jesus asks that Peter take on the penance of humility, the penance of leadership, the penance of obedience, obedience even unto death, death on a cross. Jesus challenges Peter to become like Him.

What can we take from this powerful exchange? What's our lesson? John's gospel is loaded with allegory – so let's dig a little deeper here. Peter represents the Church. When this gospel was written, Peter had been dead for at least 40 years and already acknowledged as the first leader of the Christian Way. To go fishing is seen as analogous to evangelization, to fishing for people. At the start of the reading, Peter declares that he is going fishing, presumably by himself. Regardless of whether or not he has company, his fishing expedition fails. Why? Again, speaking in allegorical terms, he is unsuccessful because he is fishing in the dark. He is relying solely on his own skill, and that is simply not going to get the job done! When Jesus shows up, he addresses them as "children" for that's what they are – naïve and a little foolish. Jesus comes with the dawn of light and tells them what to do. Lo and behold, they are successful, and did you catch this? They net *153 fish*. Why is that significant? The best suggestion I've heard is that at the time of John's writing, there were 153 known nations in the world. The point? With the help of Jesus, the Church will catch *everyone*.

Peter leaps into the water and swims to shore, to join Jesus. If you were here on Easter Vigil night, you witnessed three people who likewise entered the water in order to meet Jesus. Peter is fed by Jesus on the shore. Likewise, our newly baptized were fed by Jesus in the Eucharist. Once washed in the water and fed by the Lord, Peter is challenged to go out and tend to the sheep, to tend to the ones who need to hear the voice of care, of leadership, of direction. As those baptized and fed, we as Church are also called to tend the sheep, to make a difference, to witness to the reason why we are here each Sunday.

The message in the Gospel is clear. *We* cannot do it alone. *We* cannot save the world. In fact, we cannot even save ourselves. Jesus is the only way. If you want to see what happens when we invite Jesus in, look at the first reading from Acts. Even though it's the first reading, this event happens after the Gospel encounter. This Peter is hardly the uncertain, go-it-alone, compulsive Peter that we see in the Gospel. The Sanhedrin insists that Peter and the apostles stop teaching in the name of Jesus. Peter speaks with clarity and authority, challenging the Sanhedrin: "We must obey God rather than men." This statement echoes the words of the martyrs throughout the ages, defying civil authority, defying contemporary culture, speaking as one whose beacon is not of this world. Can we do the same? Yes, but only if we have been fed by Jesus first. Let's get fed.

The Perfect Gift

Scriptures Referenced: Jn 14:23-29

Peace I leave with you; my peace I give to you. Not as the world gives do I give it to you. Do not let your hearts be troubled or afraid.

It usually starts around Labor Day, but has been known to start earlier. Some people do it all year round. Many, however, wait until the last minute. What am I talking about? Christmas shopping of course! We search the stores and the Internet with a person in mind, carefully weighing what we know of that person, trying to anticipate if the item will please them. Women are really good at this. When my wife and I go shopping, or better stated, when I accompany her to the store while she does the shopping, at least a dozen times during the excursion, I will hear this exclamation: "Oh, this would be *perfect* for Cheryl." Or, "this would be *perfect* for your Mom." Then comes the pause. "What do you think?" I nod my head and agree. It's a *good* system.

Now, wouldn't it be fantastic to give someone a gift that is so perfect that nothing else will ever match it again? A gift so perfect that the receiver will desire nothing more? Jesus gives us this gift today – the gift of his peace. It is not as the world gives it, he tells us, so we're invited to consider what he means by this peace. We tend to think of peace as the absence of war, a respite of calm between periods of violence. We're so accustomed to war that we label our history with war markers – Civil War, War of 1812, World War II, Iraq war, and so on. Wouldn't it be better to label our history with peace markers?

But this kind of peace is not what Jesus is referring to. The peace he references goes much deeper, and has broader implications. The peace of Jesus is quite personal – one may say *relational*. It flows from a relationship with our Creator God, our Abba. This is how Jesus draws the strength to face the cross mere hours after he delivers these words. Jesus so intimately knows the Father that he understands himself as literally channeling the Father's words, channeling the Father's actions. Jesus and the Father breathe as one.

Would you like to know what that feels like? Let's try it right now. What is the word for God in Jewish scripture? Yahweh. This word is so sacred to the Jews that they wouldn't even say it aloud. We're not going to say it aloud either. We're going to *breathe* it. Try breathing in on the first syllable and breathing out on the second: Yah – weh. The breath we take is the name of God – over and over. Close your eyes and breathe in peace. Are you troubled or afraid right now? Take a moment and feel His peace. It is right here now. It always is. Yah-weh. Is it any surprise that all of the contemplative traditions, Christian and non-Christian, emphasize a focus on breathing? We are born to breathe, we breathe to live, when we cease breathing, we die. Our origin is God, and in focused breathing we remind ourselves of that first and ever-present relationship.

So here's how it works – the intense relationship between Jesus and the Father is passed on to us through the Spirit, and one of the fruits of the Spirit is peace. It is interesting that Jesus gives this gift before the Spirit is sent upon the disciples, so clearly this gift is very precious indeed. We experience the gift of peace by developing our relationship with Jesus. The stronger that relationship, the more that we walk in the steps and words of Jesus, the more readily will we find peace in our lives. Now note carefully that Jesus does not promise uneventful or calm lives! What he does promise is freedom from fear, freedom from anxiety, because with Jesus walking by our side, what more could you ask?

So once we experience this perfect gift, can we give this gift of peace to one another? What do you think? Is it possible? Follow the relationship chain. God and Jesus are one in peaceful relationship, and we are invited to share in that relationship by following Jesus. So how would we bring peace to others? That's correct – through relationship, through what Pope Paul VI called *right* relationship. In other words, it's not a matter of being aware of the other person, but in holding that person in *right* relationship.

What is meant by *right* relationship? At its most general level, the world of human beings, right relationship is marked by an acknowledgement of everyone's basic human dignity. It is seeing in everyone, friend or stranger, the spark of God incarnate. It is seeing the face of God in the poor, the immigrant, the prisoner, the other color, the aged, and the ill. Right relationship is justice borne of the simple reality that we are all children of God. All of us.

Closer to home, among our families, friends, and acquaintances, right relationships are marked by a willingness to understand, to forgive, to see another's point of view without feeling threatened. I have very close friends who reflect entirely opposite sides of the political spectrum. In my email last week, I received invitations to attend both pro and anti-immigration events. The temptation is to take a side, dig in with both hands and feet, and immediately demonize the other. This is what talk radio, Internet blogs, and political power mongers want. Take a side. Fight the others! Win the battle.

Brothers and sisters, this is not what is meant by right relationships! Dualistic, either/or thinking is as far from the teachings of Jesus as you can get. Have you ever noticed that Jesus never condemns sinners in the Gospels? Never. Check it out – he forgives, and calls them to new life, to a new relationship. The only people Jesus complains about are those who think that they have all of the answers, who are never wrong. Yes, the Pharisees – who are so convinced that their viewpoint is correct, and that everyone else is beneath them, that they miss the very presence of God walking among them. There's a warning here – to the degree that you are locked into a position that completely closes out what the other side is saying, that has claimed your identity, then you are not in right relationship, and consequently, you are not in peace.

When I wrote the first draft of this homily last weekend, I was not at peace. Changes in my work environment had me all roiled up. I felt far from the peace of Christ, and yet, somehow I had to write in celebration of this gift from Jesus. That afternoon, in the mail, I received a calendar/bookmark from Spiritual Director's International. Who sends out calendars in May?! But on the other side of the calendar was a poem by a woman named Jennifer Hoffman. Guess what the title was? Peace. May I read it to you?

> There is a peace that passes understanding, a peace that need not control.
>
> Though life is uncertain and random and chaos is ever present, there is a peace.

There is a peace, an intuitive knowing that fits like pieces of a jigsaw puzzle into a coherent whole, a peace that seeks and finds Peace.

There is Peace longing to be present in all the world, Peace that desires nothing more than quiet forgiveness, acceptance and recognition of the sameness and differences that make us all human.

When peace and Peace connect, as if God's hand on the Sistine Chapel finally reaches Adam's, the world will breathe a sigh of relief, and the thank you will reverberate through eternity.

Peace be with you.

The God of Relationships

Scripture Referenced: Dt 4:32-34,39-40; Mt 28:16-20

> *This is why you must now know, and fix in your heart, that the Lord is God in the heavens above and on earth below, and that there is no other.*

The doctrine of the Trinity reflects many years of theological reflection by the Church Fathers to explain who God is and how God acts. Because God is overwhelming in majesty, the Church does not claim to completely explain God, but teaches that there is truth in this doctrine, even if not complete understanding. The God of the Hebrew Scriptures creates the universe and seeks a covenant with His people. The first reading from Deuteronomy summarizes this covenant quite well. Keep my statutes and commandments that I enjoin on you, and you and your children will prosper and have long life. But Israel lost its way. Rather than living and rejoicing in the covenant, the Hebrew people got stuck in the commandments and laws! Life became observance to a cold, unfeeling formula.

So God, in His time, acted through His second person, Jesus Christ, and came to re-orient us to the relationship that God has always intended, not by simply telling us to change (as the prophets attempted), but by revealing much more about the nature of God. We learn through Jesus that God is not only a God of covenant, but a God of love. This love is described by Jesus as at least the love of a mother for her baby, or a father for his child. In fact, this love is so powerful, it is personified as the third dimension of God, the Spirit. As St. John tells us in his first letter, God is love. Clearly, love is only possible if there's an "other" to love – so God the Father loves the Son and from that love proceeds the Holy Spirit. We further know that God is engaged in the world, wholly and completely, to our benefit. As Father, he maintains us in creation; as Son, he continually redeems us in relationship; as Spirit, he sanctifies us to realize our full potential as human beings.

But now is the harder question, "so what?" Let's remember that we are made in the image and likeness of God. That means that we have all three of God's persons active in our lives. By our presence in this Church today, we seek to cooperate with God's action in our lives – how do we do that in light of our understanding of the Trinity?

Let's take each Person in turn. Because the Father is "creator" it is tempting to associate God the Father with the creative arts such as sculpture, painting, and music in seeking our answer. But the word *creation* implies a broader meaning, a bringing forth of something from nothing. Keeping in mind that God is a relationship among three persons, I would propose that God wants us to also create *relationships*. This is truly creation in the deepest sense, in that where before there was nothing, there is now a relationship that is itself a potentially life-changing, life enhancing, "something". Consider the excitement you feel when you create a new friendship when before there was only two people.

Creating relationships may indeed mirror the Father, but simply generating friendships is not enough. This is where reflection on the Son is appropriate. In all of the relationships Jesus initiates or responds to, Jesus offers *redemption* in some overt or subtle way. Whether it is delivering a person from a lifelong illness, or challenging a sinner to repent, or pointing out the path to salvation, Jesus shows us that relationship is only meaningful if it leads to freedom and love. By modeling a life of authentic engagement, Jesus demonstrates that *we too* can change lives by creating relationships based on the inherent dignity of the other person. My mother told me to marry the person who will help me get to heaven. Sage advice that brings a smile, but it is truly a Jesus-message. If we all looked at each other and asked, "how can I help that person get to heaven?", what a different world this would be!

Creating relationships that are liberating and redemptive is a laudable goal, but the task seems daunting. How do we accomplish such a feat in the complex world we live in? Here it is valuable to consider the Person of the Holy Spirit and take heart. We've all experienced the feeling of *synergy* in our lives, that force that takes a one-plus-one relationship and somehow generates the power of three. This tends to happen especially in situations where our goal is redemptive in nature. By freely entering into the suffering of another, we most profoundly experience the power of the Spirit. Perhaps tentatively at first, we gradually find ourselves *impelled* to partake in ministries to the poor, the sick, the imprisoned.

Our Deacons in the past have led us in ministries such as the St. Leo's clinic, the Thrift Store, ministry to the race track employees, Mission Circle, and many others.

So what can we take from this mysterious theological concept called the Trinity? Let's summarize:

- God is love. Love implies relationship, deep sharing, and the sense of synergy that happens when two people loving each other take on the power of three.
- We are made in the image of God. We can ignore that if we choose, or we can be open to God's presence in us and cooperate with God's plan.
- A good way to do this is by entering into relationship with other human beings in a very deliberate way. It's not simply about making friends. It's about building relationships that are redemptive, that save people. That's why we are called to those who are poor, marginalized, imprisoned, or lost in sin.
- Ironically, by giving ourselves to such redemptive actions, we save *our* lives. Jesus tells us emphatically, "If you lose your life for my sake, you will find it!"
- We can't possibly do this without help – the Holy Spirit will do the hard work through us.

I ask you in the weeks ahead to consider how you can cooperate with the power of the Triune God in your lives. The world needs saving. But we are not alone – as the Gospel says, "Jesus is with us always, until the end of the age."

It's Decision Time!

Scripture Referenced: Jos 24:1-2,15-18; Jn 6:60-69

Now, therefore, fear the Lord and serve him completely and sincerely. Cast out the gods your fathers served beyond the River and in Egypt, and serve the Lord.

If it does not please you to serve the Lord, decide today whom you will serve, the gods your fathers served beyond the River or the gods of the Amorites in whose country you are dwelling. As for me and my household, we will serve the Lord.

In the first reading, Joshua is at the end of his life. He has led his people into the Promised Land and has subdued it. The people have carved up the territory and things are going well. But somehow sensing that the people don't really appreciate the situation, Joshua decides it is time to renew the great covenant between Yahweh and the people. The Israelite people must choose – the gods of the surrounding countryside, or the one true God. Joshua, knowing where his allegiance lies, gives us that wonderful phrase, "as for me and my household, we will serve the Lord."

The people say "Yes, we will also serve the Lord, for he is our God!" It's too bad the reading ends there, for the next verse has Joshua saying, "You may not be able to serve the Lord, for he is a holy God; he is a jealous God…" In other words, do you know what you are saying? Oh yes, the people say. Yet, they had great difficulty as the Bible shows us.

Now to John's gospel – more decisions! The reading starts with a non sequitur. Many said, "This saying is hard; who can accept it?" What saying are they talking about? Last week, Jesus says "I am the living bread that came down from heaven; whoever eats this bread will live forever; and the bread that I give is my flesh for the life of the world." It's not the flesh part that repels them, it is the implication, the challenge in the words. Jesus is saying that he is the way, the only way. You want food, I'll give you food – I'll give you everlasting life! Just follow me, follow my way.

Many turn away at this time. It's tempting for us to think, "those poor stupid people. Why don't they get it? If I were there, I certainly would be right there with Peter." I'm sure many of you have been to a new housing development – there seems to be one going up everywhere you look. What I love is the part when you walk out to a home site and the realtor says "imagine the house right here, with a swimming pool in the back, and your bedroom looking out over this view, on and on." Part of you is saying, yes, yes, and part of you is saying, you've got to be kidding.

The same is true of Jesus' followers here. Jesus says follow me – everlasting life is yours! But understand that this is pre-Resurrection. This is an unfinished book. This is a half-built bridge over the river. This is a foundation without a house. So the people leave. It has to hurt. After a long time of "getting" things, maybe food, maybe the thrill of seeing a miracle, maybe their own healing, they are challenged to give something of themselves. Oops. Is there any more poignant a question than Jesus to the apostles? "Do you also want to leave?"

Peter, paralleling the other gospels, makes his great leap of faith, "Master, to whom shall we go? You have the words of eternal life." How can Peter say this? What allows him to make this statement? In short, he had a personal relationship with Jesus Christ.

Please, people, understand. Christianity is not a philosophy, or a theory, or a pledge of allegiance. It's a personal response to Jesus Christ. It has to come first!! You know that old song, "you'll know they are Christians by their love". But it's true – it starts with love. One of the unfortunate drawbacks of our Catholic faith tradition is that we are rarely challenged to make an *adult* decision about our faith direction. For many of us, it's made for us at baptism as children and we ride the rails ever after. Is your religious practice based on fear of going to hell? Or a desire to please a fickle God? Or is it based on a love of Jesus and the desire to follow him?

Brother and sisters, if your faith is based on a love of Jesus and his mission, there is nothing inside or outside the Church that can affect you in the least way. If you are walking the path with Jesus, all of the little annoyances, the foibles of our fellow parishioners and priests, the confusing political landscape – all of that stuff is (as St. Paul says) nothing but rubbish. Jesus walks with us and more importantly, within us.

Here's a little test for you. How often are you offended in a given day? How often are you irritated by someone else's action? How often do you lose your temper? The answer tells you something about the peace and turmoil that's within you. Jesus can help you transform that inner turmoil if you ask Him to. He's waiting to be asked. It's decision time.

Chapter 6 – Prayer and Detachment

Ask and you will receive. Seek and you will find. Knock and the door will be opened to you. But, it may not be what you expect!

Detachment is a matter of perspective. Paul tells us that if we give everything to God, the peace that surpasses all understanding will guard our hearts and minds. By replacing the material things of this world with the glorious riches in Christ, you've invested your life into a bank account that will never go dry, and best of all, will be waiting for you when it's time to end the drama in this life. Christ's love – you *can* take that with you!

A Walk by the Golf Course

Scripture Referenced: Zep 3:14-18; Phil 4:4-7; Lk 3:10-18

Rejoice in the Lord always. I shall say it again: rejoice!

I'm sure that you noted the rose colored candle that we have lit today. Hmmm, there must be something different about this Advent Sunday. What is it?

Well, we hear from Zephaniah, a minor prophet, who appears on the scene just 20 years prior to the destruction of Jerusalem and the subsequent exile in Babylon – about 587 years before Christ. There are only 3 chapters in this book, all doom and gloom except for a last bit tacked on the end that we hear today. Some scholars wonder if Zephaniah actually wrote it at all. Regardless, it is a beautiful hymn of hope and joy, very appropriate to Gaudete Sunday, our Sunday to rejoice within Advent. Thus the rose colored candle – the call to hope, the call to joy.

The word Gaudete is the first word of Paul's letter to the Philippians that we hear today– "*Gaudete in Domino semper*" in Latin. Rejoice in the Lord always. The Lord is near. Despite the wearing of violet as in Lent, Advent is not a gloomy season. Rather, it is a build-up of excitement, an eager anticipation. Do you feel the build-up? I know the kids sure do!

I have a favorite walk that I take from my house. It starts out up a hill and through some rather boring parts and ends up after a mile or so at the golf course that is nearby. The last half mile along the course is an absolutely beautiful stroll, very flat, with an occasional golf ball sitting on the path like a little gift. Someone recently asked me why I don't simply take the walk in reverse order, starting with the golf course and then turning around at the boring part and retracing my steps through the golf course again. That way I'd get nothing but beauty, right? So I tried it once or twice and it was indeed beautiful, but I very quickly went back to my old route. Why? In short, I found that I appreciated the beauty of the golf course much more when I could anticipate that it was coming. In a way, I needed to walk some Advent before I could celebrate Christmas. This 3rd Sunday of Advent is that last quarter mile before I hit the golf course. In a way, I'm getting a free glimpse of the golf course in the distance through the trees.

This 3rd Sunday once again features John the Baptist in his familiar role, baptizing and calling for repentance. But this Sunday is a bit different – the people ask John to get specific. "What should we do?" His answer is surprising. You would think that he might say, "Put on sack cloth and ashes and pray for forgiveness." Or "Sell what you have and give to the poor." Or something similar. But he takes a different tack. He tells them first of all to simply share, share your food, share your extra clothes with those who have little. Lest we discount this directive as no big deal, recall that most people of that time did not know where their next meal was coming from, and to lose your cloak probably meant death to exposure. Sharing from whatever surplus you had means that you were essentially giving up some of your nest egg.

Then John gives specific advice to the two most hated groups of the time, tax collectors and soldiers, who often traveled together. Again, surprise - he doesn't tell them to quit their jobs – after all, if that was what they did, someone new would simply take their place. Rather, he implicitly applauds them for their effort in seeking the right action, and challenges them to change what it means to be a tax collector and a soldier – to work for change from within, to be just and fair. Jesus himself would later speak of being yeast in the dough, of being salt of the earth. This is the same basic message. Our lives are not necessarily about making dramatic changes. Our life purpose is to be authentic, to be light to the world, to be noticeable in the good we do within a world that seems to have far too much evil at work.

There is something more here, however, that's hidden a bit. At face value, John's recommendations seem kind of simplistic and mundane. After all his calls for repentance, this is it? The hard part of this message is not "doing the right thing". The hard part is the persistence, the day in, day out, persistence in doing the right thing in the face of a world that expects quite the opposite. In fact, our morality and upright nature may seem like an invitation for any unscrupulous person to take advantage of us, to rob us or bilk us, and laugh all the way to the bank. You've probably heard the cynical saying, "no good deed goes unpunished"? So we stop doing good deeds? We measure the potential outcome first? We do a risk analysis? Peter tried this with Jesus on the road to Jerusalem you may recall – and Jesus wasn't very pleased with the exercise. The core to John's call to repentance is to be persistent in our good actions, to act and not measure the cost, to give even if the gift will be thrown away or misused. That is not easy. That is not trite, simplistic, or mundane. It is Christ-like, and therefore the duty of we, his followers.

That doesn't sound very joyful, though, does it? How does this tough message of repentance and persistence bring us to joy?

Our friend, St. Paul gives us the answer. As Christmas rapidly approaches, it is so easy to get caught up in the busy-ness of it all, to get pulled into the rapid current of commercialism, parties, buying, wrapping, and doing, doing, doing. There seems to be a competition, especially among the ladies, to outdo the other. My mother in law says that when she is reincarnated, she wants to come back as a man at Christmas time.

However, the Lord is reminding us today that he doesn't want a human *doing*, he wants a human *being*. He asks us to take some time with him, to recognize that he is near. Paul's words today are so appropriate. "The Lord is near. Have no anxiety at all, but in everything, by prayer and petition, make your requests known to God. Then the peace of God that surpasses all understanding will guard your hearts and minds in Christ Jesus." Where peace is found, brothers and sisters, joy is right next door. Gaudete! Rejoice! The formula for joy is right here in the midst of our duty as leaven in the world. We are in a season of hope – and that is a God-given virtue.

Enjoy these last few days of Advent. The golf course is just around the corner.

Ask and You Will Receive?

Scriptures Referenced: Gn 18:20-32; Lk 11:1-13

And I tell you, ask and you will receive; seek and you will find; knock and the door will be opened to you.

For everyone who asks, receives; and the one who seeks, finds; and to the one who knocks, the door will be opened.

When I was a young boy, I heard today's gospel reading in my religion class, and Sister emphasized the point that all we needed to do was "ask and you will receive". I thought about this for a while and decided that it was time to test the theory. So I prayed that night before bed, and the next morning as well, and whenever it came to mind, I prayed. I prayed fervently for the one thing that I wanted most of all at the age of nine – *money*. Getting off the school bus that afternoon, I happened to look down at the side of the road and what did I see but a gleaming silver dime. Was I ever excited – it was equal to my weekly allowance, so this was quite a windfall. I told my mother about it and she stunned me by saying, "Well, if it is from God, I'm sure that he would want you to give it to the Church this Sunday!" Seeing my look of dismay, she quickly added, "God rewards us ten times over for our generosity." Another theory to test! So I popped that dime in the collection basket on Sunday and waited to see what would happen. The next day, I received a card in the mail from my grandparents – I don't remember the reason exactly, but what I do remember is that in the card was a one-dollar bill. This prayer stuff was pretty neat. Then I stopped cold – what do I do now? Give this money away? There seemed to be a flaw in these theories. The only one getting richer was the Church! After pondering this carefully, I decided that God and I would make a deal. We'd split the winnings 50-50. So, I got change for the dollar and next Sunday, put 50 cents in the collection basket. Where would that five dollar bill come from, I wondered.

Doesn't this sound a little bit like Abraham in the first reading? God and Abraham are bargaining back and forth like a buyer and seller in the market, and it would be quite amusing if the subject weren't so dire –

the fate of two cities and the presumably thousands of inhabitants living there. Jesus runs with the same theme in the Gospel, telling the story of the annoying neighbor who won't stop pounding on your door in the middle of the night for some food. It seems that *persistence* is the theme of the day – that somehow if we keep pestering God, wearing him down, we'll eventually get what we want.

I probably get asked to pray for some intention or another every day. They're all good intentions, healing for a sick relative, or for a new job, or to calm a troubled marriage. I never refuse – goodness, how would that sound in someone's ears – but it is also very apparent that many of these prayerful wishes don't seem to come true. The patient dies, the marriage crumbles, the job offer doesn't arrive. What's going on here? People are asking, seeking, knocking on doors, but the requested result doesn't occur. I know some very good Catholics who are brought to the threshold of despair because a prayer is simply not being answered. They ask me, "Am I doing it wrong? Does God not like me? I'm being persistent, why isn't it working?"

When my younger brother Steve was dying of cancer in 2001, we had everyone praying for him. We had priests and nuns praying for him. We had novenas going on all over the place, we pulled out all of the stops. A priest from a local parish in the vicinity took this challenge on as a personal ministry, fasting and praying at all hours. He'd call the house and ask expectantly, "how's Steve doing?" We'd respond with more bad news, and he'd pause in dismay and then say, "we're just not praying hard enough!" At first, I would agree with him, and then, eventually, as Steve's condition continued to worsen, I began to realize that just maybe, we were praying for the wrong thing. The answer is in the Our Father that we pray every day, the second line. Your kingdom come, your will be done… Note "*your* will". Not "*my* will". When that realization struck, I became the nine year old boy again and I decided to test this theory. I prayed for God's will to be done with regard to Steven and then added, "and please show me how your will is being done." And suddenly, as if a veil were parted, God began to show me, show the family, His will. A friend of my sister's, a talented musician, was discerning her next step in life. At the family's invitation, she came to Steven's bedside and played spiritual songs for 3 hours, her voice filling the room, bringing everyone to tears. She left that evening, went home, and didn't sleep a wink, so moved was she by the experience. She wrote my sister an email and told her that God had answered a prayer and she was going to dedicate her life to ministering with music.

My parents' neighbor John across the street had ALS, or Lou Gehrig's disease, and was slowly dying from the feet up, paralysis taking a little bit of him each day. Steven asked if he could pay him a visit, and on entering John's house told him, "I know that I have it bad, and then I think of you." John made it to Steven's funeral in the freezing cold of January in Boston, bundled in a wheelchair. He lived another six months before joining my brother in heaven. God's will be done, not mine.

So if God's will is always done, and it is, why bother to pray for anything? Why does Jesus tell us to knock, ask, seek, and so forth? It's simple really. Asking, seeking, knocking, *praying* is the beginning of relationship. It's the open door to understanding the heart of God, to beginning to see that God's will is always good, even if not always obvious, even if not always about *us* specifically. Sometimes we're the answer to someone else's prayer. Can you see that?

So, if you're praying for something you really, really want, and it seems to be going nowhere, try my theory. Pray your intention and then ask for God's will to be done - and then *ask to see His will be done*. Look for it. It may be surprising, for God likes big surprises.

If you read on in Genesis, by the way, you'll see that Abraham was not able to find 10 innocent people in Sodom and Gomorrah, and God destroyed the cities. But God and Abraham were building quite a relationship, weren't they? One that would change salvation history. Did my fifty cent contribution to the collection plate bring me five dollars as I hoped? Not exactly, no. But something else happened. God and I began to talk a lot more often, and I continued my bargaining ways, which I'm sure drove him nuts. But understand, God took me where I was, and as I slowly grew up, our relationship matured as well. I wouldn't give it up for all of the money in the world. It's priceless.

Ask and you will receive. Seek and you will find. Knock and the door will be opened to you. But, it may not be what you expect!

The Monopoly Game

Scripture Referenced: Lk 12:13-21

> *But God said to him, 'You fool, this night your life will be demanded of you; and the things you have prepared, to whom will they belong?'*
>
> *Thus will it be for the one who stores up treasure for himself but is not rich in what matters to God.*

How many of you have played the game *Monopoly*? As a boy growing up with 3 brothers, this was one of our favorite rainy day pastimes. One of my brothers, once he had built up some cash, would slide a $500 bill under the game board in front of him, unbeknownst to the rest of us. If luck turned against him, and the rest of us were poised to knock him out of the game, he would suddenly reach under the board and pull out the $500 with a sly "look what I've found" comment. The rest of us were ready to kill him, but my Dad would intervene and tell us that our brother was smart to save up for a rainy day. There's not a financial advisor anywhere who wouldn't agree, and most will be happy to tell you exactly how much to store away, and what investment vehicle to use.

Today's Gospel is usually called the "parable of the rich fool". But let's be honest. If you were in his shoes, wouldn't you do the same thing? If you received a windfall, wouldn't your first thought be what new car to buy, or where to invest it, or can I now retire? Oh yes, being good folks, we'd certainly give some away, but studies show that it's highly unlikely we'd give more than 5 percent. I remember distinctly a man I knew in Seattle who worked very hard right up to the day he retired at age 65. He had the pension, the savings, and a hankering to go fishing every day. He died two weeks after his 65th birthday from a heart attack. So here's the question, "was he a fool?" Heck, are we all fools for saving money for retirement, for a rainy day?

God certainly doesn't want us to be foolish with our resources, or become a burden to others. The earth's bounty is to be mastered by mankind and subdued. The shrewdest among us figure out how to do this in a way that naturally brings them more goodies than others. We're

116

wired to achieve, to compete, to make our mark in the world. Even St. Paul says that those who won't work shouldn't eat! That's pretty tough. But clearly at some point we move from attaining what is *sensible* to working for what is *foolish*. There's a line that's been crossed by the rich man in the parable, and given *our* wealth and material goods, it would be wise for us to consider where that line is.

Notice that the man in the Gospel is already rich, even before the bountiful harvest comes in. Here's a classic case of the rich getting richer. The interesting thing about greed is that it is a hunger that is *never* satisfied. It's the Monopoly game. You win when you own it *all*, when everyone else owns nothing. Greed is a very sneaky devil – it disguises itself with many innocent sounding platitudes: I'm working hard for my family. Once I have X dollars in the bank, I'll retire. Buying a boat is a good investment. I need to save money so that my kids can go the college of their choice. Let's get a bigger storage unit – this stuff is too nice to give away. My neighbor bought a car that he would use for airport parking only. Any of this sound familiar?

About four years ago, my wife and I bought the current house we own. When we put our money down, the house was not yet built (it was part of a new development), so we were forced to move into a rental for 9 months. We packed everything carefully – actually Katie packed everything carefully – and we selected out the minimum we would need to live. Pots, pans, dishes, towels, and so forth. Everything else went into storage. Without intentionally thinking about, it was an interesting experiment in living simply. What amazed both of us over time was how little we missed most of the stuff in the boxes. In fact, we completely forgot what was in many of them.

What irritates God about greed is that it misuses our time and our talent as well as our treasure. Feeding the greed machine takes up tremendous time and energy. If we have the wisdom and the perspective to stop and say "enough is enough", and re-direct our time and talent toward helping those without the ability to make it on their own, then we've beaten the greed machine and begun to store up treasures that matter to God. So how do we get that perspective? What concrete actions can we take?

Some thoughts for you to consider:

- Look at your consumption. Look at what you buy. Is it always more, more, more? If I were to tell you that you could go the rest of your life simply replacing what you wore out, would your life suffer much?

- Make a distinction between what you *want* and what you *need*. Ask that question before every major purchase. Do I *need* this, or simply *want* it?
- Practice aggressive simplification. If something hasn't been used in a year, it's unlikely to ever be used again. Give it away, even if it was a gift from your favorite aunt, or has some other emotional significance.
- Look at how you spend your free time. If you have a choice between working with things and working with people, always choose people. Things can't love you back.
- Give more away. More money, more stuff, more time. Practice donating – it's the absolute best antidote to greed that's available. It will give you perspective.

There's a modern day extension to today's parable. The rich man meets St. Peter at the pearly gates and pleads with St. Peter to let him go back to earth for one day, so he can gather up his wealth with and bring it with him to heaven. St. Peter agrees, with the stipulation that it all fit in one suitcase. So the guy heads back to earth for one more day, sells everything he has, and buys gold bars that he packs into one very sturdy suitcase. On returning to heaven, he proudly opens the suitcase to show St. Peter. Peter looks in the suitcase with astonishment and asks him, "Why did you bring bricks with you? We've got plenty of these – the streets are paved with them."

Don't be a rich fool. The only thing you can take with you to heaven's gate is love, for love never dies. How can it? *God is love*. What matters to God in the final analysis is how much we love, not how much we have. Love is the only "thing" that truly satisfies. All else, as we hear today, is simply vanity.

Detachment

Scripture Referenced: Phil 4:12-14, 19-20

> *I have learned, in whatever situation I find myself, to be self-sufficient.*
>
> *I know indeed how to live in humble circumstances; I know also how to live with abundance. In every circumstance and in all things I have learned the secret of being well fed and of going hungry, of living in abundance and of being in need.*

Has this last week been a challenge for you? It seems like every turn of the economy is an exercise in breathless anxiety. We're told that the market is a delicate balance of greed and fear – that's what is meant by "managing risk". Right now, fear seems to be winning. I've never seen so many people rattled and upset over a little number that bounces up and down called the Dow. The drumbeat from the media is thunderous and rarely helpful. I didn't expect to be up here today talking about the economy, but we need to face the issue.

The passage from St. Paul's letter to the Philippians that we read today is remarkably appropriate. In a brief sentence, he expresses a quiet conviction that is just as striking now as it was 2000 years ago. Listen again to what he says: "In every circumstance and in all things I have learned the secret of being well fed and of going hungry, of living in abundance and of being in need." What is this secret to which he refers? Apparently, whether he is well fed or hungry, surrounded by stuff or has nothing, Paul does not vary, does not change. Despite the fact that Paul is writing this from prison, is facing death, he is completely at peace.

Paul's secret is one that many deeply spiritual people have discovered as well. This secret is *detachment*. Detachment is a term that is easily misunderstood. It doesn't mean that you don't care, or that you stand aloof from the world. Detachment is a practice as much as it is an attitude. Detachment comes from perspective, and perspective is a grace from God.

Let me tell you a story that illustrates detachment born of perspective. A man is taking a walk with his wife one morning in July and suddenly notices two one-dollar bills on the ground. He picks them up and announces to his wife that he will take the money and bet it on a horse at Del Mar. She says okay and off he goes. He bets on a 50 to 1 long shot and the horse wins! Taking the $100 that he won, he puts it all on another long shot the next race. And guess what? The horse wins! He now has $5000. Feeling pretty good about things he heads home and finds himself passing a casino. It's my lucky day, he thinks, so he enters the casino, and bets the entire $5000 on the roulette wheel, number 14. The wheel spins and the number comes up – 27. So the man goes home. His wife greets him at the door and asks, "well, how did it go?" He smiles and answers, "well, honey, I lost the two dollars." You see, we all start out life with nothing, and we all end our life with nothing. Everything in between is drama! Awareness of that reality is called perspective, and perspective leads to a sense of appropriate detachment.

Now, all that drama in life can be a bit disconcerting. It isn't easy to live each hour of each day in an attitude of detachment. Does Paul have an answer for this as well? You bet he does: "My God will fully supply whatever you need, in accord with his glorious riches in Christ Jesus." In other words, to live a life of total peace and detachment, you turn it over to Christ Jesus. Paul doesn't say a word about material things here – it's not pertinent. Whether you have a lot of money in the bank or you're wondering how you're going to get through the next week, the goal is to hold on to the riches of Christ – and trust it will all be well.

So let's get practical. How do we begin to cultivate this sense of detachment, this overriding relationship with Christ Jesus? There are 3 stages to the strategy.

First of all, pull away from the commotion, the false sense of urgency. If you're caught up in the blitz of information that pours into our homes, it's virtually impossible to detach. The media are very good at getting your attention – that's what they're paid to do – and with all of the sources of data out there, you can be bombarded from the moment you wake until the moment you fall asleep. Heck, I know people who can't sleep unless the television is on. I'm sorry, that's not detachment, that's exhaustion. So, simple advice – turn off the television, take a day and never check email or the Internet. Grab the newspaper and only read the comics. (There are limits!) Amazingly enough, the world will move along just fine without you.

Secondly, re-engage with God. Now this can take many forms, of course. All of us have special places that open our hearts to God quickly and effectively. For some, it's entering a church. For others, it's a walk on the beach. Whatever it is for you, do a lot more of it when the drama gets a bit too intense.

Thirdly, re-engage with God's people. Nothing does more to detach us from our worries and concerns than to seek out Christ's presence in others. Children can be a great source for this, especially youngsters. Loved ones, friends, people of faith, energizing people, these are the ones to seek. But don't forget that a great source of detachment is where Christ is especially present – the poor, the sick, the imprisoned, the elderly, the ones who probably have a bit too much drama in their lives right now. Share some of that peace that you've gained with them. In return, you'll gain perspective.

Finally, if life is a bit too much to handle right now, do yourself a favor and get some help! Don't carry it alone. It may be spiritual guidance or psychological counseling – it's all good if it helps you.

Detachment is a matter of perspective. Paul tells us that if we give everything to God, the peace that surpasses all understanding will guard our hearts and minds. By replacing the material things of this world with the glorious riches in Christ, you've invested your life into a bank account that will never go dry, and best of all, will be waiting for you when it's time to end the drama in this life. Christ's love – you *can* take that with you!

Sheep and Goats

Scripture Referenced: Mt 25:31-46

> *Then the king will say to those on his right, 'Come, you who are blessed by my Father. Inherit the kingdom prepared for you from the foundation of the world.*
>
> *For I was hungry and you gave me food, I was thirsty and you gave me drink, a stranger and you welcomed me, naked and you clothed me, ill and you cared for me, in prison and you visited me.'*

The story you've just heard from Jesus is striking for a number of reasons. It is an apocalyptic narrative, full of end-times imagery, featuring a dramatic final judgment of all the nations. Apparently, neither the sheep nor the goats are entirely clear on what to expect. The King pronounces the criteria for salvation and here's the first surprise. Unlike our modern society where we are judged on *what* you know or *who* you know or what *title* you hold or how much *stuff* you have – in the eyes of the King, salvation is about caring for the hungry, the thirsty, the naked, the ill, and the imprisoned. And here's the second surprise - to care for these least is to care directly for Jesus Himself.

But wait, say the goats, if we had known that it was you, Jesus, we certainly would have helped! And you know what? These goats are quite sincere. They definitely would have helped if they knew that Jesus, their God and King, was in need of assistance. Heck, just do the cost-benefit analysis. But equally striking is the fact that the sheep didn't make the connection either! They didn't equate Jesus and those who are in need. They simply helped without any calculation about who they were helping.

It's very easy to get a little concerned and depressed about this reading, because we all feel that we don't do enough. If only I had more time. If only I had some special skills. If only I had more money, if only, if only. Well stop it! You see, the danger is in thinking that the only way to be saved is by doing something grand and dramatic. So we put things off, we admire others who do great things, and we muddle along making excuses for ourselves and our busy lives. We end up doing *nothing*. Note that the goats are goats not because they do bad things, but because they do *nothing*. One of the key points of this reading is that judgment is based on very simple actions, actions that the good sheep *take for granted*.

When my wife and I were first married, we moved to Seattle for my graduate school work. We were very young, very poor, and didn't know anyone when we got there. Well, the young and the poor part didn't change, but we did meet some wonderful people, mostly other graduate students. Seattle at that time was not a hotbed of religion, and we soon discovered that we were the only church going people in our entire circle of friends. Katie and I would minister in the Parish, acting as lectors and assisting with the youth group. But what surprised us was how many of our unchurched friends did very "Christian" actions. Some served the poor in soup kitchens, others acted as foster parents for troubled kids, others volunteered as big brothers or big sisters to inner city youth. When we asked for their motivation, typically it was shrugged off as simply "the right thing to do". Sometimes you find sheep where you least expect!

So, why *do* we squirm a little when we hear this reading proclaimed? Part of the challenge for us is the stark words used in the gospel: the hungry, the thirsty, the naked, the ill, and so on. In the time of Jesus, these sufferings were day to day realities. There's no doubt that in our society today we've made tremendous progress in eliminating hunger, thirst, nakedness, and poor health. But that doesn't mean we're off the hook! These problems have simply morphed into other challenges. So let's re-imagine these terms in our society and see what comes to mind.

Hunger and thirst in the time of Jesus was certainly real, and did indeed mean lack of food and water. And yes, there are many hungry and thirsty people in our world today, many in foreign lands. But let's stay out of the trap - let's keep it simple and local. What does hunger and thirst look like here in North County San Diego? It could be loneliness, a lack of companionship. Is there a person on your street that lives alone? Perhaps a widow? Perhaps a young man or woman striving to make it? Loneliness can eat you up just like hunger, can't it? People hunger for meaning, for affection, for parenting, for a kind word. Maybe it's a person at work who needs to go to lunch with you. Keep it simple, keep it real.

What about clothing the naked? Again, that sounds way too dramatic. Here's a thought – when was the last time you donated clothing to the thrift store? A homeless shelter in Oceanside has a sock drive every year. Socks! Can't get much simpler than that. We're heading into winter – time to take a good look in your closets and ask the question, what haven't I worn in the last year? What's been hanging here since last Thanksgiving, untouched? Time to donate it! And I don't want to hear that your things are "too nice to donate".

What about caring for the sick? Again, our tendency is to shoot too high and think about volunteering at hospitals and hospice centers and other health care facilities. Nothing wrong with that, and some do this well, but there can be lots of obstacles in volunteering. Perhaps it's as simple as being nice to our spouse who's on day 14 of their cold. Or chipping in at work when a co-worker is having a really bad hair day.

And now for my favorite, visiting the imprisoned. This is a ministry that I find very rewarding, but it's not for everyone. Prisons can be difficult places to minister, and there are many logistical challenges in getting authorization. But we shouldn't limit ourselves. Prisons take many forms, don't they? People are imprisoned by drugs, alcohol, unemployment, sadness, and fear. They may be living in your own households, or where you work or go to school. Visiting the imprisoned is a simple word of encouragement, a smile of welcome, an invitation to share a coffee. Keep it unobtrusive, quiet, simple. Never underestimate the power of a simple, every day act of kindness.

When that day comes when we meet Jesus and he places us with the sheep, and tells everyone of the kind deeds we did in this world, our response may be, "Gee, it was no big deal. It was just the right thing to do." Then Jesus will say, "Yes, it was a big deal, because it was a big deal to *me*. Welcome!"

Chapter 7 - Journey

Look for the unexpected, look for the invitation, look for the interruption --maybe you'll hear it or see it today.

Seek the truth wherever it may take you.

You will meet hostility, indifference, and evil along the way.

Listen for truth even amongst those who seem to have a very different agenda.

Bring your gifts to the search.

When you find truth, be not surprised by its simplicity and profound depth.

The spiritual journey is not a solo journey, made by each of us one by one. It is a *communal* journey, a journey made with others. We cannot avoid this. We must not avoid this. People who tell me that they are *spiritual* and not religious are in danger of missing a critical point. God's relationship is always two dimensional – vertical between ourselves and God, horizontal from ourselves to others. Yes, the cross. It's possible for someone to have only a vertical dimension at first, but it must sprout wings for it to be truly a God relationship.

Pilgrimage, Journey, Quest

Scripture Referenced: Mt 2:1-12

When Jesus was born in Bethlehem of Judea, in the days of King Herod, behold, magi from the east arrived in Jerusalem, saying, "Where is the newborn king of the Jews? We saw his star at its rising and have come to do him homage."

In seeking a metaphor for the spiritual life, many of our great mystics and authors use the term "journey" or "pilgrimage" to describe the movement from spiritual darkness to dawning light. Did you ever notice how many popular works of fiction feature a quest? The mega-hit Lord of the Rings is one such example, where our heroes must overcome daunting odds to achieve peace in a land overcome by great evil. Our imaginations are continually fired up by people who do the same in real life, whether it's climbing a mountain or overcoming a physical malady or getting that college degree at an advanced age. This restless yearning and struggle to better ourselves and our families is from the same root, the desire to beat down anxiety, push back evil, and find a measure of peace in our lives. This feast of the Epiphany, so often misunderstood, is the feast that celebrates the quest, the journey to enlightenment.

The journey of the Magi appears only in Matthew's gospel. The Magi were likely from Persia, and were known at this time to be men skilled in philosophy, science, and medicine. They were typically employed as teachers to the Persian nobility, and their advice was sought for everything from when to plant crops to the interpretation of dreams.

So here's the first key point – these "wise men" saw no contradiction between science and religion, no battle of ideologies, no need to choose one or the other. In their eyes, the natural world was saturated with the divine, and when they saw the natural world produce something unexpected, an incredibly bright star where none was before, they didn't congratulate themselves and name the star Caspar or Balthazar. No, instead, they asked themselves what God was pointing out to them in this natural event, and began to seek understanding. Like many of us, their journey to enlightenment starts with the unexpected. God acts first, we see the action, and choose to seek further. Think on your lives for a moment. Do you remember that first contact from God? Or are you still waiting for it?

Now the journey begins. The Magi consult their libraries and come to the proposition that Judea is the source of this new king who is heralded by the star. They act, they move, they take some chances, they risk ridicule, and they obey the yearning in their heart. On reaching Jerusalem, they realize that they are close and unlike most men, they stop and ask for directions! In doing so, they clearly upset King Herod and all Jerusalem by extension. Understand that Herod is near the end of his 40 year reign and has become an increasingly fearful and vengeful king. If a powerful and paranoid king is threatened, we are not at all surprised that the people are quaking in their boots. Herod calls in his priests and scribes and hears the prophecy repeated. In his fear, in his grasping, Herod hatches a plot to discover this new king and destroy him.

So here's the second key point – the spiritual journey is not appreciated by everyone we encounter. Some, like Herod, will be devious and sly, seeking a way to use your journey for personal gain or evil intention. Perhaps they will offer you wisdom in exchange for money or your material goods. Perhaps they will try to convince you that you should be following them. Think of Jim Jones, think of David Koresh.

Moreover, some, like the priests and scribes in Jerusalem, who *should* be interested in your journey, will react with total indifference. Why? They have all of the answers already. Just follow the rules, the rubrics, the motions, and all is taken care of. The lesson for us is simple: beware the person, political or economic system, or religious expert who claims to have all of the answers. Always seek the humble person who is still seeking.

Oddly enough it seems, the Magi get good information from the scribes and move on to Bethlehem, the city where prophecy places the ruler who is to shepherd Israel. Here's the third point already – God will use everything on earth to give us guidance and revelation. God is so above all of this that he can even draw truth from sources that seem to have evil intent. Have you ever noticed that at times evil is a better revealer of truth than truth is? After all, we only truly appreciate the light when we have spent some time in darkness.

So the Magi finally arrive at the place where Jesus, Mary, and Joseph are camped and they recognize Christ the King in this little child. How remarkable! These learned men, so well educated, so honored, so upper class, have discovered through the grace of God that the prince of peace is a baby lying in a feeding trough, a manger. And yes, this is the fourth point – the revelation when it comes, will be profoundly simple and utterly correct, known in a gut sense, down to the toes in your shoes. You will laugh, you will cry, you will do homage, you will immediately give whatever you have to acknowledge the gift given to you. The Magi, we are told, lay down on the muddy ground in a gesture of utter humility, and give of their treasure.

I'm sure some of you are wondering, what is this revelation he's talking about? That's a good question to ask. Paul gives us a tantalizing clue in his letter to the Ephesians we just heard. He tells us that the Gentiles are co-heirs with the Jews in the promise of Christ Jesus. He tells us that God has expanded the notion of a chosen people to everyone in the universe. The revelation is not reserved for just a few. Paul is telling us that the journey to enlightenment is a wide open road – all we need to do is to embark on the journey. What will you find? Well, just like the Magi:

- Look for the unexpected, look for the invitation, look for the interruption --maybe you'll hear it or see it today
- Seek the truth wherever it may take you
- You will meet hostility, indifference, and evil along the way
- Listen for truth even amongst those who seem to have a very different agenda
- Bring your gifts to the search
- When you find truth, be not surprised by its simplicity and profound depth
- When you find truth, you will be compelled to share your gifts to spread the truth

If you read the lives of many of our saints, you will see this journey lived out in vivid detail. Read the life of St. Augustine, read the life of St. Francis, read the life of St. Ignatius, read the life of Mother Teresa. Even though they are saints, their journey is our journey. We honor them for their humility and honesty. What you will discover is that the revelation that they arrive it is each uniquely their own, tailored to their lives and circumstances. You will see this as well. Your understanding of the truth is ultimately part of who you are, the inner being that God knows and cherishes.

Would you like to know the one common denominator, the key element among those who find revelation, both then and now? The path is always through Christ Jesus. Always.

The Beatitudes

Scripture Referenced: Mt 5:1-12a

> *Blessed are the poor in spirit, for theirs is the kingdom of heaven.*
>
> *Blessed are they who mourn, for they will be comforted.*
>
> *Blessed are the meek, for they will inherit the land.*
>
> *Blessed are they who hunger and thirst for righteousness, for they will be satisfied.*
>
> *Blessed are the merciful, for they will be shown mercy.*
>
> *Blessed are the clean of heart, for they will see God.*
>
> *Blessed are the peacemakers, for they will be called children of God.*
>
> *Blessed are they who are persecuted for the sake of righteousness, for theirs is the kingdom of heaven.*
>
> *Blessed are you when they insult you and persecute you and utter every kind of evil against you (falsely) because of me. Rejoice and be glad, for your reward will be great in heaven.*

A little over two years ago, I had the opportunity to stand at the foot of a hillside in Galilee and hear this gospel proclaimed. On the top of the hill is the Church of the Beatitudes, a striking chapel that has eight-sides, one wall for each beatitude. The setting is peaceful and serene; one can easily imagine Jesus preaching in the sunshine overlooking the Sea of Galilee. Our gospel author Matthew places Jesus "up the mountain" to emphasize to his Jewish audience that Jesus is the new Moses, bringing truth and wisdom down from on high, just as Moses did. So what are these beatitudes anyway?

The Beatitudes, given their convenient list format, are often compared to the ten commandments, which is useful to a certain extent. The ten commandments are the core of Mosaic law, deeply engrained in the Judaic character. The eight beatitudes don't line up in exact relation to the ten commandments, but many note that the 10 commandments generally tell us what *not* to do, whereas the 8 beatitudes tell us what we *can* do, what a life in Christ looks like.

So what do we hear today? There are a number of common themes:

- In the first and third beatitudes, the poor in spirit and the meek receive the kingdom of heaven and inherit the land respectively. Jesus is telling us that we need to get a grip on how material goods affect us. If we are simply striving for stuff, or the money to get stuff, we will be unhappy. Oh yes, it may seem like that new video game or gold bracelet will satisfy, but the satisfaction is woefully brief, and we are off to the races again. When we break the hold that stuff has on us, we are truly free. And so we are blessed.

- In the second and fourth beatitudes, those who mourn and those who hunger and thirst for justice are equally comforted and satisfied. What Jesus is telling us is that we need to see the world as God does. If we insulate our lives and barrier ourselves behind our gates so that nothing bad ever enters, we are missing Jesus. When we see the world with eyes of compassion and cry for our brothers and sisters, when we hunger and thirst to have the world change for the better and act in response to that hunger, we mimic Christ. And in mimicking Christ, we share in the reward – for God has promised that justice will reign in the end. That's good news, that's a blessing.

- In the fifth, sixth, and seventh beatitudes, those who are merciful, clean of heart, and peacemakers will receive equal measure in return. It is very countercultural to demonstrate any of these traits. Mercy? Our society would tell us that the answer to crime is to build more prisons. Clean of heart? Our society would agree to a point, but if the other person is playing dirty, you need to do the same. Peacemaker? We send armies to kill others so that we will have peace. The dirty lie is that the peace we seek is really nothing more than *control*. You can't change the dogs of war into the doves of peace by control. True people of Christ are not fooled by claims that war leads to peace.

- The eighth beatitude tells us the consequences of speaking the truth – insult, standing alone in your convictions, marginalization, and death. And oh yes, the kingdom of heaven is yours if you live such a life filled with truth.

Taken as a whole and studied carefully, it is easy to get a little depressed. How can we possibly live up to these expectations? Remember that the beatitudes are not laws. Despite the connection

Matthew draws to Moses and the mountain, these are more appropriately seen as ideals, as wisdom teachings. They illustrate what to anticipate if you follow Jesus. In many ways, this list of beatitudes can be seen as a guide for our journey. To what degree do these behaviors resonate with us? If they do, you are following Jesus. If they don't, some reflection, some assessment is needed.

And if you're like me, it takes about 10 seconds to realize that some soul work is indeed needed. Where to start?

St. Augustine felt that the best way to approach the beatitudes was in the order presented. "Blessed are the poor in spirit" is our first challenge. The lure of possessions is just as pervasive and insidious today as it was in Jesus' time. Do you remember what Jesus tells the rich young man who was doing everything right but desired a guaranteed ticket to heaven? Sell all that you have and give to the poor. Then follow me. Note the order of events!

It seems that we can't truly follow Jesus until we completely detach from our goods and possessions. Ironically, by doing so and giving to the poor, we begin to see the true shape of the world and yes, we mourn as Christ would, and the second beatitude is realized. Then we recognize our smallness, our insignificance, our total reliance on God, and we realize what it means to be humble, to be meek. And the third beatitude makes sense. And once we are poor in spirit, and mourn for the world, and give ourselves humbly to God, we are suddenly fired up with a desire to change the world, to seek justice with the heart of a prophet. We live the 4th beatitude. But, we are only heard if we show mercy, if we live lives of purity, if we have peace as our goal. The 5th through 7th beatitudes. And then, once all of these beatitudes describe us, only then can we walk into the jaws of death and give our life for others without hesitation.

How can we possibly do all of this? Note that each beatitude, in describing its unique challenge, has a corresponding joy, or fulfillment with it. The simple reality? The Holy Spirit accompanies us on the journey, giving us exactly what we need as we open ourselves to the spiritual test, to the inherent challenge in following Christ, who incidentally personifies each and every one of these beatitudes perfectly.

Take a few moments this week and read the eight beatitudes. Which of these do you live? What do you need to work on? The recipe for following Christ is right here.

Blindfolded

Scripture Referenced: Jn 9:1-41

As he passed by he saw a man blind from birth.

His disciples asked him, "Rabbi, who sinned, this man or his parents, that he was born blind?"

Jesus answered, "Neither he nor his parents sinned; it is so that the works of God might be made visible through him.

When I was ten years old, I was given a pocket knife by my grandfather. I was delighted. My parents were not so delighted for some reason, probably because I was known to be a bit accident prone. Included with the gift was a flat black stone, which puzzled me greatly. My grandfather explained that this was called a whet stone, and was used to sharpen the knife. You put a little drop of 3-in-1 oil on the stone and rubbed the knife against it to sharpen it. At the time, I remember thinking how strange it was that to sharpen a knife, you had to sort of test it, you had to match it against something harsh and unyielding. This reading from John features a character who learns that this lesson is true in life as well.

Our hero of the story, we are told, is blind from birth – he is completely unaware of what sight and light are all about. He is quite literally in darkness. Notice that he does not ask to be healed. But Jesus heals him anyway. Why? What John is trying to emphasize is that this man is not fully created – he is not quite fully alive. Jesus makes clay with his saliva and rubs it on the man's eyes. It sounds kind of gross until we realize that the book of Genesis has God creating man from the clay of the earth and breathing life into him. The point is that Jesus is completing this man's creation – he is finishing the job! John invites us to continue the thought process. Don't stop there – Jesus was sent by the Father to complete creation, to finish the job with *all* of us, to make us fully alive!

Now the story shifts. Jesus exits stage left and the remainder of this marvelous story consists of a running dialogue between the man with new sight and a skeptical, hostile group of Pharisees who believe that they have the answers, that they are the ones with complete vision of how the world works. The dialogue starts simply enough but eventually escalates into an increasingly absurd debate that ends up with our formerly blind hero back out in the streets where he started, kicked out of the temple.

Notice how the blind man grows in his understanding of who Jesus is. He is asked by the Pharisees four times, "how were your eyes opened?" The first answer he gives is "the man called Jesus". The second time? "He is a prophet." The third time? "A man from God." The fourth time? The Son of Man who he worships. The man born blind comes to understand who Jesus is by pondering the meaning of his healing and reacting to the badgering of the Pharisees. It's almost as if he needs to be disbelieved and insulted to come to the amazing conclusion that God himself has touched him.

Isn't this true of us too? When our faith is challenged, we can either deny Jesus or we can stop and ask the question, "what do I really believe?" If nothing else happens in your lives, I sincerely hope that each of you at some point is asked what you really believe. We all fear that test, we all fear that we will melt under the glare. But I strongly believe that God allows us to be tested for the same reason it worked with the blind man. You must come to understand and own your faith. It can only be honed and polished if it is rubbed against something unyielding and harsh, just like my pocket knife. In a very real way, you must be willing to be insulted to hold your beliefs. If not, as St. Paul says, it's just rubbish. It's dull and useless.

What about the Pharisees? In direct contrast to the man born blind, they *think* that they are in the light. What frustrates Jesus is when the Pharisees are shown the true light, are given stark evidence of the truth, and still cling to false beliefs, cling to the darkness, stubbornly refusing to believe their own eyes. They are shown a wonderful alternative to their rigid moralism and they simply will not see it. It's as if the Pharisees tie a scarf around their eyes and choose to walk the earth blindfolded. The harsh reality is that we often do the same thing. Jesus invites us to walk with him, to engage in a life of service, and we persist in our path. We walk in self-imposed darkness –and the light is shining right nearby.

At this time of year, as spring is approaching, I like to take a walk around the neighborhood and look carefully at the trees. Do you see the buds at the ends of each branch? Do you see them opening? Take a good look today. The point is that spring can catch us completely unaware and surprised – "look, it's spring – how did that get here?" Or, we can delight in each and every day of awakening. The blind man was given his spring in one shocking moment of revelation. But we have the opportunity to see revelation at each simple step, at each moment of encounter along the way. Lent is about the journey to Easter, the journey to new life, the journey to light. Today, Laetare Sunday, in the middle of Lent, is a reminder to us that the journey culminates in glory – it's not all gloom and doom. See how God works his wonders. See it each day. Open your eyes – and your hearts. Take off the blindfold.

The Beloved Disciple

Scripture Referenced: Jn 20:1-9

> *When Simon Peter arrived after him, he went into the tomb and saw the burial cloths there, and the cloth that had covered his head, not with the burial cloths but rolled up in a separate place.*
>
> *Then the other disciple also went in, the one who had arrived at the tomb first, and he saw and believed.*

Do you ever watch nature shows on television? Like Animal Planet or National Geographic? The shows that always draw the biggest TV audiences are the ones that feature animal babies. Right? We delight in seeing animal mothers and fathers treating their young in much the same way we do. The mother lion goes out "shopping", oops, hunting for food while Dad lies on the grass watching the gazelles. And the cubs jump all over him until he casually whacks them away with a big paw and what happens next? They come bouncing back and it starts all over again. The lion cubs are utterly trustful and utterly alive. We human beings are the same. Childhood experts tell us that unless a child is loved, that child will never thrive, never grow up normally, never trust anyone.

Our gospel reading today features an unnamed follower of Jesus who is known simply as the "disciple who Jesus loved". Much debate has occurred about who this may be. Some say it was John, the writer of the gospel, who was embarrassed to use his own name in the text. Given John's tendency to use symbols in his writings, many scholars think he meant us to go deeper. Quite frankly, the so called "beloved disciple" can easily be interpreted to mean you and me. The disciple is a stand-in, a *proxy*, that represents each of us.

Let's try that for a moment, let's relive this story with us playing the role of the beloved disciple. So, after following Jesus for three years, you've just witnessed a most horrible sight – Jesus has been crucified like a common criminal outside the city walls. Three days later -- you've spent another sleepless night with the other disciples, mourning your loss. Suddenly, as dawn breaks, Mary Magdalene comes running in and tells you that the body of Jesus is gone! You and Peter race out to the tomb, heart pounding, emotions churning. What is going through your mind? You get there and yes, the tomb is indeed open. You look inside, but then respectfully wait for Peter, your leader, to catch up to you. He, in typical Peter fashion, charges in and begins to examine the burial cloths. You then go in, look at everything, and then as the Gospel says, you *believe!*

But, *what* do you believe? Remember you haven't seen Jesus yet. What *could* you believe? You could believe the body has been stolen. But the cloths are a big problem. Why would someone unwrap the body, leaving the cloths behind, folded up even, and then steal it? It makes no sense. There's one other explanation, however. Jesus said he would rise from the dead. You heard him say it. And suddenly, like a blinding light, it explodes into your brain - Jesus is *alive!!* You look at Peter – he's clearly puzzled. What do you say to him?

Recall that the Gospel writer John uses symbols. Peter, who was given the keys to the kingdom, represents the Church in John's gospel. The beloved disciple is the person on the faith journey, you and me. John's message here is simple – the path of faith is a journey of companionship, a journey that is walked not alone, but in the company of the Church. And what is the Church? It's all of the beloved disciples who have been likewise touched by the presence of God. It's clergy, religious, single people, married people, young, old, and everyone in between. We're all beloved disciples journeying together.

We need each other. We're all sinners, top to bottom. This past year, our Church family has been pounded over and over in the press, the sins of our leaders splattered everywhere. Innocent people have been damaged, some irreparably. Many of us have been discouraged, dismayed, heart-broken by the abuse scandals. At a time like this, all we can do is ask ourselves, "what do I believe?" If you can answer, "Jesus is alive," then you are okay, you will survive, and the Church, all of us beloved disciples, will survive too. Because if you can answer that Jesus is alive, then you can trust his other promises too, because all of the other promises of Jesus are meaningless if he remains dead in the tomb. If that sounds a little harsh, read St. Paul's first letter to the Corinthians – "if Christ has not been raised, your faith is vain...(and) we are the most pitiable people of all." (1Cor 15:16-19)

Easter celebrates Christ *alive*. Christ alive is the *Church* alive. Why? Because Christ is the head of the Church. Not the Pope, not the bishop, not the clergy, but Jesus the Christ. Our Church is a human family, featuring lots of us trying to figure out how to navigate through the choppy seas of our lives. Somehow we know that it all belongs, somehow we know that evil will *NOT WIN*. But we need each other. We need more saints. We need all of God's beloved disciples working together. Each one of you is a beloved disciple. Each one of you has been touched by God or you wouldn't be here. It is not about being perfect all of the time, it is about journeying together, loving God and neighbor both.

As beloved disciples, just like those lion cubs, just like a infant in its doting mother's arms, we can trust God, we can *thrive*, we know that we are loved right down to our bones. And with that love secure, there's nothing on this earth, even death, that should frighten us.

Easter is our celebration of that hope, that promise, that reality.

We celebrate it every Sunday.

What To Do With the Pain

Scripture Referenced: Mk 16:1-7

> *On entering the tomb they saw a young man sitting on the right side, clothed in a white robe, and they were utterly amazed.*
>
> *He said to them, "Do not be amazed! You seek Jesus of Nazareth, the crucified. He has been raised; he is not here. Behold the place where they laid him.*

I'm going to guess that the vast majority of you here today were baptized as infants. Is that a fair assumption? If you were baptized as an infant, raise your hand. The rest of you presumably were baptized later on – perhaps as teens or adults. Out of curiosity, how many of you fall into that category? Any here not yet baptized? OK, see me after Mass!

The point of my question is that for most of us, our Catholic faith was handed to us, probably by our parents, so we dutifully attended CCD, or were taught in a Catholic school. Whether we were well-educated in the faith or not, at some point – usually young adulthood – we begin to ask the question, "does my being Catholic matter?" Does my religion speak to the problems of life I'm facing, the challenges, the joys, and the sorrows? If not, then we simply slip slide away, falling into the pattern of so many who claim a Catholic identity, but see little real world application. This is a classic pattern, lived by virtually every person who has walked the earth.

After all, life is not a bowl of cherries. There are high points, for sure, but much of life consists of many mundane day-to-day issues that dominate our time. Work, school, family – this is the life we have. And then, ever so often, we hit a crisis. Crisis sounds kind of dramatic, so let me define crisis as situations when we find ourselves in some kind of pain and not in control. The kind of pain that comes when our child is hospitalized. Or a parent is slipping into dementia. Or we ourselves suffer an emotional loss due to a broken relationship – perhaps someone we love leaves us. Many people today are suffering acute anxiety over financial matters, fear of losing a job or a home. It is at times like this, when we're in crisis, that religion is put to the test. Theologian Richard

Rohr puts it quite well: "If we don't learn how to *transform* our pain, we are bound to *transmit* it to someone else." Great religion tells us what to do with our pain.

Easter is about resurrection of course – that is a central tenet of our faith. But Easter is about transformation as well. How does the resurrection of Jesus help us to transform our pain? The answer is deceptively simple – Jesus is the model of how to transform pain. When Jesus accepted the cross, he was completely innocent of every charge trumped up against him. It's one thing to suffer pain because of something stupid that we've done – it's quite another thing to suffer when it is completely undeserved. Not once did Jesus lash back, not once did he scream at his tormentors in anger, not once did he transmit the pain he was suffering to another person. He absorbed it, and even though he tasted death, he utterly transformed that horror into resurrected life. Jesus models what to do with the pain. You hold it in, hold it together. The buck stops with you. Like a closely woven sieve, you filter out the bad and hold it until it transforms *you*.

Not so easy, you say? Yes, that's correct. It's not easy at all. It takes lots of practice. But here is where our Catholic tradition stands tall. Being Catholic is not about the Pope, the Bishop, or the clergy. It's not simply about the institution we see. What the Catholic Church offers to her people is a long history of incredible wisdom for the spiritual journey, a wisdom we believe is a direct influence of the Holy Spirit down through the ages. There are literally dozens of prayer practices, from lectio divina to the rosary to contemplative prayer to healing prayer to the ultimate prayer of the Church, the Mass. There are dozens of spiritual traditions, from Jesuit to Franciscan to Augustinian to Benedictine to Carmelite to Eudist and more. These practices and traditions are like jewels in a crown – ready and waiting for the seeker to ask, "may I try?" Why all of these traditions and practices? Because we are all so different in our backgrounds, in what makes us tick, our personalities, our life circumstances. Each of these prayer spiritualties and traditions is designed to open you to *encounter*, to the presence of God. Because once you have experienced a relationship with God, you will begin to transform, to become someone who *can* transform pain, instead of transmitting it.

A friend of mine who has been deeply transformed by the presence of God in his life wrote an email two weeks ago. He said, "I am contacting you to let you know that your prayers are especially appreciated at this time for my family. This past Friday I was laid off by my company where I have worked for 7 years. Like so many, I lost my job because company revenue was down about 25%." Note the classic crisis here. He is in some pain due to a loss of job that was outside of his control. So does he complain about his hard luck? Does he curse the banking system or AIG? Here's what he goes on to say: "We were prepared in case something like this was to happen, so we are doing fine in many ways, but I will be looking for new opportunities with much help from the Holy Spirit, our Mother Mary and Jesus. We trust that God has something very special waiting for us...we can't wait to see what it is!" Only a transformed person can write an email like that. By the way, he got a new job offer the next week.

Today's gospel reading from Mark features very little detail. An open tomb, amazed women, a stranger dressed in white, and an astonishing statement that the Jesus you seek has been raised. This is where Christianity started. The crisis of Good Friday and the transformation of Easter morning. A simple beginning. Starting small. Most of started small, as infants, each given a simple gift of grace and a community to dwell within. Pray, explore, seek a spiritual tradition or prayer practice that you can embrace. Ask for God to say hello. Get ready for a surprise – you'll find joy, real joy, and a peace that the world cannot give. Wouldn't it be nice not to worry? It'll feel like resurrection.

Three Strikes?

Scripture Referenced: Mt 18:15-20

> *If your brother sins (against you), go and tell him his fault between you and him alone. If he listens to you, you have won over your brother.*
>
> *If he does not listen, take one or two others along with you, so that 'every fact may be established on the testimony of two or three witnesses.'*
>
> *If he refuses to listen to them, tell the church. If he refuses to listen even to the church, then treat him as you would a Gentile or a tax collector.*

Did you see the article in the paper a couple of weeks ago about the woman in Carlsbad who painted her home bright sea foam green? Apparently, the house practically glows in the dark. There is no homeowner's association there, and no city laws were broken, but some of the neighbors are a bit upset. More recently, I was having a discussion with a good friend of mine about politics. As you all know, politics is a risky discussion topic these days, since people tend to grab onto strong viewpoints and woe to you if you don't agree. It's been said that you should never discuss politics, sex, or religion in polite company. I don't think it's possible to turn on the television news without at least one of these topics being discussed. Actually, it's usually all three being discussed at the same time! As elections approach, there is much discussion about what a good Catholic should do.

Our first reading and gospel have something to say about this challenge. Ezekiel, preaching from Babylonian exile, hears the word of God with great clarity – it's a stern message. If a person is doing something wicked, they will be punished. If you see the person doing something wicked and don't speak out to dissuade them, then God will hold you equally responsible for his death! Yikes! But if you do warn the person and they ignore you, you're off the hook. The key is that you have to try, to make the attempt to turn them back to the right path.

Matthew's gospel updates this mandate with some interesting details. Jesus describes an intervention approach – first, you speak to the sinner one on one. If the sinner ignores you, you bring in reinforcements (one or two others) and try again. If still no change of behavior, you get the whole community engaged in an attempt to turn this sinner around. If all this fails, you must reluctantly let them go, treating them as you would an outsider. This is the basis of the term *excommunication* – meaning "out of the community." So, it's three strikes and you're out.

Scripture scholars have a hard time with this part of Matthew's gospel because it doesn't sound like something Jesus would say. How do you reconcile this three strikes mentality with forgiving the sinner seventy times seven times? How does this gibe with a shepherd who will seek out the lost lamb and leave the 99 behind? Of all of Jesus' teachings, the mandate to forgive is probably the most unique and compelling. Jesus is forgiving people even while hanging on a cross! How do we resolve this seeming contradiction?

Remember that Matthew is writing his gospel with a particular community in mind, a community of Jewish converts. These early Christians were struggling with the reality of communal living, the nuts and bolts of disputes, confrontations, and justice. As people of Jewish background, they wanted clear laws to govern themselves, so Matthew responds by taking some sayings of Jesus and molding them into a conflict resolution process. Matthew's use of the term *church* is a telling detail here – this is a post-resurrection concept. Don't be alarmed that Matthew did this – the other three gospel writers take similar liberties – remember that they were each writing to a distinct community of believers with different issues and challenges.

Sound familiar? We have issues and challenges as well. So, what is our direction here? What are we being asked to do? Here are some guiding principles:

1. First, the spiritual journey is not a solo journey, made by each of us one by one. It is a *communal* journey, a journey made with others. We cannot avoid this. We must not avoid this. People who tell me that they are *spiritual* and not religious are in danger of missing a critical point. God's relationship is always two dimensional – vertical between ourselves and God, horizontal from ourselves to others. Yes, the cross. It's possible for someone to have only a vertical dimension at first, but it must sprout wings for it to be truly a God relationship.

2. Second, we are responsible for each other! We're here to help, to listen, to guide, and yes, sometimes to correct each other. This is critical. As human beings, we are flawed, we don't get it right every time. No one, from the Pope on down, gets it right every time!

3. Third, when we see someone in our community going astray, or taking a position that we know is dangerously flawed, we are obliged to speak up. But this is important. We don't correct the person by yelling at them in public, or telling Father Howard to go speak to them. It's easy to waggle a finger from afar. Jesus tells us to speak to the person ourselves, one on one, to engage in dialogue. Essentially, we ask them quietly because we might not have all of the details, we might not understand their circumstances, we might be missing a key to their behavior.

4. Fourth, there is power in numbers. If the person persists in wrongdoing, we can add the weight of others to our concern. Few people can withstand community disapproval for very long, if (*importantly*) they see themselves as belonging to that community in the first place!

And yes, above all, we must put on the mind and heart of Jesus, slow to anger, full of kindness and compassion. We must be quicker to seek understanding than to react in anger. We must honor the dignity of each human being and respect their individual freedom just as God respects ours.

By the way, the bright green house in Carlsbad is owned by a woman who has terminal cancer. She loves colors, the more vivid the better. She wanted to express her joy of color one last time – and chose this method to do so. We can certainly question her judgment, but knowing her motivation, can we fully condemn her? There are worse things in the world than a bright green neighborhood house. And what about politics? By all means, get involved. Learn the issues, listen to what our bishops say, how our most important community, our Catholic community of faith, is framing the issues. Pray to God, our vertical dimension. Pray for and with others, our horizontal dimension. And above all, be quick to forgive, quick to be understanding, quick to walk in the shoes of the person who has a different opinion from ours. Try some dialogue – you might both be surprised by what is heard, and you may win over a brother or a sister.

Ascent and Descent

Scripture Referenced: Mk 9:30-37

They left from there and began a journey through Galilee, but he did not wish anyone to know about it.

He was teaching his disciples and telling them, "The Son of Man is to be handed over to men and they will kill him, and three days after his death he will rise."

But they did not understand the saying, and they were afraid to question him.

They came to Capernaum and, once inside the house, he began to ask them, "What were you arguing about on the way?"

But they remained silent. They had been discussing among themselves on the way who was the greatest.

Like many of you out there, I'm an avid reader. I love books of all sorts, from novels to history to biography to spiritual texts. Someone once said that if you took all of the novels ever published and condensed each of them down to the basics, you would find considerable similarity among them. In fact, I've been told that there are only about a dozen unique plotlines that have ever been written, and we recycle them over and over. You know what I'm talking about – boy meets girl, boy loses girl, boy gets girl back. Or, team of lovable losers find inspiration through tragedy and go on to win the state championship. Or, hero from poor background goes on an heroic quest, overcomes incredible odds and daunting setbacks to find the holy grail, whatever that means. Virtually every biography follows that same formula, and we enjoy reading the book, because we anticipate the ending and love to relish the details of their journey.

Our gospel today finds Jesus and his disciples on a journey. Whenever we see the word *journey* in the Bible, we need to perk up and notice. Although the story may be describing a physical movement from one place to another, we are always invited to take a step deeper and see this journey as a metaphor for the spiritual journey that we are all on.

Reading this brief passage in Mark, we soon realize that although Jesus and the disciples are physically journeying through Galilee together, their *individual*, spiritual journeys are going in completely opposite directions! Jesus speaks of his impending death, foretelling the details in stark terms, and the disciples are struck dumb, lost in confusion, and afraid to learn more. They don't want to talk about such things! They'd rather discuss who is the greatest among them (after Jesus, of course). You could say that Jesus is on a journey of *descent*, and the disciples are on a journey of *ascent*. The apostles are looking at the plot line, and fully expect that it will end where all plot lines end – in victory for the underdog, the little team, against the big bad Roman occupiers. They've got Jesus the miracle worker on their side, the guy who calms seas and raises people from the dead. How can they lose? All they have to worry about is who stands next to Jesus on the victory podium.

Most of us are taught from a very young age to do our best, work hard, and expect to be rewarded. We see others as competitors for the same crown, and we carefully construct our ladders, slap them up against the wall, and climb, baby, climb. It seems to be built into our genetic makeup somehow, this striving for the top. Our world encourages this behavior, in business, sports, house size, and nursery schools. Only the best, only the brightest, only the strongest survive, thrive, and go on to create new little strivers. If you see yourself in this picture, I'm here to tell you without hesitation that this is NOT how the spiritual journey unfolds. Not that we don't try to make it this way.

When I was a child, I decided that getting to heaven was like following a formula, or a roadmap, or a game like Candyland or Life. Go to church each Sunday, say a prayer now and then, throw a nickel in the collection, avoid mortal sins, and give up cookies for Lent. If I did all of that without whining, God would like me, and I was in. When I reached adulthood, I realized that life wasn't that simple, that it was possible to slip into some seriously sinful practices, and I figured that I needed to up the ante. So I did some volunteer work, helped out at the parish now and then, smiled at the pastor, gave to the building fund and demonstrated that I was a good Catholic. I was climbing that spiritual ladder. God would really like me now.

So here I was climbing the business ladder, climbing the spiritual ladder, and doing everything correctly. No problemo, right? So, why wasn't I happy? Why wasn't I happy? Not that I was deeply depressed or anything, but there was definitely very little peace in my life. The work ladder required more and more from me. Our son was reaching adolescence and that wasn't a picnic, and I began to question why I wasn't getting the appropriate payback from my religious practice. Where was this peace the world cannot give? Where was the joy? All of this love talk struck me as empty and hollow. Where was the return on investment? The big ROI?

So I began to investigate, to look around, to ask questions, to listen to some people who had reputations as wisdom teachers. Three startling revelations came to me. First of all, some of the most peaceful, spiritually grounded people I met had passed through some horrible life challenges, physical, mental, emotional, and spiritual. They had suffered, and not only had they made it through and survived, but they had actually blossomed into the flower of happiness and joy. Secondly, another contingent of spiritually blessed people I met had not necessarily suffered themselves, but were completely immersed into caring for the lives of the poor, the marginalized, and the suffering. The idea of climbing a spiritual ladder was laughable to them. They were actually grabbing their ladder, taking it off the wall, putting it into the pit, and climbing *down* to be with those who had fallen there. The third revelation? The real eye opener for me? These people, those who have the authority gained through suffering, and those who help the suffering, are people of peace and joy because they have both come to understand a powerful reality- that God in his infinite wisdom, mercy, and power, loved them utterly, completely, and without any need for payback. You don't *earn* God's favor, you *rely* on it – and once you realize that it is solid and never-ending, you step out and spread it around.

Jesus said, "If anyone wishes to be first, he shall be the last of all and the servant of all." The way up the spiritual ladder is paradoxically achieved by going down. This is very hard for us to understand, especially those of us who continue to receive the goodies of life by our hard work and striving. I actually feel kind of sorry for people who continue to win, win, win. They'll never find true inner peace. It seems that we must fall and/or live among and aid the fallen to truly understand the radical news of Jesus, to witness miracles, to see life resurrect from certain death.

Lest I sound like a hypocrite, I admit that I continue to work in the business world, and I play the corporate ladder game, but my heart is not there. I see it more and more like Candyland or Chutes and Ladders, you win some, you lose some, it matters so little. But put me in a jail, or in a classroom, or in a counseling situation with recovering addicts, and I'm at home. Put me among children, family, and the body of Christ, and I'm home. Why? Because God is there, and my heart is there, and where God and my heart mutually abide, peace and joy are inevitable.

If you'd like a taste of this joy, our parish outreach programs are taking on volunteers – volunteers in all sorts of ministries. Come on *down!* Your story is still being written.

Chapter 8 - Gifts

Brother and sisters, you are all gifted. The Holy Spirit gives all to all. Use your gifts – you are the hands, the feet, the body of Christ in this world. We don't need special certificates or diplomas or licenses. All we need is Christ living within us.

Give and gifts will be given you, Jesus says. And, more importantly, the measure with which you measure your gift will in return be measured out to you. So if you expect to receive abundantly when you stand in front of God on your last day, I certainly hope that you have given abundantly in this world. You are creating your own measuring cup with each and every gift, a cup that grows and shrinks with each gift given and each gift withheld each and every day.

Your Gifts

Scripture Referenced: 1Cor 12:4-11

> *There are different kinds of spiritual gifts but the same Spirit;*
> *there are different forms of service but the same Lord; there are*
> *different workings but the same God who produces all of them*
> *in everyone.*

I don't know about you, but I love gifts! It's not hard to imagine the excitement experienced by the Corinthians when one by one they began to demonstrate the gifts, the "charisms" of the Holy Spirit. What before was a life of emptiness became, with the help of God's grace, a life of fullness. But much like children at Christmas, it wasn't long before they began to compare their gifts, and as we know, this one-upmanship reached divisive levels in the Corinthian community. Paul takes care to tell them the gift is not as important as the Giver – and, each gift is important, not for what it grants the individual, but for how it serves the community.

So, what are your gifts? What are your gifts? This question makes us uncomfortable, doesn't it? If we answer too quickly – "I have the gift of prophecy!" – we sound conceited or presumptuous. We may stay silent out of false humility, after all, isn't it obvious what our gifts are? But I suspect the reason we don't readily answer is because a little voice in our head says "You don't have any gifts!" Beware that voice, brothers and sisters. It's the prince of lies speaking. See how he distorts these charisms:

- Do you have the gift of wisdom and knowledge? Is it indeed necessary to have a deep understanding of all things theological to speak of Jesus?
- What about the gift of healing? We can't help but conjure up images of sweaty preachers in a big tent beckoning the lame to walk in dramatic tones.
- Mighty deeds? As hard as I try, not once has the weather changed or a mountain moved because of my efforts.
- What about the gift of prophecy? I leave a lot of money at the racetrack.

- Tongues? I have a hard enough time with English. So, I guess I'm lacking these gifts…

But let's look again. Paul tells us that there is a Trinitarian aspect to these gifts. They reveal the presence of God in us in three different manners. First, they are workings of God the Father; i.e., they are creative and life giving. Second, they are forms of service from the Lord Jesus. Third, they come to us from the Spirit. As Jesus lives in us, (no longer I, but Christ who lives in me, says Paul), all of these gifts present themselves in various ways. So let's look again.

- Do you have the gift of wisdom and knowledge? In the eyes of a child, a troubled teen, an incarcerated person, a sick relative, your witness of Christ Jesus can astound like the wisdom of Solomon.
- What about the gift of healing? When we listen with loving compassion to a person who is struggling and offer a word of comfort – we are healers.
- Mighty deeds? Any time we perform a truly selfless action in the name of Jesus, we perform a mighty deed. From little actions ripple forward other little actions and the world can indeed shift. A mountain of misunderstanding and anger can move.
- What about the gift of prophecy? Remember that prophecy is not foretelling the future. Rather it is speaking the word of God to a people who need to hear. Our words can afflict the comfortable and comfort the afflicted. That is prophecy in the true Biblical sense.
- Tongues? Yes, this is a hard one. Those who speak in tongues are sincere, but it does seem like meaningless babble to me. Let me offer another interpretation. We speak in tongues when words do not suffice. A timely touch, a hug to the hurting, our presence at a graduation ceremony, a smile to a stranger – we speak in volumes at these times without saying a word!

Brother and sisters, you are all gifted. The Holy Spirit gives all to all. Use your gifts – you are the hands, the feet, the body of Christ in this world. We don't need special certificates or diplomas or licenses. All we need is Christ living within us.

Get a Cake!

Scriptures Referenced: Lk 15:1-32

My son, you are here with me always; everything I have is yours.

But now we must celebrate and rejoice, because your brother was dead and has come to life again; he was lost and has been found.

Six years ago I was in Donovan State Prison and heard this reading proclaimed. The occasion was a men's retreat for the inmates and I was on the leadership team conducting the reflection. As you can imagine, the 36 inmates had little difficulty relating to the younger son featured in this perfect short story of God's mercy, the story of the Prodigal Son. The younger son is impetuous, greedy, rude, and foolish. The men all nod their heads when they hear the stupid things he does. They continue to nod ruefully when they hear that the son comes to his senses and sees the folly of his ways. When the story describes the father's forgiveness and joy at the son's return, however, they grow quiet and stone-faced. Why? It's simply not believable to them. These men who have done some very bad things have rarely been offered forgiveness – they don't know what that feels like. The job of the prison retreat team is to convince them that they are indeed forgiven, if not by men, then certainly by God the Father. When that message finally sinks in, the reaction is incredible – grown men sobbing and shaking, their hearts bursting with a combination of regret and incredulous awareness of God's love.

Can *you* relate to the younger son? Or does someone else catch your attention?

Perhaps as a parent, especially an "experienced" parent, you relate to the father in the story, whose extravagant love for his son seems counterintuitive. How could he treat this rude and foolish boy so generously and compassionately? He clearly hasn't read any bestselling books on tough love. This can't be realistic – or can it?

A number of years ago when my own son, Joe, was in high school, he got behind in his English class and we received a note from the teacher that he was in danger of flunking the course. Joe reassured us that he had everything under control, so we said okay and let it be. Two weeks later, a letter appeared in the mail from the school and you guessed it, he was still behind. My wife Katie read the letter and was torn with anger, frustration, and confusion. Joe wasn't home from school yet – what was she to do? She prayed to God and at that moment, the prodigal, extravagant parent in this parable spoke to her. God said, "Get a cake." Huh? "Get a cake." So Katie, still a bit puzzled, went down to Ralph's supermarket and bought one of those triple chocolate layer cakes, the type that she knew Joe loved. She put it on the kitchen counter with the letter. When my son got home, his face lit up when he saw the cake and fell when he saw the letter. He was very confused. In words inspired by the Holy Spirit, Katie said to him, "This letter came today, but I want you to know that whatever happens, we'll always love you – that's what the cake is about." It hit home. My son Joe was given a taste of that extravagant forgiveness that Jesus speaks of today – and it continues to resonate in our family relationship, 10 years later.

(If you're wondering where I was in all of this drama – well, I was on a business trip! All the good stuff happens when Dad is on a business trip.)

But there's a third person in this story, the person you really don't like at all - perhaps because we relate to him the easiest. That person, of course, is the older brother. He is the one who does it right all of the time, the law-abiding, dutiful, obedient, responsible, church-going one. Put yourself in his shoes for a moment. He witnesses this idiot younger brother taking everything he had, his whole inheritance, and blowing it all in Vegas. Then this loser hitchhikes home with nothing but the clothes on his back and what does Dad do? He not only welcomes him home, but throws a big party! Where's the justice? Where's the righteous indignation? Where's the swift kick in the posterior? What is Dad thinking? So the older son lets Dad have it, spewing out his resentment and anger, referring to his brother not by name, but by the scornful term "this son of yours".

Can you imagine standing at heaven's gate with everyone else who has died that same day as you and witnessing God inviting into his embrace all sorts of people we don't like? Fill in the blank – terrorists, pedophiles, criminals, gang members, drug addicts? Do we react like the older brother and ask God what in heaven's name is He doing?

Apparently, what God treasures much more than "eye for an eye" justice is humility and honesty. The younger brother came back because he saw the light, he realized the folly of material things, the emptiness of wealth, the shock of a poor decision. Moreover, the younger son came to the Father in humility and repentance. This simple act of contrition is more important to God than anything else, so important that it completely trumps the sin, completely erases the damage done, the insult caused. God clearly values *humility* over our sense of reward and justified punishment.

Don't get me wrong, the father clearly loves the older son for his faithfulness. If the older son would just open his eyes, he would see the beauty of the father's house in which he dwells. And if you've been a good person, faithful and true, God will say, "My son, my daughter, you are here with me always, everything I have is yours. But now, we must celebrate and rejoice, because your humble brother terrorist, pedophile, criminal, gang member, drug addict was dead and has come to life again, was lost and has been found."

Let us take delight that the extravagantly merciful God the Father is the one doing the judging on the last day, and not one of us!

Love Your Enemies?

Scripture Referenced: Lk 6:27-38

> *But to you who hear I say, love your enemies, do good to those who hate you, bless those who curse you, pray for those who mistreat you.*

For those of us on the spiritual journey, these instructions from Jesus are very hard indeed. Love your enemies. Bless those who curse you. Pray for those who mistreat you. Give to everyone who asks of you. After the consolation of the Beatitudes, when we who are poor, hungry, weeping, and mistreated will apparently be lifted up, this is cold water splashing us in the face. How does Jesus expect us to do these things? Can he really be serious?

Let's deal with the hardest one first – love your enemies. What is meant by an enemy? In the time of Jesus, an enemy was anyone outside the tribe, that is, anyone who wasn't a Jew. This was common usage and fully understood by everyone. Your family and your tribe were the two greatest sources of security in a very unsafe world. So an enemy could be a Roman soldier, a Samaritan, or an Egyptian. They could live right next door. It doesn't mean that they were in open warfare against you – it was simply a way of relating, a basic impenetrable distrust.

In our world, we tend to associate the word enemy with a nation at war with us. We might think of terrorists, or Osama bin Laden, or whoever seems to be the most dangerous to our national interests. Unfortunately, that definition of enemy excuses us from the key intent of Jesus' teaching. If the enemy is out there halfway across the world, we don't need to think very hard about what Jesus is saying. But understand that by "enemy" Jesus means simply "the other", someone not in our immediate circle of friends and family, anyone who is outside. By "enemy" Jesus means that homeless person at the bottom of the freeway ramp, that sales clerk who ignores you, that co-worker who drives you crazy, that illegal immigrant on the street corner, that neighbor with the obnoxious dog – these are the "enemies" he wants us to love. How? Why?

As the book of Genesis tells us, God created all things, including us, and finds it all very, very good. His love maintains all in creation. So, understand, that as much as we may not like it, God loves Osama bin Laden. He loves the obnoxious neighbor. He loves the barking dog. He loves us. That doesn't quite describe it however. He not only loves us and the whole world, he loves us *abundantly* and with incredible patience.

I saw this exemplified at Von's just the other day. This two-year old was having a meltdown and Mom was as calm as could be. She stood by while the tantrum proceeded and at just the right moment, she picked up the sobbing boy and simply held him close, stroking his head and whispering in his ear. The tantrum stopped and two aisles later, the boy was busily sorting cans in the bottom of the shopping cart. The mother's patience, her ability to block out the words, the screams, the scene – that was what impressed me. She was God-like in that moment.

In today's reading, Jesus wants us to act like God the Father does. Jesus wants us to treat everyone as if they are our children, our sons, daughters, and close family members. Jesus wants us to treat everyone as if they are part of our own body.

But wait, how does this behavior, this generosity, lead to peace and happiness, to God's kingdom? Here's the secret. If you give abundantly to someone, there is no way that that person can stay an enemy, an "other", an outsider. The homeless person at the traffic light, the neighbor with the obnoxious dog, the co-worker who drives you crazy, the sales clerk who ignores you – all of these people upset us. Why? Because they seem wrapped up in themselves, oblivious to their surroundings, perhaps a bit scary. They are seemingly dismissive of us. How do we follow Jesus' words here?

Jesus' solution is actually wonderfully simple and very effective. You get their attention by your generosity, by your gift, by your act of love. To the obnoxious neighbor, you bring the first fruit from your tree. To the co-worker who drives you crazy you give a birthday card or take them to lunch. To the sales clerk who is lost in their IPod, you ask them what music they like and offer them a stick of gum. To the homeless and the immigrant you offer a McDonald's gift certificate. Do you see the pattern? What you give to them, freely and thoughtfully, wakes them up too! More than that, it changes the dynamic. The gift freely given forces the receiver to consider how to respond – and the more abundant the gift, the more abundantly the receiver feels an obligation to respond in kind. What was once distrust becomes mutual investment in each other's well-being.

My friend Steve tells the story of going to lunch with two coworkers in his car just last week and encountering a begging man at the bottom of the freeway ramp. Without hesitation, Steve dumped a handful of loose change in the man's hand and drove on. The people in the car scolded Steve and told him that he was simply allowing this beggar to buy drugs and alcohol. Steve listened quietly to this for a while and then asked them, "did you hear what the man said to me after I gave him the money?" One of the passengers said, "Yes. The man said 'God bless you.'" Steve smiled and replied, "That's right. And that's probably the only blessing I'll get from anyone today."

To move from loving your family to loving the outsider is an act of will, an act of self-sacrifice, a freely chosen intent to change the dynamic. It is an act of the cross by definition. This is how the world is changed – acts of outrageous kindness and generosity.

Give and gifts will be given you, Jesus says. And, more importantly, the measure with which you measure your gift will in return be measured out to you. So if you expect to receive abundantly when you stand in front of God on your last day, I certainly hope that you have given abundantly in this world. You are creating your own measuring cup with each and every gift, a cup that grows and shrinks with each gift given and each gift withheld each and every day.

How big is your measuring cup? How many former "enemies" are now your friends by your acts of love? That's what Jesus is talking about. That's what a follower of Jesus does. Lent starts this week. Instead of giving up chocolate, love an enemy, love an outsider into friendship this Lent and help change the world.

Awareness and Compassion

Scripture Referenced: Jer 23:1-6, Mk 6:30-34

> *The apostles gathered together with Jesus and reported all they had done and taught.*
>
> *He said to them, "Come away by yourselves to a deserted place and rest a while."*

A couple of months ago I was offered a new position at work. Along with the new position is a new boss. After working for the same management for nearly 10 years, I'm suddenly in a brand new world. It's kind of a shock, and mildly depressing, to have to prove myself all over again, but then I realized that part of my new job is to manage 30 people I've never met before. I'll bet that they are just as concerned about me as their new manager. You've heard the saying, "do unto others as you would have them do unto you." Well, in management, it's "manage others as you'd like to be managed." Did you notice that the readings today speak to the topic of management in a very real way?

Now in case you're wondering if you've wandered into a Dale Carnegie course, let's broaden our definition of management. If you're in any position of authority at all – a parent, a neighborhood watch captain, a volunteer coordinator, or the chairman of the cleanup committee for the parish festival, then these readings have something for you. Heck, most of us wear multiple management hats, don't we? If you're a baby boomer, you're probably managing your kids and your parents both. The only people off the hook are those under 7 years old.

In our first reading, Jeremiah speaks in a prophetic voice, which means that he speaks God's truth. It's a harsh message, one that certainly did not make Jeremiah a very popular guy. At this time in Hebrew history, a long sequence of very bad kings have ruled Israel, and things aren't getting any better. Jeremiah uses a very simple metaphor, that of a shepherd and his sheep, to make his point. A bad shepherd is coldly indifferent, lazy, or downright corrupt. He has no sense of his flock, no awareness of their fears, their concerns, their basic needs. The sheep wander off and he doesn't bother trying to find them. Without care and feeding, the flock dies off, and those that remain are constantly in fear, trembling at any distraction. It's an ugly picture, and the people of the time certainly made the connection. That Jeremiah managed to keep his head is a wonder in itself.

A long time ago, when I was about 30 years old, I was working for a consulting firm back east. After a year on the job, as my annual review approached, I decided that I deserved a raise. My boss was the chief accounting guy of the company I worked for, so I knew that this would take some negotiation. So I prepared a memo with all of my accomplishments duly noted, and summed up by asking for a rather exorbitant increase. My motto was, "if you want the moon, ask for the sun!" I figured we'd eventually settle for something a bit lower than my demand and everything would be great. So I handed off the memo to my boss and a day later we met. Well, it seems that I misread the situation. My boss reacted with anger and coldness, and basically knocked me flat. I was devastated – my pride was deeply wounded, and I felt about as big as a flea. I was basically young, naïve, and stupid – and he made sure that I knew it.

Contrast this picture with our gospel reading. Jesus welcomes the apostles back from their first missionary journey and he immediately sees that they are in need of rest, in need of some simple refreshment. So a key point – Jesus is tuned in to their mood, their youthful exuberance, and their fatigue. He is aware. So off they go on a picnic across the lake and in a wonderful comic twist, who should meet them there but the very people they were escaping from. You can imagine the apostles' comments, can't you? But here's the second key point – Jesus models for them a critical management trait – compassion. Jesus sees beyond the simple need of these people for the basics and gives them the gift of his wisdom and teachings. He feels for them.

Let's go back once again, all those years ago, to poor pitiful me, badly burned, feeling quite depressed. I couldn't quit, the economy was poor, and I had a wife and young baby son. What was I to do with my Jeremiahan boss? Fortunately, I did something right – I went over his head to the president of the company and asked to be transferred. God smiled on me in my frustration and brokenness. My new manager was a middle-aged Jewish lady with a team of about 10 people. For the first time, I was given the experience of working for someone who demonstrated the two traits that Jesus did – awareness and compassion. From day one she recognized my damaged state as she reached out with gentleness and allowed me to talk about what I needed to share. More importantly, she made me feel significant, and I slowly re-opened my closed door of trust. One day I walked into work and there was a birthday cake and presents – for me! I knew it was my birthday, but I was flabbergasted that anyone at work would know. It had never happened before. Awareness and compassion – Mayde Rosen, that gentle compassionate lady, had those traits and I still think of her as a model for my management style. Sometimes I get it right, often I don't.

Think back on the best leaders you've ever had – would you agree that their two top traits were awareness and compassion? A manager can be the smartest person in the room, but if they are dense and cold, heaven help their workers. As you can see, in my career, I've had experience of both types, and many in between. But the ones that stand out, the real stars, were alert to the moods of their team and compassionate to the utmost. Those managers you can count on two or three fingers in 40 years of work.

So if you're called to manage others in any capacity, remember these two tips – awareness and compassion. Note that awareness and compassion have nothing to do with your agenda, and everything to do with the hearts of the people you're managing. Put them first, yourself second, and it's amazing what a good shepherd you'll be.

Humility

Scripture Referenced: Lk 18:9-14

> *Two people went up to the temple area to pray; one was a Pharisee and the other was a tax collector. The Pharisee took up his position and spoke this prayer to himself, 'O God, I thank you that I am not like the rest of humanity--greedy, dishonest, adulterous--or even like this tax collector. I fast twice a week, and I pay tithes on my whole income.'*
>
> *But the tax collector stood off at a distance and would not even raise his eyes to heaven but beat his breast and prayed, 'O God, be merciful to me a sinner.'*
>
> *I tell you, the latter went home justified, not the former; for everyone who exalts himself will be humbled, and the one who humbles himself will be exalted.*

So, are you a Pharisee or a tax collector? It's a bit of an unfair question because each of these characters represent an extreme end on the spectrum we would call humility. On the end where humility is completely lacking is our self-righteous Pharisee. He thanks God for giving him the wisdom and strength to avoid sin and do all the right things. His arrogant stance repulses us, especially when he compares himself with other people he considers less worthy than him. One of these people, the tax collector, is the complete opposite on the humility scale, not daring to even lift his eyes to heaven as he prays in simple contrition for God's mercy. If pressed, I would expect that most of us would claim to fall in between these two extremes – somewhat leaning toward humility, of course!

I grew up the second of four boys, all born within five years of each other. We had a rough and tumble existence, marked by many a bruise and Band-Aid, as each of us egged the other on to more extreme physical feats of daring and manliness. I don't think I was injury-free until high school. We competed on every level, whether sports, school, or how long you could hold your breath underwater. The winner of each contest made certain that his victory was loudly proclaimed, in terms that would make that Pharisee take notice. Now before you ladies get too self-righteous, I've been told by many a woman that competition is just as fierce on your side. You ladies may not crow as much as the guys do, but a quiet superiority can be just as exasperating.

It seems that competition and a desire to distinguish ourselves is absolutely hard-wired into our human existence. We want to be different, to be special, to stand out, to be famous, to walk down the street with our head high. Certainly God made us this way, certainly he wants us to use our talents to better ourselves, so why would Jesus point out that it is the person who hides in the shadows as – well, the one to be exalted?

The danger with competition and goal attainment is not the achieving, the striving, the hard work, it's the achievement itself, the winning of the "prize". The danger with success is that it leads us to a false sense of independence, a sense that we got to where we are by our own qualities alone. As my favorite guru Richard Rohr says, after the age of 35 or so, success teaches us absolutely nothing. The Pharisee is a great example of someone who has done everything right; in fact, he has gone above and beyond the law, and has achieved the goal of religious perfection. The result is a false sense of independence, a false sense of importance, and worse yet, a complete alienation from the rest of God's people. He will be humbled eventually – not because God is vengeful, but because humans are inherently flawed and broken. In his alienated state, his fall will be painful and lonely, excruciating to endure.

Humility, however, is a different story. By definition, humility comes from the Latin word for earth, *humus*. One who is humble is of the earth, one with the universe, so to speak. One who is humble is in solidarity with humanity, by definition *interdependent*. Note that what makes the tax collector remarkable is his acknowledgment of his sinful nature, his shared responsibility for the poor condition of the world. We aren't told whether he was a cheat or an honest tax collector – he simply asks for God's compassion. In a very real sense, he is one with us all – we all make mistakes, we are all part of a sinful world, and he is one with our humanity. This quality is what God is looking for.

So, can you be humble and achieve great goals at the same time? You bet! I'm sure that many of you can think of co-workers or family members who have achieved great success in life yet remain completely humble and self-effacing. They have detached themselves from needing to succeed, and simply allow their gifts to speak out. The best salesman I ever witnessed in action never sold anything in a conventional, in-your-face, aggressive way. His goal was to create a relationship with each customer, period. On a one hour sales call, he would spend 45 minutes sharing life with the person and simply being a friend. The customer would eventually wake up and ask, "what are you selling again?" Whether the sale happened at that point or not was completely immaterial to this guy. But more often than not, the sale would take place. People responded to his genuine concern for them, his honesty, and his simple humility.

Now be careful, you can't decide to start being humble tomorrow and expect people to buy into it. Golda Meir, the famous Israeli prime minister, once said to a fellow politician, "Don't be so humble, you're not that great". Humility is a quality of perspective, of seeing the world clearly, of seeing how absurd our little ego games are. True humility comes from the true self within, the sure knowledge that God loves us in our sinfulness, in our simple humanity. When we are confident in that love, we don't need games, we can just be real and let our gifts shine. Humility starts with little actions, with small things that put others before ourselves. Letting someone in front of us while we're in line, pausing to ask a waitress how her day is going, helping a senior find his car in the parking lot – whatever the moment calls for.

Are you a Pharisee or a tax collector? The right answer? We are both at the same time, achieving and arrogant, failing and sorrowful. When we see both of these characters acting in *our* lives, and *accept* that reality, we can then open ourselves to God's mercy and forgiveness. Only then are we able to be *exalted* as God wills. Try to see the two sides of yourself this week. Being humble starts there. *Living* as a humble person is day to day, action by action, interdependent with the world. Great humility identifies with the world and embraces it, just as Jesus did.

Chapter 9 - Troubles

The hole in our heart is God-sized. It is only filled when we allow God in through his Son, Jesus. Jesus the good shepherd makes himself available to us in the Scripture, in the Eucharist, and in the Christian people that we surround ourselves with. With these three dimensions of Christ in our lives, we find food for the soul, we find guidance in how to deal with life's challenges, and we find safety and support from our friends and neighbors in Christ.

Christianity teaches that every misfortune in our lives is an opportunity for resurrection. By asking ourselves what God is trying to show us during the bad times, we can gain enough clarity to abide with the suffering and see it through to the resurrection moment that will *always* occur.

The Eternity Business

Scripture Referenced: Jn 3:14-21

> *For God so loved the world that he gave his only Son, so that everyone who believes in him might not perish but might have eternal life.*
>
> *For God did not send his Son into the world to condemn the world, but that the world might be saved through him.*
>
> *Whoever believes in him will not be condemned, but whoever does not believe has already been condemned, because he has not believed in the name of the only Son of God.*

In the past three years, I have often been asked how I like being in the "deacon business". Since the question is meant to be a bit facetious, I usually reply "interesting", or "a blessing" or "so far so good". As many of you know, I work for a high-tech company during the daylight hours, and someone surprised me the other day by asking how I like being in the software business. The identical question, different business. It got me thinking about the similarities between the deacon business and the software business. You could say that being a deacon is about the world of spirit and religion, and software is about the world of electronics and science. But that's way too simple. The reality is that I'm straddling both worlds, the physical and the spiritual, and I bring something of each domain to the other. And if you think for a moment, I'm sure that's true for you too. You're spiritual beings in a physical world. We're really all in the same business – what I call the *eternity* business.

Our gospel reading from John, particularly the early portion, is so familiar to us that we may skim right over it. John 3:16 – "For God so loved the world that he gave his only Son, so that everyone who believes in him might not perish but have eternal life." That one sentence summarizes the Gospel message of Jesus succinctly and clearly. It is no surprise that we see signs waving John 3:16 everywhere we look. It's a very hope filled, very comforting phrase, and I'm sure that you are just as reassured as I am to hear it. This is the kind of God that resonates with the desire of my heart and soul.

166

But then, two verses later, we are a bit depressed to read that "… whoever does not believe has already been condemned, because he has not believed in the name of the only Son of God." Part of our dismay is the word "condemned", which sounds very final and harsh, and part of it is our own realization that we are hardly ideal believers. We can't help but wonder where on the sliding scale of belief we score – is it enough to be saved, or are we already condemned? Am I falling short in the eternity business? Fortunately, John does not leave us here. He goes on to explain about light and darkness, and the fact that evil prefers darkness, and those in the truth prefer the light of God.

A theologian I heard speak some years ago said something very interesting that has always stuck with me. He proposed that heaven and hell are the *exact same place*. Huh? But wait, let's go with this a bit and see if it makes sense. When we die, we will find ourselves in God's presence – is that a fair assumption? If we are people of the light already, we will find this a very satisfying, very positive, very ecstatic experience. What more could we want than to drink in the warmth and goodness of that light? But, if we are people of darkness, of works of evil and wickedness, how would that light feel? I bet it would feel very harsh, very intense, very much like fire. It would be quite painful. Same God, same place, same light, two totally different reactions. One would feel saved, the other condemned.

Note that God simply continues being God – *we* make the choices day in and day out that predispose us to either embrace the light or hide in the darkness. The judgment of God is simply an endorsement of what we've already made clear, a choice made for eternity. I hope you see the implicit comfort in this interpretation. God does not play "gotcha" games, attempting to trip us up, especially on the last day of our lives. My religion teacher used to terrify us 3rd graders by asking, "wouldn't it be awful to miss Mass and get hit by a bus Sunday afternoon?" That's "gotcha" thinking, and doesn't sound like the God of Jesus in the least. God wants the whole world to be saved, not just a few fastidious perfectionists.

But, I can hear you think, I'm not even close to perfect – I may want the light, but I'm not light through and through. There's definitely darkness in me. Where does purgatory fit in? Well, think about it. The light of God has often been compared to a refiner's fire, burning out the impurities in our soul, allowing us to shine and reflect the glorious light of the Savior. I believe that each of us will face the light of God and see our entire life in stark clarity. It may feel like hell for a while, but the light is there just the same, and we will be able to embrace it eventually.

Now we can spend a lot of mental and emotional energy pondering the end times and what will happen. My point today is to convince you that if you are leading a life of sincere desire to respond to God's love and grace, you truly have nothing to fear. Fear is such a debilitating emotion, isn't it? Fear freezes us like a deer in the headlights, unable to move, unable to act, even to the point of losing our lives. St. Augustine tells us to love God, love your neighbor, and do as you please. In other words, if we center our lives on God and neighbor, taking the two great commandments as our guiding principles, we should act with boldness and audacity, for we have nothing to fear.

Three weeks ago, I heard Jim Wallis, a social activist, speak at a gathering of several thousand Catholics at L.A. Congress in Anaheim. Reflecting on the signs of the times, he said, "a big crisis is a terrible thing to waste". Many of us know people who are living in fear, fear of losing a job, or their savings, or their health insurance. As people of the light, what is our response? What does love of neighbor nudge us to do? Raise your antenna – scan the neighborhood. Who is hurting? What can you do? Maybe a well-timed meal, or a donation would help. Perhaps a simple offer to email their resume to business contacts you have. At a minimum, you can pray for them. Please don't lose hope in the power of prayer. I've personally seen two people become amazingly blessed in the past week – due in no small way to the power of prayer.

We're all in the eternity business – you don't need to be a deacon or a priest or a religious to be employed. Whether you have a job, or not, whether you're retired, or still in school, you never get laid off from the eternity business. The job description is pretty simple actually – spread the good news. As we hear in John's gospel – "God so loved the world..." As we hear in Paul's letter today, " For by grace you have been saved, and this is not from you; it is the gift of God..." No wonder the Church calls this Laetare Sunday, the Sunday of joy in the midst of Lent. Can you imagine better news than a gift from God?

Choose a Cross

Scripture Referenced: Jn 18:1-19:42

Jesus, knowing everything that was going to happen to him, went out and said to them, "Whom are you looking for?"

They answered him, "Jesus the Nazorean." He said to them, "I AM."

Five days ago we heard Luke's version of the Passion on Sunday, and you have certainly noticed that John's version is different in many subtle ways. Luke goes out of his way to emphasize that Jesus is innocent, that all of this is undeserved. And yet, despite his victimization, Jesus moves through the horror in the same way he moved through life, healing and forgiving. By contrast, John's version features Jesus as completely in control of the situation, not a victim at all. Note the betrayal in the garden. Jesus doesn't wait for Judas' kiss, but boldly asks who they are looking for. When told "Jesus of Nazareth," he states clearly, "I am he." At the words "I am", which we recall as the name for God, the soldiers fall flat on the ground. This sense of control and barely hidden power permeates the account. John is inviting us to see Jesus in all of his cosmic glory, even in the midst of suffering.

Whenever something bad happens to us or someone else, especially if it seems tragic or undeserved, the phrase "he or she is carrying a cross" comes out in conversation, doesn't it? Perhaps an illness, or a disabled child, or a house burned down, or a lost job – all of these seem like stand-ins for the cross in our Christian culture. To a certain degree, this reaction is understandable – after all, when victimized, we tend to seek release and perspective, and there is no better one than Jesus to emulate in suffering. Just as he suffered without a word of complaint and ultimately forgave his torturers, we are likewise encouraged to transform our suffering lest we transmit it to someone else.

But John invites a very different identification with Jesus in his Passion account and ironically, it ties back to words spoken by Jesus in Luke Chapter 9, "If anyone wishes to come after me, he must deny himself and take up his cross daily and follow me." These aren't words of victimhood, these are words of *intention*. To John, the cross is something you choose, not something that chooses you. This is considerably more challenging, isn't it? Now be careful, John is not advocating some kind of masochistic behavior here, although some in the past have read just such guidance. No, the point is not that we choose something painful for the sake of pain, but that we choose something painful for the sake of the Kingdom! How does this look in real life?

Perhaps it is giving of your time to an elderly or sick neighbor, especially on a weekend. Perhaps it is an intentional downsizing of your life, a turning away from our consumer society, and a turning toward the poor and the vulnerable in solidarity and financial support. Perhaps it is sponsoring one of our seminarians, or volunteering to teach in our Faith Formation program. There are many, many crosses out there that are waiting to be picked up and carried. Start with a small one and increase the size each time. You'll be surprised at how your spiritual life changes with each subsequent yes. Keep it in perspective – you may not be thanked. You may not be recognized. And if you really are inspired, you may choose to be the anonymous donor. After all, it is not about you, but the Kingdom.

Choose a cross and walk with the Lord.

Easter is About Hope

Scripture Referenced: Lk 24:1-12

Peter got up and ran to the tomb, bent down, and saw the burial cloths alone; then he went home amazed at what had happened.

For an Easter Sunday gospel, this reading leaves a lot to be desired. There isn't a lot of evidence here that Jesus has been raised. We have an empty tomb, puzzled women, some very odd words from two men in white garments, and skeptical apostles. Peter runs to the tomb, checks it out, and goes home amazed at what had happened. Jesus doesn't even appear on the scene until two verses later, after this Gospel passage ends. Why does the Church stop the reading here, leaving us hanging, wondering?

Well, Easter is all about *hope*. You could reasonably say that it is about faith or love, and you wouldn't be wrong, but hope rings as the most authentic virtue at work here. Why? To answer that, let's approach it from the dark side. What is the opposite of hope? (repeat) The most common answer is *despair*. But that's not quite accurate. Despair is too dramatic a term. The opposite of hope is actually *anxiety*. Anxiety. Does that surprise you? Let's look at it this way. On one end of the spectrum you have despair. On the other end of the spectrum you have the carefree presumption that nothing can ever go wrong. Neither end is the place to be. Hope lives in the middle, sliding up and down the scale, matched in perfect opposition to anxiety, which also slides up and down the scale. As hope goes up, anxiety goes down. As anxiety goes up, a feeling of hopelessness permeates us. If we lose all hope, we are so filled with anxiety that we are in despair. If we are completely worry free, we err on the side of recklessness, which is just as dangerous. So a well-balanced person is in the middle somewhere, holding the tension of hope and anxiety together.

Peter, in our Gospel, is exactly at this point, isn't he? A good word for it is "amazed". Amazement carries a tinge of excitement, danger, and the hope for something more, something better. After the last three days of near-despair for Peter, and the great anxiety that death by crucifixion

171

may be waiting for him too, Peter looking at that empty tomb is now faced with a completely different possibility. Are the women who reported back to the apostles right? Is it possible that Jesus has actually risen?! Can he believe it? Dare he hope for it? What happens next? He is quivering with excitement, amazement, hope, and yes, maybe even some anxiety.

We're over two thousand years from this event. I would dare to say that life is exactly like this for all of us. Whether we are people of deep faith, or simply people of engrained habit, we come to the Easter celebration because we want to be reassured that life has a purpose, that it doesn't end here, that something incredible is in store. We so much want that to be true, yet we wonder, we are concerned, we worry. Maybe you are on the lower end of that sliding scale, a little too close to despair. Perhaps you've had some hard knocks lately, you wonder if this Gospel, like so many come-ons in life, is too good to be true.

Easter is about hope. If you're over-indulging in alcohol, if you're experimenting with drugs, if you're fighting addictions to any number of seemingly good things that have a nasty way of hooking you, this day is for you. If you're working too hard, buying stuff you don't need, eating too much, envying too much, this day is for you. All of these bad habits are manifestations of anxiety, all of them stem from an uneasy sense that we're not complete, that something important is missing.

Easter is about hope. If you're battling anxiety for any number of good reasons – kids, jobs, parents, school – take a moment to consider the other side of the scale. Hope springs eternal, we are told. That's a very theological statement, actually. And just as darkness can never overwhelm the light, so anxiety can never truly overwhelm hope in God. If you can truly come to believe that God loves you without any hesitation, without any conditions, without any need for you to prove yourself, how can you be anxious? How can you be anxious? See? I just saved you several thousand dollars of therapy!

Easter is about hope. Through the saving act of Jesus, we are assured that the world has been saved, but it seems that God wants each of us to come to that discovery on our own. The Kingdom of God is both here and not yet here. It is finished and yet in process. It is a paradox, because God is so above us that we cannot understand it all. A famous theologian puts it well: "The Resurrection of Jesus is the first fruits of the kingdom, God's *down payment* on the promise." As all of us know, a down payment is made to guarantee the rest. This down payment, the resurrection of Jesus, shows God at work in the most hopeless of human situations, the crucifixion of his innocent Son. If God can bring life from death, is there anything we can bring before God that he cannot likewise transform? If God can raise Jesus, can't he also raise the dead in us?

Easter is about hope. God is not "up there" in the clouds. He is "in here", in our hearts, in our soul, inviting us forward. Hope implies a future reality different from our present, doesn't it? As that other famous theologian Scarlett O'Hara said so well, "tomorrow is another day!" God forgives us not because he is a nice guy, but because he wants to pull us out of our mud and have us help him change the world. God can't work with people who are moping around saying "woe is me!", or frozen solid from anxiety. He wants us to work with him, to cooperate, to listen and act, and spread the word. There's something ahead to look forward to, a Kingdom we don't completely understand today, but if the Resurrection of Jesus is just the down payment, imagine that Kingdom where all our anxieties are gone. That's something to hope for. That's what Easter means.

Easter is about hope.

Stay on the Vine

Scripture Referenced: Jn 15:1-8

> *"I am the true vine, and my Father is the vine grower.*
>
> *He takes away every branch in me that does not bear fruit, and everyone that does he prunes so that it bears more fruit.*

Do you may recall Jesus claiming that he is the good shepherd? John loves these metaphors about Jesus, and he has many more – the bread of life, the light of the world, the gate for the sheep, and my personal favorite: the way, and the truth, and the life. Each of these metaphors tells us something about God, about how the Christ is to be understood, how to relate to the risen Lord. This Sunday, Jesus makes the claim that he is the true vine. The image that always comes to mind, of course, is that of a grape vine. The vineyard is a very typical metaphor in Hebrew scriptures, since vineyards were so important to the region. But notice that the word "grape" does not appear in the Gospel reading at all. So allow me to alter the image in your mind a bit and instead of a grape vine, consider another plant, the rose bush.

How many of you have rose bushes? You can tell by the scratches on your arms! I have two rose bushes in the form of mini-trees, like a rose bush on a stick. I also have a bunch of so-called knock-out roses that form a low hedge in the front yard. When I first began to grow roses, I was taken by their beauty and delicacy. With a little fertilizer, water, and direct sunlight, the bushes will produce roses for most of the year. Since I was new at this, I took advice from many rose growers – one told me to prune the bush back dramatically each January, to no bigger than a man's head, and strip off every leaf. Prune the branches so that none grew inward, but all pointed outward. I was a little shocked – this seemed a bit much. But every one of these expert rose growers seemed to agree, so I did exactly that. When I was done, my poor rose bush was nothing but bare, stubby sticks. Oh well, I thought, that's that.

But, within two weeks, little buds appeared, and by mid-February, leaves were sprouting all over the bush. By the first day of spring, I had a dozen beautiful roses, with more buds peeking out. The rose bushes were not only alive, but bursting with renewed life and beauty.

The words of Jesus tells us that to follow him means that we will be pruned by the Father, the master grower. Pruning is always about cutting back, sometimes dramatically. Pruning hurts. Many of us are being pruned right now. We're suffering from job losses, bank account shrinkage, postponed dreams, mounting mortgage or credit card debt. We're being pruned, asked to reconsider what is truly important, what god we truly worship. But here's the key point of this gospel, one that we often miss as we think about grape vines. Jesus says, "Whoever remains in me and I in him will bear much fruit, because without me you can do nothing."

Remember that we are the body of Christ. We all get pruned at various times in our lives, but rarely are we all being pruned at once. As long as we remain on the vine, we can bear fruit. The key is to stay on the vine! Don't go it alone!

Abortion Changes You

Scriptures Referenced: 2 Sm 12:7-10,13; Lk 7:36-8:3

He said to her, "Your sins are forgiven."

The others at table said to themselves, "Who is this who even forgives sins?"

But he said to the woman, "Your faith has saved you; go in peace."

The Gospel of Luke has been the favorite of many women over the years and here is a prime example of why that is the case. We are presented with the touching, poignant story of a so-called "sinful" woman who despite her life as an apparent outcast, has braved ridicule and rejection to seek forgiveness and healing from the one person she somehow knows will accept her, Jesus. She never says a word – she doesn't have to. Her sobs, her tears, her gentle caress of Jesus' feet as she anoints them speak volumes. Put yourself in the scene. She realizes that she has no towel, perhaps looking for something to use, anything, and in utter abandonment, uses her long hair, the very mark of a fallen woman in that era, to dry the feet of Jesus. And Jesus, moved by the woman's humility and likewise irritated at the pomposity of Simon the Pharisee, says the words that He knows will bring peace to the woman and horrify the righteous guests. "Your sins are forgiven." "Go in peace."

We're not told what the woman's sin was – we assume adultery, of course, for what else would drive this woman to such a state? It's interesting to bring this story into the 21st century and ask the same question. What would drive a woman to such a state? I'm not sure the answer today would still be adultery. Adultery is practically celebrated these days, especially in our overheated entertainment media.

But I think that there is one that has taken its place in our day and age – an act that despite its legality is never celebrated, and often mourned long after it is done. I'm talking about *abortion*. It's interesting to see the collective tension in the Church rise at that word, and immediately the three elephants of politics, morality, and polarized thinking enter the room. I'm going to ask those elephants to leave, however, because I'm not here to discuss those points today. I'm here to talk about *healing*. I'm here to talk about forgiveness and new life.

About six million women in the US become pregnant every year; of these pregnancies, 1.2 million end in abortion, about 20 percent. I'm not telling this to you to shock you, but to point out that there is a very high likelihood that every adult in this Church knows a woman who has had an abortion, whether you realize it or not. There is growing evidence that despite the woman's conviction at the time of the abortion that it was the right thing to do, many suffer from depression and related anxiety disorders for years following the event. Worse yet, women who abort their pregnancies are less likely to obtain professional help than women who have had stillbirths. My point is simple: there is a large population of women in our very real world who are in pain, who are suffering, who feel that they cannot seek help – all the consequence of a poor choice at a vulnerable moment. Their pain transfers to their spouses, their significant others, many of whom suffer beside them in solidarity. There's an awful lot of weeping going on. So here's the question: how can we be like Jesus to these women?

Reread the first reading. David, accused of murder by Nathan the prophet, acknowledges his deed and what does God do? He forgives David. Reread this gospel. Does Jesus shun this woman? No. Does he condemn her? No. Does he demand that she do penance? No. You can bet that this sinful woman would not have taken the immense risk she did if there was any hint of Jesus rejecting her. Somehow she knew that Jesus was a safe place to seek peace. This is the first step we need to take as well. Can we be a safe place for the woman who has had an abortion? Can we be there for her without causing additional grief and pain? I invite you to examine your emotional state, your own feelings on the matter. If a woman came to you today and divulged that she has had an abortion, how would you react? What if she wants to justify herself? What if she is depressed and angry? What if she simply needs to share?

Here are some things to consider:

- A person going through a grieving process often displays many complicated emotions. Don't get wrapped up in the emotions. See the grieving person inside.
- Healing takes a long time, marked by many, often messy, setbacks.

- As a disciple of Jesus, make the distinction between public rhetoric and the reality of a person who is sitting in front of you in pain. Once the abortion is a reality, a done deed, what good is there in labels, party politics, and talking points?
- If the person comes from a strong religious background, understand that the shame and guilt can be doubly crippling. She can feel hopelessly condemned, to the point where she cannot imagine that she can be forgiven. Can you be the first one to say, "I am so sorry for your loss. I know it must have been difficult. How can I help you find peace?"
- Don't try to fix the situation or force healing. Use a method that works in prison – listen, listen, love, love. Communicate compassion.
- Offer support resources. I'll leave you with one resource to remember. There is an excellent web site called Abortion Changes You.com. This is a simple, completely non-political web site that offers resources for women who have had abortions and those who care about them. There is also a link to local counselors that requires only a zip code.

What if you know someone who you suspect is suffering from an abortion experience? Or who has confided to you in the past and you had nothing to offer? How do you approach them? Here's a simple way. Mention that you read a homily about post-abortion healing and you thought of her. Give her a copy of this book! Or, as I mentioned above, point her to Abortion Changes You.com. Above all, if you open the door, prepare to walk through it with her. We're not into hit-and-run compassion!

This homily is not sponsored by a political party. There is no hidden agenda here. There is a difference between the container and the contents. This is about the content that is Jesus. Jesus demonstrates how to be in relationship with a person in intense pain. He is a safe place, he is available, he listens, he forgives, he heals, he sends in peace.

There is a difference between fighting evil -- and caring for the wounded, just as we distinguish between justice and charity. We are called to do both if we're to be credible followers of Jesus. After all, they'll know we are Christians by our love. And love transforms the world.

Shepherding

Scripture Referenced: Mk 6:30-34

> *He said to them, "Come away by yourselves to a deserted place and rest a while." People were coming and going in great numbers, and they had no opportunity even to eat.*
>
> *So they went off in the boat by themselves to a deserted place.*
>
> *People saw them leaving and many came to know about it. They hastened there on foot from all the towns and arrived at the place before them.*
>
> *When he disembarked and saw the vast crowd, his heart was moved with pity for them, for they were like sheep without a shepherd; and he began to teach them many things.*

Did this Gospel reading make you smile a little? The plot sounds like something out of a summer time family movie that we've all seen before. The apostles come back from their first mission (which we heard about in last week's Gospel) and you can see that they're excited by their results, ready to talk about it, and quite frankly, a little tired as well. However, the crowds around Jesus in Nazareth are growing larger all the time, and the apostles can't even get a bite to eat with all the commotion. Jesus, ever the good leader, sees their fatigue and suggests that he and the twelve head across the Sea of Galilee to a nice little cove on the other side for a picnic. So they pile on board a couple of fishing boats, pack up some loaves of bread and dried fish and set sail. Whether it was poor sailing conditions or distracted sailors, it takes a while to get to their secret camping spot. And lo and behold, what's in store when they hit the shore? The same crowd that they were trying to escape has followed them around the lake on foot and there they are, 5000 strong! I'm sure that the apostles had some interesting comments as they saw this welcoming committee!

But Jesus sees something different in the crowd, something that makes him think of sheep without a shepherd. What does he see? Remember that sheep are simple animals, domesticated for their wool, milk, and meat. In Jesus' time, they were highly valuable animals. Wealth was often measured by the number of sheep in your herd. However, sheep without a shepherd are completely at the mercy of the world. Sheep without a shepherd cannot find food unless they stumble across it. Sheep without a shepherd have no defense against danger – whether robbers or wolves or steep cliffs. Sheep without a shepherd face lives that are painful, brutish, and short.

So Jesus takes pity on them and teaches them. We don't know what he tells them exactly (wouldn't you love to know?), but he clearly takes the time to be a good shepherd for them. The story ends with a picture in our minds of Jesus holding forth to the crowd on the shore of this deserted place, the apostles laying on the ground beside him (maybe taking a nap?) and the crowd hanging on his every word.

So how do we relate to this story? I can't speak for you, but I know that I have trouble identifying with the people on the shore. After all, I'm a pretty well educated individual with a decent job, a place to live, and a nice car. I'm pretty sure I know where my next meal is coming from, and I don't feel as if I'm in danger of being robbed or attacked by wolves. I certainly don't think of myself as a sheep! Do you?

But if we're honest, we may admit that at various times in our lives, we are indeed like sheep. Maybe not in a physical sense, but definitely in a spiritual sense. Sheep are always hungry, always seeking to fill the hole in their bellies. We are hungry too, always seeking to fill another hole, the hole in our hearts. As we go through life with this hole in our hearts, we seek out all sorts of ways to fill it. Some seek material goods – the more stuff I acquire the happier and more secure I'll feel. Some seek fame – if everyone looks up to me, I'll feel important and loved. Some seek control – if I'm in charge, then nothing can sneak up on me and hurt me. Our mass media culture is very clever in this regard as well – notice how every advertisement subtly plays on the hole in our hearts, our basic uneasiness and lack of security. Do I look OK, smell OK, eat OK, drive the right car, follow the right political agenda, - oh my, it never ends, does it? We're milling around, bumping into each other, each individually seeking to fill the hole in our hearts. Kind of like sheep, maybe?

The hole in our heart is God-sized. It is only filled when we allow God in through his Son, Jesus. Jesus the good shepherd makes himself available to us in the Scripture, in the Eucharist, and in the Christian people that we surround ourselves with. With these three dimensions of Christ in our lives, we find food for the soul, we find guidance in how to deal with life's challenges, and we find safety and support from our friends and neighbors in Christ. Have you ever noticed how people who have a strong spiritual life seem the most happy and at peace, even in the most trying of circumstances? They are following the Good Shepherd.

There's another part of this story, however, that's very easy to miss. Don't you wonder what the apostles were thinking? Remember that they just returned from a mission to the surrounding villages in which they found themselves able to drive out demons and cure sick people in the name of Jesus. They saw Jesus do this many, many times before he gave them the same power. Now they're seeing Jesus preaching and teaching the people, feeding their spiritual hunger. Seeing how their Master is acting, I wonder how many of them asked the question – does Jesus expect me to do this too?

I think you know the answer. Yes, he did expect the disciples to do this too. At this moment of the Gospel, they weren't capable yet. They had more to learn. The story wasn't complete – and isn't until it culminates with the Resurrection. Ultimately, the power of the Holy Spirit, the power of love manifested at Pentecost, drives them to be good shepherds too. And from the good shepherding of these eleven men called apostles is born the Church -- an unbroken line of bishops that continue in our day to channel the shepherding power of Christ. But it's not simply the bishops – we are called to be shepherds too! It is not as obvious as within the hierarchy of the Church, but we are shepherds any time we come across a person with a hole in their heart and fill it with Christ's word, touch, and example.

The final irony -- as we act as shepherds to the children of God, the hole in our heart is not only filled, but overflows. From this overflow comes the power and the impetus to go out into the broken world filled with hungry sheep and feed them. At the end of John's gospel Jesus challenges Peter three times – "do you love me?" At each of Peter's insistent replies that he does, Jesus says what? "Feed my lambs, tend my sheep, feed my sheep." We're asked to do the same.

During our lifetime, we will find ourselves as sheep at times. This is what being human is all about. Jesus, as human as the rest of us, is tempted by the devil in exactly the same ways that we are tempted – by wealth, security, and power. But he has overcome the world and shows us His way to the Father. As we enjoy His love, as we should, we will find ourselves nudged to share that good news, to help someone else who is bumping around as a hungry sheep. Try being a shepherd – I think you'll surprise yourself. Jesus shows us how – give that person your time, especially when it is inconvenient for you. The words mean more when there's a sacrifice attached, when paired with a good example. Let's look for a chance to be a shepherd this week....

Sin

Scripture Referenced: Mk 9:38-48

> *If your hand causes you to sin, cut it off. It is better for you to enter into life maimed than with two hands to go into Gehenna, into the unquenchable fire.*
>
> *And if your foot causes you to sin, cut it off. It is better for you to enter into life crippled than with two feet to be thrown into Gehenna.*
>
> *And if your eye causes you to sin, pluck it out. Better for you to enter into the kingdom of God with one eye than with two eyes to be thrown into Gehenna, where 'their worm does not die, and the fire is not quenched.*

Wow, those are some strong words that Jesus proclaims! If your hand causes you sin, cut it off! If your foot causes you sin, cut it off! If your eye causes you sin, pluck it out! By these measures, Captain Hook is one of our greatest saints!

But all joking aside, just what is Jesus talking about here? In the first century Middle East, the body was seen as the instrument of sin, to the point that various parts of the body were associated with various sins. For example, the hand was associated with theft. The eyes were associated with adultery. The feet were associated with highway robbery. Kind of makes sense, doesn't it? To this day, the fundamentalist Islamic law called Sharia (sha-ree-uh) mandates amputation of the hand as punishment for theft and amputation of the foot as punishment for robbery. We in the West recoil in horror at this, but understand that these practices are rooted in the same cultural heritage Jesus references in today's gospel!

So, what is sin? At the fundamental level, sin is a turning away from God. But it's more than that, actually. All sin is fundamentally something that we *choose* to place *above* God in our lives. In a word, it is idolatry, that is, a *false* god. Many sins are blatantly obvious – we all know what it means to steal something of value. We all know what it means to kill someone. We all know what it means to lie. These are all spelled out in the ten commandments in stark words. But here's the interesting part. Many sins are not so obvious, or seem so insignificant that we really don't even think about them. Breaking a minor traffic law, telling a lie to get something you want, cheating a little on your taxes, gossiping about someone, an unkind word or two.

These little, insignificant sins have a way of adding up, of slowly but surely dulling our conscience until they become a pattern in our life. These life patterns have names. They're called addiction, prejudice, materialism, racism, greed. These life patterns start to own us, to become as comfortable to us as our arm, our leg, and our eye. This is what Jesus is talking about.

What needs to be cut out of your life so that you can live more fully? What sin is so comfortable to you that it's basically a part of who you are? Let me give you an example. My grandparents were wonderful people. I was always so excited as a child when they would come to visit. My grandmother was a great cook, and my grandfather would fix my bicycle. But they had this quirk, this annoying habit -- they constantly bickered. I knew that they loved each other, but their bickering would drive me crazy. I remember asking my Dad about it when I was a child, and he said, "that's just the way they are". Their bickering had become a part of their relationship, an acceptable way of interacting that they were blind to. Unfortunately, this sin had permeated their lives. Even a child could see it. When I asked myself how did they get that way, I realized that it took a long time, made up of millions of little, insignificant, unkind words.

Each of us can think of an example in our own lives. The most difficult sins to identify are those that start out as good things. We can all agree that hands, feet, and eyes are very good things, absolutely integral to the human body. Well, shopping for necessities is a good thing. But what if it becomes shopping for the heck of it, which isn't that bad a thing, but if it leads to shopping to look better than anyone else, then oops, now it's become vanity and greed. A good thing can become a bad thing slowly but insidiously. Hard work in our job begets higher salaries, which encourages more work, which leads to 80 hour weeks, which leads to losing touch with spouse and kids, which leads to a breakdown in our families. As St. James so vividly states in the second reading, "your wealth has rotted away, your clothes have become moth-eaten, your gold and silver have corroded…" The best intentions, the seeming good, when overdone becomes the disguised sin, only realized when the painful result occurs.

Brothers and sisters, excising these behaviors from our lives is going to hurt. It going to feel like amputation if it's really engrained.

So let's take a hard look at ourselves for a few moments and ask God to help us see the sin that has become so comfortable, so much a part of our lives, that it's hard for us to see. You may ask a child what they see in you! And then ask for the courage and the grace to change, to pull back from the brink before the devil gets the last laugh. Jesus is here to help, after all, he came to save sinners. If we make a humble effort to see the sin, to ask for forgiveness, and work to rid it from our lives, Jesus will help. And the best part is that he loves us throughout the whole process, as undeserving of that as we are. Good news, isn't it?

Divorce

Scripture Referenced: Mk 10:2-16

He said to them, "Whoever divorces his wife and marries another commits adultery against her; and if she divorces her husband and marries another, she commits adultery."

Are you ready for a test? OK, here goes. According to the National Center for Health Statistics, which state has the highest divorce rate in the US? I'll give you a hint, it's not California. Whoever said Nevada is correct. Which state has the lowest divorce rate in the nation? I'll give you a hint, it's not California. The correct answer is Massachusetts. Final question, is California above or below the national average for divorce rates? Surprisingly (to me), California is below the national average! Let's not applaud, it's still nearly double that of Massachusetts.

Does being Catholic make a difference? Somewhat – Catholics and Lutherans have the lowest divorce rates among all Christian denominations, but it isn't a big difference. One of the problems with many of these surveys is that they don't measure the degree of religious commitment. Studies do show that people who have a strong sense of religious identification are more likely to stay married. But here's what I found fascinating. When people who are currently divorced were asked, "do you wish that you and your ex-spouse had worked harder to save your marriage", over 2/3rds said yes. Isn't that sad! But hold that thought.

Jesus' teaching on the permanence of marriage is crystal clear in Mark's gospel. "What God has joined together, no human being must separate." It's interesting -- Jesus rarely gives a direct answer to a challenge by the Pharisees. He often answers their question with a question, and he does the same here today. But the direction he takes surprises them. When they quote Mosaic law to him (that yes, you can divorce), Jesus rejects the law and appeals to a higher law, the law of creation itself. In the very constitution of the universe marriage is meant to be an absolute – it should be permanent and united, as if she is bone of his bone and flesh of his flesh. The disciples are also surprised, for the reading goes on to report that after they get Jesus behind closed doors, they probe him again. "Do you really mean that?" He takes it one step further – you see, in 1st century Palestine, women were considered property. But Jesus takes the universal law of marriage and applies it to both parties – the marriage is one in both relationship and responsibility. Jesus raises the status of women to the same level of commitment as men. This is radical stuff for the time!

But here we are in 21st century America. How are we to take such an instruction from Jesus? Are things really so black and white? What about marital situations of abuse and clear incompatibility? What if one of the partners is unfaithful? What then? People do make mistakes, don't they?

If we study the scriptures on divorce carefully, we find that the Bible, especially the New Testament, is not so black and white after all. Mark's gospel is the clearest and most severe. Matthew reports the same discussion, but has Jesus say that divorce is prohibited except in cases of adultery. St. Paul says that divorce and remarriage are permissible if a Christian is divorcing an unbaptized person, a pagan. This is the so-called "Pauline Privilege". So even the New Testament itself makes it clear that it is not so clear! The Church honors this tension in an interesting way. While keeping Jesus' absolute prohibition against divorce before us, the Church has the authority to make concessions that are pastorally necessary.. If we fall short of the ideal, we are in sin. But we are also graced with forgiveness – and given the importance of marriage in the eyes of God and society, the Church takes it very seriously and acts to annul a marriage only after great deliberation and only if it is quite necessary.

Some may say that annulments are too easy in the Church today. Some may say that annulments are too difficult. Brothers and sisters, it's not about easy or difficult. I had the great pleasure of taking a class in canon law from a priest who has served on the Diocesan tribunal for years. What struck me was his attitude toward annulment. He told us that the roots of marital success are evident while the couple is dating. The issues that may drive them apart or throw them into each other's arms are present from day one. That is why the Church emphasizes pre-marital preparation. If an engaged encounter weekend reveals the elements of the relationship that will keep it together for years and years, that is good. If it likewise brings pause to a couple who realize that there are serious incompatibilities, that is good too.

An effective annulment process takes the couple back to their early times and with the benefit of hindsight, shows them the roots of their marital discord. Yes, it can be painful. But if the attitude of the couple is open and honest, the annulment is also about healing, about mercy, and hopefully about forgiveness. How easy or hard it is depends on the attitude of the couple. Remember, the Church is not here to punish, it is here to heal.

I'm sure that all of us know couples who are struggling with their marriage. However, as members of the Body of Christ, we are a community committed to commitment. This means that all marriages are important to us, not just our own. What are we doing to promote the good of these families? How can we insure the stability of parents and the good of children? Remember, if we can help people work a little harder to save their marriages, we may be able to help them avoid some future regrets and considerable pain. We're all in this together.

Offer It Up

Scripture Referenced: Is 53:10-11; Mk 10:35-45

If he gives his life as an offering for sin, he shall see his descendants in a long life, and the will of the LORD shall be accomplished through him.

Because of his affliction he shall see the light in fullness of days; Through his suffering, my servant shall justify many, and their guilt he shall bear.

You might be surprised to hear that our first two readings are also featured at one of our holiest days of the year – yes, Good Friday. Our first reading features a description of an unnamed servant of the Lord who is afflicted with suffering. To this day, we're not sure who Isaiah had in mind when he wrote these words – remember that it was written 400 years before Jesus' birth – but early Christians quickly saw Isaiah's description as a very clear prophecy describing Jesus. The key point to remember from this prophecy is that the servant's suffering is not meaningless. Somehow the servant's suffering saves others – it is *redemptive*.

Now fast forward to the Gospel. Here's James and John, two out of the three apostles that Jesus seems to favor. (Who's the third? Yes, that's right – Peter. Where was he in all of this? Is this a subtle bid by James and John to usurp Peter's leadership?) They ask Jesus to appoint them as vice presidents, one on his right and one on his left. With our knowledge of what is to come, we can't help but smile at the silliness of this request, but they are completely serious. And Jesus takes them seriously. He gently asks if they really think that they can follow in his footsteps, drinking the cup that he must drink. "Sure we can" they say. Then you *will* drink the cup I drink, he tells them. Be careful what you ask for, boys!

It's intriguing to wonder how Jesus came to the understanding that his mission would lead to the cross. Did God the Father simply tell him it would? Or was it more subtle, more gradual, an unfolding of the truth? I opt for the latter explanation mostly because it is more realistic from a human point of view – and we must not forget that Jesus was completely human as much as he was completely God. We can be certain, for example, that Jesus read the prophet Isaiah – Luke has Jesus reading Isaiah in the synagogue early in his gospel. Did Jesus read about the suffering servant and in a moment of searing clarity, see himself as that servant? Talk about an "aha" moment! But it makes sense – note the last words of Jesus in today's gospel – "For the Son of Man did not come to be served but to serve and to give his life as a ransom for many." In short, Jesus sees himself as the servant who is to die so that others may be freed – he's the ransom to free the captives. Doesn't that sound like Isaiah?

Here's the kicker though. We hear Jesus say this and we think – "well, thank goodness Jesus came and suffered and saved us. Hooray for Jesus!" Yes, indeed. But Jesus also challenges us to walk the same walk, to drink the same cup, to be submerged into the same muck of the world that he was – in short, to follow his example. That's a bit of a challenge, isn't it?

I don't know about you, but I don't like the idea of suffering at all. When I was a child and had to wait 30 minutes for my Dad to come home before eating dinner, you'd have thought I was near moments from death. But my stomach hurts, I'd wail. My mother's response? Offer it up. *Offer it up.* Those three little words I would hate to hear. But you know what? Those three little words sum up what we mean by the very big concept of redemptive suffering.

Let's be very clear. There's nothing intrinsically good about suffering. God doesn't like us to suffer any more than any of us as parents want to see our children cry. But evil, pain, and suffering seem to be inevitable outcomes of a world in which we are free to choose our path – whichever way it takes us. The price of our freedom is the reality of poor choices made, which always lead to someone in pain, often ourselves. We can either scream at the injustice of it all, or somehow, in some way, offer it up. Jesus did not try to explain suffering – he simply endured it, made doubly painful because he was completely innocent – and in enduring a tortured death, took on all of the sin and suffering of the world, past, present, and future. The horror of his crucifixion sent his closest friends fleeing in terror, convinced that all was lost. And for three days, it appeared that they were right – and then God fulfilled the prophecy of Isaiah, that "the will of the Lord shall be accomplished through him" and Jesus was raised. Death is an illusion – it is not the end – it is a doorway to life.

Great religion, according to Fr. Richard Rohr, tells us what to do with our pain. If we don't learn to transform it, we will simply transmit it to another, an endless cycle of escalating violence. Buddhism tells us that the best way to avoid pain is to become completely detached from the world – to own nothing and thereby have nothing own us. Christianity asks us to give suffering a meaning, to grow through it, to become ennobled by it. How?

First of all, for those who are suffering from physical pain here and now, my heart goes out to you and I pray for your relief. Your patience as you navigate this difficult road i s all that Jesus asks. He's walking it with you. For the rest of us, recognize that as we go through the prime years of our lives, suffering does not typically mean *physical* pain. Suffering is usually emotional and psychological, a response to the whipsawing nature of the world, our families, and our friends. We often feel like we're on a roller coaster that we can't get off, and we can grow resentful, angry, and cynical. This is where our faith can really help. Christianity teaches that every misfortune in our lives is an opportunity for resurrection. By asking ourselves what God is trying to show us during the bad times, we can gain enough clarity to abide with the suffering and see it through to the resurrection moment that will *always* occur. Losing a job sounds awful, until we find the next job that is a perfect fit. Losing our money in the stock market sounds awful, until we realize that what is truly important is the love of our family and friends, a love that can't be bought. Delaying supper for 30 minutes didn't cause my death, and boy, that meat loaf sure tasted great that night.

If we offer it up, we ask God to show us the resurrection moment. That's how God redeems suffering, by taking it from us, teaching us a truth about ourselves, and making the world a better place for our self-realization. Ideally, we take our knowledge and use it to tell others, to *serve them*. That's not so hard, is it? So where are you on the roller coaster right now? Up in the clouds? Down in the dumps? Going up or going down? God is in these times – most assuredly. What is he trying to teach you? Pray for that guidance. Pray for that patience. Resurrection is coming!!

Chapter 10 – Eucharist

We believe the body and blood of Christ is present in three different ways. First of all, we have the actual human person of Jesus. Second, he is present in the form of bread and wine, allowing us to literally consume him, to share his essence with us in a physical way. And third, Christ is present in the entire body of believers, the essence of Christ in each one of us coming together with Jesus as the head and each of us as one of a billion parts.

Eucharist is meaningless if it stops with you. The food we take at Communion is the essence of Christ, and as we take and eat, we literally make Jesus one flesh with us. As Pope Benedict tells us, adoration becomes union. As the host is broken down into its constituent parts, the molecules of nourishment that our cells need for energy, we absorb Jesus into our very being. We implicitly ask Jesus to make us just like Him. We see the world as Jesus sees it, we hear the world as Jesus hears it, and we become the body of Christ on the earth to serve those who cry out. We become part of the transformation this world desperately needs.

Let's Get Washed

Scriptures Referenced: Jn 13:1-15

> *He came to Simon Peter, who said to him, "Master, are you going to wash my feet?"*
>
> *Jesus answered and said to him, "What I am doing, you do not understand now, but you will understand later."*
>
> *Peter said to him, "You will never wash my feet." Jesus answered him, "Unless I wash you, you will have no inheritance with me."*
>
> *Simon Peter said to him, "Master, then not only my feet, but my hands and head as well."*

Welcome to the Sacred Triduum! Yes, Lent is officially over – it ended at sunset this evening - and now we embark on the 3-day liturgical journey that culminates on Easter Vigil with our celebration of Christ's resurrection. The Triduum celebration goes back to the fifth century. Prior to that time, Christians celebrated Easter Vigil only, staying up all night from sunset until the dawn of Easter Sunday. In the very early years, pilgrims to the Holy Land would re-live the final days of Jesus over the course of a week (they called it the Great Week originally), and would walk from Jerusalem to Bethany to Gethsemane to Golgotha sharing Scripture and prayer. From the very beginning, the Triduum focused on those to be baptized, since it was seen that sharing in the death and rising of Jesus mirrored the catechumen's journey from death to life.

Holy Thursday, the beginning of the Triduum, asks us to go even further back in time and make some connections to our Jewish roots. The first reading spells out the directions for the Passover feast, the Seder meal, which marks the final night that the Hebrew people were held in bondage by the Egyptians. The blood of the lamb smeared on the door post saved the lives of the Hebrew people. We are invited to see that the blood of Christ poured out for us on the cross has the same effect for each of us – saving us from the death of sin. Our second reading, Paul's letter to the Corinthians, is the earliest written account of the institution of the Eucharist, pre-dating Mark's Gospel by at least a decade, maybe more. You'll hear these words spoken by the priest tonight, but not again until Easter Vigil.

All of this theology homework is interesting, but the true message of Holy Thursday is contained in John's gospel. As someone who is privileged to present homilies, I know that we do not *own* the teaching message until an attempt is made to answer the question, "so what?" John's gospel does a pretty good job for me, doesn't it? When John wrote this gospel account, he already had access to the other gospels plus Paul's letters. He could have simply written his own version of the Last Supper with the familiar words of bread, wine, body, blood and covenant. But John's community needed something we all need – a resounding answer to the question, SO WHAT?

Jesus, the master and teacher of them all, the acknowledged Messiah, the miracle worker and healer of the sick, the one who raises people from the dead, performs the most basic, simple action that anyone of that time would perform. He does what a servant would do and washes their feet. It's hard for us to find a suitable equivalent in today's world that conveys the same impact. But I'll try…

I was getting my hair cut a few weeks ago and in a ritual that is actually still pretty new to us guys, the stylist shampooed my hair first. The gal who did this had very strong fingers and she massaged my scalp like she was scrubbing a melon. It was great! I remember thinking that this was a taste of heaven. And suddenly, I knew that in heaven it would be Jesus Himself who would be washing my hair just like this. It gave me the chills. So the stylist asked me, "is the water too cold?"

John's point is that Eucharist is meaningless if it stops with you. The food we take at Communion time is the essence of Christ, and as we take and eat, we literally make Jesus one flesh with us. As Pope Benedict tells us, adoration becomes union. As the host is broken down into its constituent parts, the molecules of nourishment that our cells need for energy, we absorb Jesus into our very being. We implicitly ask Jesus to make us just like Him. We see the world as Jesus sees it, we hear the world as Jesus hears it, and we become the body of Christ on the earth to serve those who cry out. We become part of the transformation this world desperately needs.

At Mass this evening, we are all invited to re-enact this self-gift of Jesus. The order is a little backward – ideally we'd receive Christ in the

Eucharist first and then respond in service to each other. But let's give Jesus a gift tonight. Let's serve each other first and offer our humble gesture to our Lord and Savior. I invite you to come forward and form a line by each basin. I know that many of you like to come forward as couples and wash each other's feet. Instead, please consider simply washing the feet of the person behind you in line – that way everyone here can participate in this simple sharing as one family. And you may just meet a new friend!

Jesus the Christ

Scripture Referenced: Lk 24:35-48

> *So they set out at once and returned to Jerusalem where they found gathered together the eleven and those with them who were saying, "The Lord has truly been raised and has appeared to Simon!"*
>
> *Then the two recounted what had taken place on the way and how he was made known to them in the breaking of the bread.*
>
> *While they were still speaking about this, he stood in their midst and said to them, "Peace be with you."*

As we begin the third week of the Easter Season, you'll notice that the Church provides us with many readings from the gospel of John and from the Acts of the Apostles. Remember that the purpose of the seven weeks after Easter is to rejoice in the good news of the Resurrection and to ponder its meaning for our lives. Today we hear from Luke's gospel, in a scene that transpires shortly after two disciples have hurried back to Jerusalem from Emmaus. In the middle of their exciting story about seeing Jesus, pow! There he is, in their midst! The gospel tells us that the apostles are startled and terrified, and Jesus takes great pains to reassure them of his reality. It seems to work – they go from terror to joy and amazement, which is certainly an improvement. Clearly, the apostles are trying to come to grips with the notion of a resurrected Jesus – who seems to be who he was – and yet something much, much more.

How many of you have lost a loved one? A close family member or friend who has died? The older we get, the more likely we are to raise our hand, true? This is why religion is so important to us as we get older – it gives us context about death, it gives us a way to think about the reality of our existence. It gives us the resurrection. Here's a more interesting question. For those who have lost a loved one, how many of you have had an experience of this person after they've died? In a way, you've experienced a *taste* of resurrection, nothing quite so

197

dramatic as happened to the disciples, but an inkling, a sense of the person living beyond our space and time. As befits the son of God, Jesus in his appearance to the disciples shows us what to expect when we are resurrected.

Back to our gospel, did you notice that Jesus refers to himself in the *past* tense when he says "These are the words that I spoke to you while I was still with you..."? Furthermore, he then refers to himself in the *present* tense as the *Christ*, which is equally significant. What's going on here? We are being challenged to recognize that a transition has taken place, that *Jesus* the historical figure has become the *Christ*, the eternal anointed one. When we express our belief in Jesus Christ, we are stating two beliefs at once – that Jesus was an historical person, as real as you and I, and that secondly, he is the Christ, ever present and timeless, changing the world through His direct action within and among us.

Words carry meaning, and mis-used words cause confusion. When we study the Gospels, we are reading about the historical Jesus, what he said, where he walked, what he did, how he treated others. This is all good. When we read Paul's letters, however, we rarely hear Paul talk about Jesus at all. Paul didn't know the historical Jesus, this was not his frame of reference. Paul talks about the *Christ* – this is who he knows. Paul's language can be very theological, because the notion of the Christ is very theological. The boundaries of space and time necessarily limit the extent to which Jesus can affect the world. The Christ has no such limits – and is immensely more powerful in the world because of this. When we speak of Jesus and we speak of the Christ, we are speaking of separate stages in a continuum – Jesus the historical being, Christ the present reality – the cross-over point being the resurrection. Do you see the distinction?

When we receive the Eucharist, what are we told? The body of Christ. The blood of Christ. We don't say "the body of *Jesus*" because it's imprecise language, it doesn't express the totality of what we are receiving. It's not that it's wrong – it's simply not saying enough! Jesus has become the Christ!

You've heard time and again that Christ is not Jesus' last name. But if it were, I would say that Jesus has a middle name too, and no, it doesn't begin with "H". To express more accurately our belief, Jesus' middle name is "the". Jesus *the* Christ. This sums up our belief in the historical and cosmic reality that is Jesus Christ, savior of the world – *present* tense.

So, what do we do with this understanding? How does it affect us? Here's some thoughts for you. Be careful not to *limit* Jesus the Christ. It's easy to get wrapped up in the study of the historical Jesus, to dissect the Gospels in minute detail, and examine the life of Jesus the way we would examine the life of Lincoln or Mohammed or Gandhi or any other historical figure. Nothing wrong with studying Scripture in this way, but if our study ends at the resurrection and never considers anything beyond this point, we've missed the most exciting part of the story, the truly life-changing event. Encountering the *Christ* is what transforms us. We've all met people who can quote the words of Jesus left and right, but by their lives there is no evidence that they have ever encountered the Christ. Many scholars, historians, and religious skeptics fall into this camp.

Next, note the significance of the term *body of Christ*. This is probably the most powerful concept that we can ponder and grasp as Christians. It is clearly a Eucharistic term as we've already mentioned – we receive the body of Christ during communion. It's also a statement of our identity! *We* are the body of Christ. It's how the Christ is made manifest to the world. If we are waiting around for the historical Jesus to come back and save the world, we're missing the point. Jesus the Christ *is* saving the world by using you and me as his physical presence. This is how the world changes – not with fire and brimstone and flying dragons. Jesus the Christ asks (never demands) to join with each of us individually, and through that relationship, we use our gifts to change the world around us, a bit at a time. As we live "in Christ" we see the mission as Jesus surely sees it.

Finally, see in the figure of Christ the promise of life, the promise of much more to come. If you can experience the on-going existence of a loved one who has died, as delicate as that seems to be, can you see the risen Christ as the first born of the dead, the archetype of everlasting life? This is why we shouldn't fear death. We do fear death just the same, but if for one moment we decided to act as if death were not an end, but simply a doorway to eternal life, would you act differently? A bit less fear, less anxiety, less tension? Ponder this during our seven-week Easter season. What does this knowledge of resurrection lead to change in me?

Eighty People

Scripture Referenced: Jn 6:51-58, Mt 1:1-25

> *"Just as the living Father sent me and I have life because of the Father, so also the one who feeds on me will have life because of me.*
>
> *This is the bread that came down from heaven. Unlike your ancestors who ate and still died, whoever eats this bread will live forever."*

On this feast of Corpus Christi, it is natural to focus on the Eucharist, the body and blood of Christ in the form of bread and wine. Yet, many Catholics are a bit uncomfortable with this doctrine, despite the fact that it is a core teaching of our faith. It's easy to get caught up in the *how*, the exact mechanism by which bread and wine become the holy Eucharist, the essence of Christ. We can blame that on our post-modern reliance on empirical evidence and scientific discovery. As one scholar put it, "God has an easier time convincing the bread and wine to become Christ than he has of convincing us!" Down to this day, many of our Protestant brothers and sisters are in serious disagreement with Catholics about what this ritual feast really means.

So, let's focus on what we agree upon. We share the belief in the reality of Jesus the person, the *actual* body and blood of Christ as it were. We believe that Jesus was a real human being, born some 2000 years ago, anointed by God to bring us to an understanding of the love that God not only offers, but defines as Himself. How many of us wistfully think about what it must have been like to walk at the side of Jesus in person?

We may feel far from the human Jesus, but consider this. Think of the one person who was most responsible for bringing you to the Catholic faith, your personal evangelizer. Maybe it was a friend, maybe your mother, maybe another relative, or maybe a priest or religious sister. Stop for a moment and think of that person. Do you have that person in your thoughts? For me, it is my Mom.

Now consider that this person who brought you the faith was similarly brought to faith by someone else. Perhaps a peer, perhaps a parent or an ancestor. But someone definitely acted in that way for your evangelizer. For my Mom, it was her mother, my grandmother. Now consider that chain going back in history, down through the ages. My mother was born in the 1920's. My grandmother was born in the 1890's. Someone evangelized her, probably born 25 years earlier. The human chain in my instance heads over to Ireland. Perhaps it goes back to St. Patrick. But he came from Rome. Who evangelized him? The chain goes back some more. Eventually, there is a person who received the message directly from one of Jesus' apostles or perhaps Jesus himself. Logically, it has to be.

Here's the shocking thing. It's not as long a chain as you may think. If we consider that a generation is 25 years in duration, and each generation produces a past evangelizer for us, then our chain is perhaps 80 people – 80 people to link us back to someone who was in the actual presence of Jesus. And if you have longevity in your family tree, it may be fewer people than that! 80 people - that's hardly enough to fill a section of pews here. We're that close to the physical body and blood of Christ.

As you know, we proclaim the Gospel of Matthew this church year. Here's a little quiz: what does Matthew feature at the very beginning of his gospel? The first 25 verses of Chapter 1? A genealogy! Matthew believed it was important to show how Jesus descended through his long line of evangelizers in the Hebrew community, right from Abraham. Likewise, we are the descendants of a long line of evangelizers, right from Jesus! So the interesting question of course is, who are you evangelizing? Who will count you in their faith genealogy? Or does the tree die with you?

So let's review. We believe the body and blood of Christ is present in three different ways. First of all, we have the actual human person of Jesus. Second, he is present in the form of bread and wine, allowing us to literally consume him, to share his essence with us in a physical way. And third, Christ is present in the entire body of believers, the essence of Christ in each one of us coming together with Jesus as the head and each of us as one of a billion parts. It's rather awe inspiring to consider the potential of the body of Christ as the sum of his believers, isn't it? If we all acted in concert as Christ would, could the kingdom of God be far from our reach?

So what holds us back? Why don't we act as the body of Christ? What stops me? What stops you? Often, it's one of three things: fear, complacency, or hopelessness:

- Fear: not in a "terrified" kind of way, but simply because action is sometimes uncomfortable, it's not that easy, it puts us at risk for ridicule or conflict or divisiveness. It means rocking the boat.
- Complacency: I'm too comfortable, too at ease in this world where I win a lot more than I lose. Why change? Do I really want Christ to transform me? How could I get any better *really*?
- Hopelessness: I'm small, insignificant, powerless. I'm just too human. Why bother?

So, why does Christ offer himself to us in the Eucharist? Why did he do this? What's the point? Simple. He offers us an *encounter* with God. He wants us to understand that God is *for* us. Encounter drives away all fear, all complacency, and all hopelessness as long as we allow God to permeate us. It's called *conversion*. Once converted, we seek out others who are similarly converted, who are likewise asking what to do once we experience this encounter with the living God. This is called *communion*. And once in communion, once we see ourselves as the body of Christ, we see our lives as *mission*. You'll know that you are a part of the body of Christ when you see the world as Christ sees it **AND** you start to do something about it. The form your action takes depends on your gifts, your talent, your treasure, your circumstances – it's different for all of us.

The promise of Christ is that if each of us strives to act as Christ would, the summation of all of those individual actions will change the world! It happens one person at a time. It happens one evangelizer at a time. That's the promise of this feast day. That's why we're called Christians. Let's earn the label!

Eat My Body!

Scripture Referenced: Jn 6:51-58

"I am the living bread that came down from heaven; whoever eats this bread will live forever; and the bread that I will give is my flesh for the life of the world."

During this sleepy time of the summer, everything seems to be in a dormant state. Yes, school will be starting soon (sorry, kids), and Halloween decorations are starting to show up in the stores, but in general, the weather is still warm and the beach inviting. Who would think that this is a time when the Church would feature a crisis in Jesus' ministry?

Yet here it is, a pivotal point in John's gospel. Remember a couple of weeks ago, the crowds were following Jesus because he was feeding them. True, it was loaves and fish, but for 90 percent of the crowd, this was better than their usual meal. Jesus realizes that in their eyes, he was simply a meal ticket, a way to get their bellies fed routinely. And as is typical of the "crowds" in the Gospels, they have it all wrong.

So Jesus says something that is kind of shocking, a bit scandalous perhaps. He says, "the bread that I will give is my flesh for the life of the world." Taken literally, we recoil at these words just as some in the crowd recoiled back then. Is he advocating cannibalism?

Let's take a step back for a moment. The Jewish religion of the time had highly developed sacrificial rituals. It was Jewish law that the first portion of any harvest belonged to Yahweh. The first bushel of grapes, the first sheaf of wheat from the field, the first lamb born from the flock – all of these were to be offered to God. So the farmer or herdsman would take his offering to the Temple and present it to the priests. If it was an animal, it was slaughtered and a portion of it was burned. The rest of it was cooked and the priests shared the flesh with the people who provided the offering. Basically, once the flesh of the sacrifice was offered to God, it was believed that God entered into it, and the worshippers in eating it were taking God into their bodies.

So, when Jesus speaks in this language, it is not all that shocking – they would certainly have seen the symbolism in his words. What shocks them is that Jesus is clearly equating himself to God – you eat the sacrifice to become like God in Jewish ritual. Jesus claims that by "eating him" you will attain life, you will become like God! To make the point even more graphically, Jesus uses a form of the verb "eat" that is not translated here. The word "eat" in John's gospel is closer to "chew" or "gnaw" or eat with gusto, as a starving person would. Jesus does not simply want you to taste, or snack, or have a tentative bite, he wants you to enthusiastically devour him! Kind of scandalous, huh? It's earthy, a little gross, invasive. God wants to get inside us, quite literally.

We need to be a little shocked, because this is pivotal to our faith.

Here's the point. God decided to take on humanity, to enter into a physical reality on this earth, a human body in all its fleshiness, locked in time and space, just as we are. That's amazing. But why? To show us how to live, how to act, how to bring God's kingdom to this painful world in which we exist. He did it for *love*, not for power, or punishment, or glory. But we have this free will. We can say no! So many seem to say no. But we who are graced with faith make the choice to get in the communion line, face the minister with the host held up, and say "amen" to the offered body and blood of Christ.

Understand that it is only meaningful if we are aware of what that "amen" is saying. It says, yes, Lord, come into me, invade me, mingle your flesh and blood with mine so that we become more alike. And since you're God and I'm not, change ME.

A number of years ago, my brother Steve was in the hospital recovering from serious abdominal surgery due to colon cancer. He was on a liquid diet for days, until finally the morning came when he could eat solid food. Well, imagine his dismay when the tray arrived and it was jello and broth once again. He asked, "wasn't I supposed to get some real food today?" The orderly checked his record and said, "yes, sorry, we'll bring you a new tray right away." Two minutes later, a knock came on his door, and who walks in but a Eucharistic minister. He asks Steve, "would you like to receive Jesus this morning?" The beautiful irony was not lost. My brother wept as he consumed the host. For to him, Jesus' flesh was indeed real food and he needed to become one with Christ in suffering and transformation.

We are a hungry people, journeying together. So let's not forget the other dimension of the Eucharist. The body of Christ is not simply the host we receive at Communion. The body of Christ is also the community that surrounds us. When we say "amen" to the host, we are also saying "amen" to the people of God. We are saying, yes, I see these people as my brothers and sisters, united and commingled with the body and blood of Christ. Do you ever wonder why the priest doesn't simply come by at 7 AM, consecrate a bunch of hosts, leave them in the tabernacle and allow each of us to drop by during the day to consume one? The reason is simple and profound. The Eucharist must always be *offered* and *received, in community.* For the body of Christ is both food and community. You cannot separate the two!

You've probably heard the Eucharist called "food for the journey". Yes it is, but perhaps a better description is food that sustains and *guides* the journey. Taking the Eucharist into our bodies allows us to see with the eyes of Christ, to act with his courage, to feel with his heart, to transform pain into peace. As our lives commingle with his, we feel a hunger for more, a craving for his blessed presence within us. We take his body and blood with enthusiastic reverence, open to the transformative power, and ready to embrace the journey, knowing that the cross awaits, but also knowing that Jesus has already conquered the cross, and he will not let us down.

So choose. Are you here for a snack, a taste, a tentative bite? Jesus wants more than that, he wants you to devour him. Come join the feast.

Drink My Blood!

Scripture Referenced: Mk 14:12-16, 22-26

> *While they were eating, he took bread, said the blessing, broke it, and gave it to them, and said, "Take it; this is my body."*
>
> *Then he took a cup, gave thanks, and gave it to them, and they all drank from it.*
>
> *He said to them, "This is my blood of the covenant, which will be shed for many."*

Last month the newspaper reported a brief story that caught my eye. Maybe you caught it too. A heart surgeon from the US was in El Salvador under the sponsorship of an organization called Heart Care International to perform a delicate surgery on an 8 year old boy. The surgeon and the team were donating their time and this particular surgery was in its 12th hour. Everything was going well except for one thing – the boy was bleeding too much and the hospital had run out of his particular blood type. Things were looking bleak.

The surgeon is alerted to the impending crisis. "What blood type is the boy?" he asks. "B-negative" he is told. The surgeon hesitates. B-negative blood is the second most rare blood type there is – only 2 percent of the population has such blood. The surgeon looks at his team. They all shake their heads. But he smiles and says to them, "that's my blood type too."

So the surgeon stops the surgery, stabilizes the boy, and lays down on a nearby gurney. In 20 minutes, the team draws a pint of his blood and gives it to the boy. The surgeon completes the surgery and hopes for the best. The patient, Francisco Fernandez of San Salvador, came off the ventilator the next day and is expected to make a full recovery. The boy's mother sought out the doctor and thanked him profusely, asking him, "Does this mean that he's going to grow up and become an American doctor?"

The surgeon, Dr. Samuel Weinstein, said, "I'm getting the attention because I'm the one who gave the blood, but there wasn't anybody on the team – I mean anybody, the nurses, the clerks – who wouldn't have done it." How fascinating – a presumably Jewish man giving his blood so that a Christian boy would live.

Today we celebrate the feast of the body and blood of another Jewish man, Jesus the Christ.

We know that blood represents life itself. Blood is a living fluid. It brings nourishment to the body and cleanses waste. Because of its unique, vital biological function the Israelites were not to touch it, drink it, nor use it for any mundane purpose. The law of Moses made it clear that blood had a *holy* purpose. We see in our first reading that blood is used by Moses to seal a covenant, to make a very strong point. Just prior to this reading, Moses has given the people the law – it takes 5 chapters of Exodus to lay it all out. This ceremony is a ratification ceremony. Whereas today we may swear on a Bible or make a solemn promise before witnesses, the Hebrews used a blood ceremony.

We see that animals are slaughtered and the blood carefully gathered in bowls. On an altar probably similar in size to what we see here, half the blood is poured out and smeared over the altar. It must have been an arresting sight! The other half of the blood is now sprinkled on the people as they make their promise, "all that the Lord has said we will heed and do!" It's a bit shocking, a bit messy, but certainly powerful imagery. The blood of life is shared between Yahweh and his people – in a sense, they are blood brothers, one God and one people.

In the second reading from the letter to the Hebrews, the author reminds us that Jesus Christ made a similar sacrificial offering, not with the blood of calves and goats, but with his own blood, and achieved eternal redemption for us.

In Mark, we hear Jesus state that "this is *my* blood of the covenant." Note the emphasis on "my". What does that mean? Jesus is telling us that the new covenant, the covenant based on love, not law, is likewise ratified by blood. But there is an important difference. The blood is not animal blood, poured on an altar and sprinkled on the people, but the blood of Christ, who as the God-Man, is the perfect intermediary between the Father and us, his sinful, stiff-necked people. Jesus gives up his life, sacrificed on a cross, and spills his blood for the redemption of the world.

So why is this important? How do we look at this mystery in a way that is down-to-earth, that is real? It's all about *transformation*!

When we commemorate and relive the Last Supper during Mass, we are re-enacting this pivotal ratification ceremony of the new covenant. The priest, through the words of institution, transforms the bread and wine into the body and blood of Christ – at the *altar* remember. And as we say AMEN to the new covenant, the priest doesn't sprinkle us with Christ's blood. No, we take an even more radical step. We come forward to take into our bodies the very body and blood of the crucified one, the living Jesus Christ. We ratify the covenant by becoming part of the body of Christ. Isn't that true of a love covenant? As in marriage, the two become as one. Christ and the Church, the bridegroom and the bride.

And just as "you are what you eat", we are implicitly stating when we take the Eucharist that we want to become just like Jesus. Be careful what you ask for! How can you tell if a person is truly present to the gift of the Eucharist? We see these people in their lives of service. We see that they are food for others, to love and live as Jesus did, giving of themselves. They don't simply receive Eucharist, they *are* Eucharist to each other. The world is so hungry, especially in our self-satisfied American enclave of wealth. Ironically, in this place where physical food is in vast abundance, the need for spiritual food is often greatest.

So the formula is simple:

- Understand the old covenant is the covenant of law
- Jesus, through his suffering and death, ratifies the new covenant of love
- We commemorate that new covenant at each Mass
- By taking Jesus into us through the form of bread and wine, we enter into that covenant and ask to be made just like Jesus
- Just as the bread and wine are transformed, we pray that we are likewise transformed
- You can tell you're making progress if you love in service just as He did

Think about it.

Science and Religion

Scripture Referenced: Jn 6:51-58

> *"I am the living bread that came down from heaven; whoever eats this bread will live forever; and the bread that I will give is my flesh for the life of the world."*
>
> *The Jews quarreled among themselves, saying, "How can this man give us (his) flesh to eat?"*

When I was a child of five, I wanted to know how the front door latch worked. So one day, I took one of my Dad's screwdrivers and proceeded to take the latch apart. My mother was a bit perturbed when she discovered me with the latch in pieces, but I reassured her that I could put it back together. To her amazement, I did, and she declared that I should be an engineer when I grew up, just like my Dad. I was well pleased with that idea, and from that point on, I naturally gravitated towards science and math, from grammar school to high school to college to graduate school. Along the way, I've met many scientists and engineers, so I'm well acquainted with the scientific mind, the never-ending quest to understand how things work.

It's fashionable these days to set up a dichotomy between science and religion, to make these terms mutually exclusive, as if to say that it is impossible to be a scientist or an technician and to be a person of faith. In my ministry as a deacon, I can't tell you how many times I've met women after Mass who tell me that their technical husbands don't want to go to Church, that they can't reconcile faith and hard reality. Religion simply doesn't speak to them, and I want to tell you, brothers and sisters, that this is a problem on both sides. We folks who love having a deeply religious identity are not clearly articulating why this works for us, and our scientific brethren are not listening very well either. This is a problem that has been stewing since the Age of the Enlightenment.

So what does this have to do with today's Gospel? One word. *How.* Jesus makes the amazing claim that the bread he will give is his *flesh* for the life of the world and what does the crowd ask? *How?* How can this man give us his flesh to eat? That's a scientific question, isn't it? How does that happen? How can that work? What mechanism is going on here, since clearly Jesus can't mean cannibalism? How, how, how? Note that Jesus doesn't answer that question – he simply restates his claim, using language stronger than before. We know what happens next, don't we? As we'll hear next week, many of his followers (presumably the practical, scientific types) return to their former way of life and no longer accompany him. The "how" question is never answered.

Now remember, I'm a trained scientist, master's degree and all. I am a strong proponent of the scientific method, of testing hypotheses, of examining evidence, and drawing conclusions. That mindset, that way of logically examining the world, is very useful, very powerful, and very much in vogue. But, *it ain't perfect.* There are four big questions that the scientific mind cannot answer, cannot get around, cannot address with logic and reason. Here they are, the four big concepts: love, death, suffering, and eternity. All four of these exist, but no one can answer how or why they do. These concepts are out of bounds as far as the calculative mind is concerned. But love, death, suffering, and eternity are critically important to address, simply because we're human beings and we know deep inside that we'd better come to grips with them, or we'll never find any peace.

The reason that the crowds can't deal with Jesus' outrageous claim is that they're asking the wrong question. The reason scientists can't explain love, death, suffering, and eternity is that they're asking the wrong questions as well. You see, it's not a question of how or why, it's a question of *who*. God loves the fact that we continually strive to understand the immensity of creation, the workings of the universe. God loves scientists and engineers! But if the questions are always *how* and *why* and *what* is the mechanism, and never *"who"*, then we've missed the point of creation entirely. God wants a relationship with us, pure and simple. He wants us to ask the question "who?" Who is behind love, death, suffering and eternity? That is the quest that will really knock your socks off. That is the question that is endlessly fascinating and endlessly teasing us forward, pulling us into a relationship that is far beyond what the scientific method can teach or explain. That is the journey that puts everything in perspective, and offers one joyful moment after another.

A note particularly to you well-educated out there. The search for God is one of the most intellectually stimulating activities you can engage in. It's like playing chess with a master, or delving into a mystery that is tantalizingly present but ultimately unanswerable. Do you want to know the true irony? The simple, the childlike, the least of our brethren, will understand the mystery of God more quickly, more intrinsically, more deeply than us folks with advanced degrees. Why? Because they understand that relationship is what truly matters, and no one needs to explain why a mother loves her child, why a man loves his wife, why the weak and the poor look forward to eternity. Because eternity is where God, the author of life, the source of relationship, the answer to the concepts of love, death, and suffering ever exists, and ever answers our pleading questions.

How does one start? How do you break down the calculating mind and open yourself to a relationship with the source of love? Many times you'll hear Jesus say, you have eyes to see, but are blind; you have ears to hear, but you don't listen. What he means is that you have senses to use, but you use them in a very limited way, in so limited a way that you miss the big picture. For example, let's say that you're out for a walk and you see a large tree. The scientific mind immediately tries to figure out what kind of a tree it is, how tall it is, whether it's healthy or not, and so on. The eyes of someone who walks with God sees all of these same things, and more – that the tree is a perfect creation, symmetrical and regal, possessing strength of limb and delicacy of leaf, that it serves a purpose as a shade provider and a home for the birds and insects of the world. The person sees the tree as a *metaphor* for God, and the viewer gives thanks and praise. It's as if the person has a third eye that goes beyond the measuring, analyzing, controlling eyes of a scientist.

When I fell in love with my wife, I didn't try to figure out what was happening scientifically. I only knew that I felt like I was out of control, and I didn't care! When my child smiled at me for the first time, and I knew it wasn't gas, my world was changed. I saw the face of God in the face of that little angel. And here's the heart of it – the best way to develop a relationship with God is to start by developing relationships with His images – those people around you. Do you see the face of God in them?

As you receive Jesus in the Eucharist during Communion, don't ask why or how this can be. Simply accept the mystery, say thanks, and invite Jesus to walk the day with you. Ask him to point out what you should be seeing and hearing – I guarantee you'll get some surprises!

Why Are You Catholic?

Scriptures Referenced: Gn 14:18-20, 1Cor 11:23-26, Lk 9:11-17

> *Then taking the five loaves and the two fish, and looking up to heaven, he said the blessing over them, broke them, and gave them to the disciples to set before the crowd.*
>
> *They all ate and were satisfied.*

A number of years ago, I was part of a dinner conversation with a group of St. James parishioners and a simple question came up, "Why are you Catholic?" Have you ever been asked that question? Like many of you, I am a so-called "cradle Catholic" – it was not my decision to become a Catholic. My parents made that decision for me and I was baptized at the ripe old age of ten days. Of course, the decision to remain Catholic and yes, to embrace my faith, was my own to make, and that decision is a daily one to make, isn't it?

Anyway, back at dinner, we discussed the various pluses and minuses of the Catholic Church for a while, and then it occurred to me that one of the dinner party was baptized as an adult. So I asked him what drew him to the Catholic Church. He had a simple, one-word answer: *Eucharist.* The belief in the true presence of Jesus Christ in the bread and wine is distinctly Catholic, - in fact, it lies at the very heart of what it means to be a Roman Catholic Christian. When he finished speaking, I remember feeling vaguely embarrassed – of course that is the key – and I took it so for granted!!

All three readings today are tied to Eucharist – after all, it is the feast of the Most Holy Body and Blood of Christ, or *Corpus Christi* for you Latin buffs. The first reading from Genesis features a mysterious figure – Melchizedek, who appears only here in the Old Testament. He is not only king of Salem, but also a priest of God Most High, and he presents Abram with bread and wine, invoking God's blessing with the gift. What makes this reading unusual is where it appears in the Bible – very, very early in Hebrew history. We believe that the Old Testament always points forward to Jesus, and this simple story of bread, wine, and blessing from a priest foreshadows Jesus by nearly two thousand years.

Melchizedek is the archetype of priesthood, the first model we see, well before Moses, the law, the Levites, and the prophets.

The second reading from Paul's letter to the Corinthians seems to be a simple retelling of the Last Supper event. But understand a significant point – this letter predates the gospels. In other words, he wasn't quoting Matthew, Mark, or Luke here. Paul was passing on what he himself was taught by witnesses, most likely by the apostles themselves. This is often referred to as oral or apostolic tradition – and it is all that the early Christians had. There were no gospels for the first 60-70 years. The fact that the Church virtually quotes Paul when the priest consecrates the bread and wine at the Mass is no accident. The Church is tying itself to the earliest eye-witness accounts of Jesus' actions and profound linking of bread and wine to his body and blood.

The Gospel, however, doesn't seem to fit as well. This story of the feeding of the five thousand appears in all four gospels, and is even told twice in Mark and Matthew. Some modern theologians have taken this story and downplayed the miracle, claiming that Jesus' action of sharing five loaves and two fish instigated a similar willingness to share among the people present and all were thereby fed through a sort of spontaneous potluck. Well, maybe. But I am inclined to take the story at face value – I don't think it would be as memorable if it was a simple matter of sharing food from five thousand backpacks. This was a shocking event, a true surprise, a public miracle in front of many, many people. But why feature this story here at the feast of Corpus Christi?

Note the words of Jesus before he distributes the food to the crowd. Listen again: "Then taking the five loaves and the two fish, and looking up to heaven, he said the blessing over them, broke them, and he gave them to the disciples to set before the crowd." Jesus is prefiguring the Last Supper; it's almost as if he is rehearsing his lines. The priest, re-enacting the words of Jesus at the consecration says, "While they were at supper, he took bread, said the blessing, broke the bread, and gave it to his disciples..." Note that the key verbs are repeated in exact order – blessed, broken, shared. Jesus feeds the five thousand in Galilee with bread and fish, the sustaining food of the time. Today, Jesus feeds the world with bread and wine, now turned into his body and blood, the sustaining food of salvation.

So how do we relate? How does this feast impact us? What should we expect when we receive the Eucharist? The last line of the gospel contains the answer – "when the leftover fragments were picked up, they filled twelve wicker baskets." In other words, there was too much food. There was food left over, there was food for others not present, there was food to be further shared. Any time we take the Eucharist into ourselves, it is simply too much. From scarcity comes abundance. The body and blood of Christ enters our reality and if we truly absorb that meaningfully, we realize that it spills over, that it is not simply about us being fed. The Eucharist compels us to share, it compels us to bring the same Eucharist to others, perhaps not in the sacramental sense of consecrated bread and wine, but certainly in the Eucharistic actions of sharing, teaching, healing, and walking with compassion. This is what Jesus is all about. If we don't do the same after receiving Him in Eucharist, we need to ask ourselves that important question, "why are you Catholic?"

Chapter 11 – Mercy and Forgiveness

What is mercy? Is it the same as forgiveness? Actually, no, it's not. Forgiveness is typically mutual. As the Our Father states so well, we are granted forgiveness as we forgive others. It is the cushion in relationships, the grease that smoothes friction, an absolute necessity in any relationship, ironically needed the most when the relationship is closest.

Mercy, by contrast, is not mutual, it is unilateral – one direction, one-way. It is always given from a person or position who has power to a receiver who has no power. And here's the important point, mercy can be exercised only when the receiver is guilty and the punishment is clear.

As Revelation, the last book in the Bible, tells us: "God will wipe every tear from their eyes, and there shall be no more death or mourning, wailing or pain, for the old order has passed away. The One who sat on the throne said, 'Behold, I make all things new.'"

Thankfully, we have a *merciful* God.

Deacon Peter Hodsdon

Blessed Are the Poor

Scripture Referenced: Lk 6:17-26

And raising his eyes toward his disciples he said: "Blessed are you who are poor, for the kingdom of God is yours.

Blessed are you who are now hungry, for you will be satisfied. Blessed are you who are now weeping, for you will laugh.

A number of years ago, I was with my family in New York City for a summer holiday vacation. It was a warm July evening, and we had just left the restaurant to walk back to our hotel in Manhattan. Full of good food, satisfied with the day, we approached the street corner to cross and waited for the light to change (unlike the native New Yorkers!). I noticed out of the corner of my eye a homeless beggar lying next to a building near the intersection. At his movement, I looked over at him and for some reason our eyes met. His were stained with tears and pain, and in a quiet, pleading voice I'll never forget, he said, "Won't you please help me?" I froze in indecision – what to do? Was he scamming me? Was he really hurt? Why was he speaking just to me? What could I do? I didn't know a soul in this big, suddenly dangerous city. At that moment, the light changed, my son, oblivious to the situation, grabbed my arm and said, "C'mon Dad, we need to cross now." I let myself be pulled across the street, and once again the beggar spoke, in words that haunt me to this day. "Won't *anyone* help me?" he asked.

If you're like most people, you heard the first words of today's Gospel, "Blessed are ..." and immediately thought, "Oh yeah, the Beatitudes". Did you tune out? I know that I did when I first glanced at this reading earlier in the week. But as I studied the gospel, some things began to jump out. Aren't there supposed to be eight beatitudes? Luke apparently only has four. What happened to the meek inheriting the earth, the merciful, the pure in heart, and the peacemakers? No mention of these in Luke's version. So first point to understand – the beatitudes that we typically hear come from Matthew's gospel, the sermon on the mount. There are no beatitudes in Mark's gospel, nor in John's. And even though Matthew and Luke take the beatitudes from the same source material, they handle it in a very different way. Why? Because they each have very different audiences in mind, and therefore very different points to make.

This becomes clear when we look at the beatitudes that Matthew and Luke have in common. In Matthew, we hear "Blessed are the poor *in spirit*, for theirs is the kingdom of heaven." Note the use of the third person, and the phrase "in spirit". Luke says, "Blessed are *you* who are poor, for *yours* is the kingdom of God." Second person, very direct, and no business about being poor in spirit, - it's just *poor*. Similarly, in Matthew, we hear "Blessed are those who hunger and thirst for righteousness, for they will be filled." In Luke, "Blessed are you who are now hungry…" Very down to earth, very immediate.

Matthew puts Jesus on the Mount, and has Him proclaim the beatitudes in a way that reminds his Jewish-Christian community of Moses. Just as Moses brought the law, what Jesus proclaims is to be understood as a new Law, a new path that is no longer focused on what you should do or not do, but how to live and be in communion with God. These are *principles*, life direction and focus, the very embodiment of what it means to be in Christ. Luke, on the other hand, puts Jesus on the *plain*, down here with the rest of us, and proffers these blessings on those who are in the worst condition, the poor, the hungry, the weeping, and the persecuted. Luke's version of the beatitudes are not principles of living, rather they are promises of justice and challenges to the status quo. Why does Luke take this tack? Because his audience is primarily wealthy first century Christians from pagan backgrounds, who were continually tempted by the world's distractions, and wanted to have it both ways. You know the type – just give me a little feel-good religion but don't ask me to change. Perhaps a bit familiar in our day and age?

Blessed are you who are poor, for yours is the kingdom of God. We think, oh, that's nice, those poor people will have it so much better in heaven. Good for them, good for God for making it up to them. That's not Luke's point! Remember what the Lucan Jesus means by the kingdom of God – it's not some place in the sky, it's here and now. A better paraphrase is, "blessed are you who are poor, for the people of the kingdom of God are going to take care of you." Picture Jesus saying this to a homeless, dirty, fellow on the street corner and then turning to you in your Lexus with the punch line. And in case you've missed it,

Luke has Jesus reinforce the message a few lines later. Did you hear it? "Woe to you who are rich, for you have received your consolation." Another translation, which I like better because it drives home the point, says "Woe to you who are rich, because you have all of the comfort you're ever going to get." Does that send a little chill up your spine? It should. The *poorest* person in this Church today has more wealth than 50 percent of the people in the world. Most of us have more wealth than 90 percent. We are the rich. That part is settled. The question is, are we the kingdom of God?

Divine Mercy

Scripture Referenced: Jn 20:19-31

(Jesus) said to them again, "Peace be with you. As the Father has sent me, so I send you."

And when he had said this, he breathed on them and said to them, "Receive the holy Spirit. Whose sins you forgive are forgiven them, and whose sins you retain are retained."

Today, the second Sunday of the Easter season, has another name as well – Divine Mercy Sunday. Pope John Paul II established this feast in the Jubilee Year 2000, as he presided at the canonization Mass for St. Faustina, a mystic from the early 20th century, who had visions of Christ spreading his mercy to the world. They say it takes hearing a message eight times for it to sink in, so right on schedule, this is the first year I've really noticed this feast! So, obvious questions – what do we mean by Divine Mercy? Why this Sunday? And finally, so what?

Let's start by defining *mercy*. What is mercy? Is it the same as forgiveness? Actually, no, it's not. Forgiveness is typically mutual. As the Our Father states so well, we are granted forgiveness as we forgive others. It is the cushion in relationships, the grease that smoothes friction, an absolute necessity in any relationship, ironically needed the most when the relationship is closest. A marriage without forgiveness is a doomed marriage, am I right?

Mercy, by contrast, is not mutual, it is unilateral – one direction, one-way. It is always given from a person or position who has power to a receiver who has no power. And here's the important point, mercy can be exercised only when the receiver is guilty and the punishment is clear. Let me give you an example from my youth. When I was about 10 years old, my family was visiting my grandparents. My brother and I were tossing the Frisbee in the front yard and sure enough, it got stuck in a big tree. So I grabbed a good sized rock and threw it at the Frisbee. It barely missed the Frisbee, kept on going, and to my horror, landed with a crash on my Dad's car, shattering the windshield. My brother immediately proclaimed, "Wow, are you in trouble! That'll cost a hundred bucks to fix!" Since my allowance at the time was 50 cents a week, I was looking at four years of hard labor. At that moment, my grandmother came outside, took in the scene, and suggested I chat with my father. At the look on my ashen face, she said to me, "don't worry, he's a good man." I wasn't worried, I was terrified. But I went in to find him, told him through my tears what had happened, and awaited punishment. So, here are the facts – he's more powerful, I am guilty, I deserve punishment, and what does he do? He goes out to check the car, sees the Frisbee still in the tree, and turns to me and said, "I understand." He shows *mercy*. He cancels the debt. It was like forgiveness, but it went beyond simple forgiveness. It was one-way and completely undeserved by me. Do you see the difference?

Why this Sunday? John's gospel has Jesus giving the apostles the power to forgive sins, to act in his stead as to whether sins should be forgiven or retained. He gives them the power from God through the breath of the Holy Spirit to exercise mercy as they saw the need. This is the scriptural basis for our sacrament of reconciliation, which celebrates God's Divine Mercy. But there's a discordant note in today's Gospel as well, a note of doubt as expressed by one of our most human apostles, Thomas. Thomas refuses to believe what he himself has not experienced. He won't take it on faith; he won't accept that Jesus has risen until he himself can touch the wounds.

But isn't he just like the rest of us? Especially on Divine Mercy Sunday? The most difficult thing that the average Christian can believe is that God is truly that merciful. This is a quid pro quo world. This is an eye for an eye world. This is a society ruled by law where actions have consequences and don't you ever forget it. We can't wait to see those arrogant politicians and business people being led from the building to the car, handcuffed, on TV, splendid in their business suits, ready to face the judgment of the courts. We expect it, and in some dark way, we love it. Brothers and sisters, we are not merciful people. And that is why we cannot believe that God is merciful. It strains credibility. As a person studying our faith once told me, it is too good to be true. Can we really believe that God would cancel our debt? Can we really believe that he would say, come into heaven, *regardless*?

Here's a simple recommendation. Practice asking God for mercy. To ask for mercy is a test of our humility. If there's one thing that Christ taught over and over, it is to pray from a humble stance. It's paradoxical, but I believe that God only grants mercy when He is asked for mercy. If we're so arrogant that we don't believe we've sinned, then we wouldn't bother asking for mercy, would we? So God would simply give us what we deserve: eternity with our own arrogance. A scary thought.

Last question, *so what*? Yes, of course, we are asked to show mercy. As we have received mercy, we need to show it to others. But let's not be too shallow here. It's not about being nice to your kid when he breaks a window. Remember that mercy is unilateral and comes from a position of power. You are all in positions of power by your social status, your relative wealth in this society, by your mastery of our culture – you show mercy by *acts of mercy*: feeding the hungry, giving drink to the thirsty, clothing the naked, sheltering the homeless, visiting the sick. The Church calls these *corporal* works of mercy. They are concrete actions that each of us take to say thank you Lord for showing *me* your mercy. And they keep us humble if given in the right spirit.

In a short while, we'll be singing the *Agnus Dei*, the Lamb of God. You'll be asking for mercy – are you humble enough to really mean it? This is the Sunday in particular that we should pay attention.

Choices

Scripture Referenced: Rev 21:1-5

I heard a loud voice from the throne saying, "Behold, God's dwelling is with the human race. He will dwell with them and they will be his people and God himself will always be with them (as their God).

He will wipe every tear from their eyes, and there shall be no more death or mourning, wailing or pain, (for) the old order has passed away."

The one who sat on the throne said, "Behold, I make all things new."

As we pray with the Church during this Easter Season, our second reading on each Sunday has featured excerpts from the book of Revelation. Of all the books in the Bible, Revelation is the one book that is probably the most difficult to grasp. With all of its fantastic imagery and scenes of dragons and plagues, it can read like a modern Hollywood movie script. Even more misguided, however, is to read it as a literal description of the end of the world. Many good intentioned people have tried to link certain creatures or images to modern day nations and events and people, with the inevitable conclusion that clearly, the end times are upon us. Maybe they're right! But that's not the intent of Revelation. It is not the cookbook of the Apocalypse.

The best way to understand Revelation is in conjunction with the first book of the Bible, Genesis, especially the first 3 chapters of Genesis. Genesis and Revelation are the two bookends of the library, and they share similarities. As you know, Genesis tells us how God created the world, the seas, dry land, plants, animals, and of course, humankind. The creation story is not science, nor is it history, it is more aptly understood as a grand parable, ancient answers to fundamental questions: where did we come from? Who made us? Why is their evil in the world? Is there any hope? Similarly, Revelation was written to answer other fundamental questions: where are we going? How does

God intend to bring things to a close? Will evil finally be dealt with?

Genesis answers the questions of origin by informing us that God is the author of life, that God made us in his image, that God imbued us with something of himself, that God cares about us. These are the truths that Genesis states if you distill the imagery to its core. Genesis also tells us that our free will is usually misused. Instead of making good choices, we desire to be little gods, and since that path is in opposition to the Creator, it always leads us to death and pain. Adam and Eve, standing in for us as the first humans, demonstrate that our condition is a direct consequence of the choices we make.

Revelation answers the questions of destiny, of ultimate outcomes, through a style of writing that was very common in the first century, a style known as *apocalyptic* writing. This kind of writing typically features the author telling us about his dream, about his vision, and just as in our own dreams, we sometimes see and do things that are impossible in real life. How many of you have had dreams of flying? Of seeing people who are long dead? Of finding yourself in frightening situations? This "dream literature" is not to be taken literally. As in Genesis, the point is one layer deeper than the story itself.

So why do we feature Revelation during Easter Season? As we celebrate the resurrection of the Lord, we are invited to ponder the meaning of that event in our lives, and to make a *choice*. The Acts of the Apostles, featured in the first reading, tells us how the first witnesses of Christ Risen lived their lives in response to this incredible experience. Revelation is featured because we are naturally curious about our own fate. What is in store for us if we keep the faith? Will we be resurrected as well? Jesus was raised over 2000 years ago – why is God waiting around? And why does evil still stalk the earth? These are not easy questions. What is our stance?

The point of Revelation is that God is very much engaged in human affairs, and he will go to great, some may say *extreme* lengths to draw every one of us to himself. From today's reading, we hear: "I heard a loud voice from the throne saying, 'Behold, God's dwelling is with the human race. He will dwell with them and they will be his people and God himself will always be with them as their God.'"

Honoring our free will, however, God will not force us to listen to him. That's up to us – we are all given the *choice*. But the key point is that God is not going to let this go on forever. At some indeterminate point in the future, God will end it. How precisely it will end is not for us to know. The book of Revelation tells us one man's vision of how it might happen. But rather than getting caught up in how it *might* happen, it is better to get caught up in how we *relate* to God and our fellow pilgrims. What *choice* have you made? Are you an instrument of his salvation or a stumbling block? Are you a sheep or a goat?

The choices we make in this life are crucial. A few months ago I was counseling a young man who was in jail. He was only 20 years old and facing the next seven years of his life in state prison for assault. He was frightened and in despair. We spoke about choices, poor choices that he had made and future choices ahead. Every choice in front of us is like facing a number of closed doors, one of which we must open. In viewing these doors, one of the doors has a star over it that says, "God's choice". It is typically the door we don't want to open because it may hurt a bit to walk through it. We may need to swallow our pride, or spend some time with someone we don't like, or give money to a cause, or forgive a relative. Typically, it's a choice that is an invitation to relationship, to deeper meaning. I challenged this young man to open the door with the star over it the next time he had that choice. Then to try it again. To get into the habit of opening that door. In his tears, I'm not sure that he understood, but he said he would try. If he has made this choice, he will be following Jesus' command in our gospel – to love one another. If he keeps this commandment, he will be known as one of Jesus' disciples. And what's in store for the disciples of Jesus?

As Revelation, the last book in the Bible, tells us: "God will wipe every tear from their eyes, and there shall be no more death or mourning, wailing or pain, for the old order has passed away. The One who sat on the throne said, 'Behold, I make all things new.'"

The Sinful Woman

Scripture Referenced: Gal 2:16,19-21; Lk 7:36-8:3

> *Now there was a sinful woman in the city who learned that he was at table in the house of the Pharisee. Bringing an alabaster flask of ointment, stood behind him at his feet weeping and began to bathe his feet with her tears. Then she wiped them with her hair, kissed them, and anointed them with the ointment.*

> *When the Pharisee who had invited him saw this he said to himself, "If this man were a prophet, he would know who and what sort of woman this is who is touching him, that she is a sinner."*

If you're a woman, you've got to love Luke's gospel. Unlike the other gospels, Luke features many stories featuring women. Mary, Martha, the widow of Nain, the daughters of Jerusalem, Mary of Magdala, and many others. Biblical scholars tell us that Luke's audience was primarily non-Jewish converts to the Christian Way, and typically people of wealth and influence. Many of these early converts were women, mainly because the early followers of Jesus treated women with respect and honor – not because they were feminists, but simply because *Jesus* treated women with respect and honor. This gospel is a prime example of that behavior.

Notice that the Pharisee, Simon, has scored quite a coup in getting Jesus to come to his home for dinner. He has undoubtedly invited all his friends to come over and meet this famous Jesus, the preacher, prophet, and miracle worker. Can you imagine Simon's embarrassment when who should come into his house but a quote "sinful" woman? Where was Security? How did this happen? But Jesus doesn't seem to even notice, doesn't seem to be the least bit bothered by this woman crying at his feet, wiping the tears away with her hair, and anointing him with ointment. Notice that she never says a word, not one, the entire time. Simon is not only shocked, he now realizes that Jesus couldn't possibly be a prophet, because he would know that this woman touching him was a *sinner*! She is unclean!

But Jesus is well aware of Simon's thoughts – you can imagine the scene – the surprise of her entrance, the uneasy quiet broken by the sobs of the woman, the smell of the ointment filling the room. Jesus turns to Simon and asks his opinion. Who is more grateful, one who is forgiven a small debt, or one who is forgiven a large debt? Simon is quick to answer, "the one whose larger debt is forgiven". Then Jesus zings it to Simon. Do you *see* this woman? Do you really *see* her? Or do you see the scarlet letter on her dress? Do you see *the person* or do you see that she is shabby, unhappy, and hungry? Do you see *the person* or do you see a drunk, a drug addict, or a petty thief? If you could see her, Simon, you would see a woman who has great love, who has great courage to come in here, and most importantly, you would see a woman of deep humility. This is action worthy of forgiveness. There is nothing in your meal, in your company, in this so-called hospitality of yours, Simon, that even comes close.

Then Jesus forgives the woman and proclaims, "your faith has saved you…" This begs two questions – where did this faith come from? And secondly, how does it save you? We're not told how this woman came to faith. We know nothing about her at all. But somehow Jesus touched something deep inside her, clearly well in advance of this scene at Simon's house. Did he cure her? Did some kind word of his penetrate her? We don't know, but we can absolutely believe that Jesus, as He always does, acted first. Whatever he did or said, he got to her in a major way. She discovered life, and her response is humble, profound gratitude, sprinkled with tears of joy.

But how does *faith* save you? Paul's letter to the Galatians we just heard contains the answer. He tells us that a person is not justified by works of the law but through faith in Jesus Christ. He goes on to tell us that in this faith, "I have been crucified with Christ, yet I live, no longer I, but Christ lives in me…" The love of Christ permeates Paul, and by that love, he is not only justified, but vindicated. He is indeed saved. An even better word is *transformed*. Likewise, the adulterous woman suffers a virtual "crucifixion" in the forum of public opinion, yet through her faith in Jesus, who loves her unconditionally, she now experiences forgiveness. Great love leads to forgiveness – the two virtues are tied together completely.

So does this mean that since I'm in Church today, and I have faith, that I have nothing to worry about? That I am saved? The answer is *yes* – after all, that is the Good News! It's pure gift, and Jesus gives it to us who have ears to hear and eyes to see. We don't earn God's grace, we accept it, we allow Christ in, we live no longer I, as Paul says, but Christ in me. So yes, you are indeed saved. But why don't I always feel *saved*? Why the anxiety, the worry, the pain, the suffering? Understand, brothers and sisters, that the way of Jesus always leads to Calvary – always to the cross. Christ living in us shows us the world as *he* sees it, with all of the pain and sorrow that exists. We weep with the world, we suffer a sort of crucifixion, we absorb pain yet we strive not to transmit it. As theologian Ronald Rohlheiser tells us, we are like a fine mesh, sifting the bad stuff that comes to us, and not letting it go further. This is not easy, and we need the help of all of our Christian brothers and sisters to do this well. We come together on Sunday to be strengthened and fed, so that when Mass is ended, we go out in peace to love and serve the Lord.

Don't you wonder what happened to the sinful woman who was transformed by Jesus? Did she go and serve the world? Heck, did she at least change professions? As many of you know, I serve as a part-time chaplain at the County Jail. I see many sinful women and men. Many of them will tell me (because I'm the chaplain) that they have changed, that they have turned over a new leaf. I ask them a simple question, "Whose fault is it that you're in here?" Some will say my boyfriend, or my ex-spouse, or my no-good friends, or a vindictive cop. The ones who really are transformed answer very simply, "The fault lies with me." The measure of our own transformation is the degree of responsibility we take for our own actions. Are you open to Jesus? Are you ready for transformation? It usually comes with tears, but the peace and joy that result are worth it completely.

If You Feed Them...

Scriptures Referenced: Jn 6:24-35

When the crowd saw that neither Jesus nor his disciples were there, they themselves got into boats and came to Capernaum looking for Jesus. And when they found him across the sea they said to him, "Rabbi, when did you get here?"

Jesus answered them and said, "Amen, amen, I say to you, you are looking for me not because you saw signs but because you ate the loaves and were filled.

Do not work for food that perishes but for the food that endures for eternal life, which the Son of Man will give you. For on him the Father, God, has set his seal."

As many of you know, I'm involved in a variety of prison ministries. One of the most interesting ministries is called Kairos, which is essentially a 3-day weekend retreat conducted in the state prison. During the five-week preparation process for Kairos, the retreat team is asked to make cookies, lots and lots of cookies, dozens of cookies, actually over 1000 dozen cookies. So all the men turn to their wives, girlfriends, mothers, and sisters and beg for some homemade cookies. When I first heard this request, I was a little puzzled. Why all of these cookies? The answer is simple – when each inmate is asked to attend, he is promised a dozen cookies per retreat day. With 35 inmate attendees, well, you can do the math.

However, I was a little bothered by this approach. Why wouldn't they come to the retreat simply because it is a good thing in itself? Do we really have to lure them with cookies? Shouldn't their motivation be pure, and not driven by a desire for sweets? Are they really sincere? Are we being upfront with them? One of the retreat masters smiles and tells me, "if you feed them, they will come".

Today's reading from John's gospel shows us that Jesus was well acquainted with this approach as well! Last week we heard of the feeding of the five thousand, a miraculous feast in which everyone present was left totally filled, totally satiated, with leftovers even. Understand that to have a full belly in first century Palestine was a rare occurrence for over 95% of the people. You can bet that the word got around quickly that following this Jesus was a good deal – you got fed!

The crowd speaks to Jesus three separate times today, and his answers show how Jesus draws them in slowly but surely to the real issue at hand. To their first question, "when did you get here?" which might be better translated, "what took you so long?", Jesus correctly names their interest: "...you are looking for me not because you saw signs but because you ate the loaves and were filled. Do not work for food that perishes, but for the food that endures for eternal life, which (I) will give you." So the crowd, once again getting it wrong, focus on the verb "work" and ask, "what can we do to accomplish the works of God?" Jesus gives his answer – there is nothing you need to do – this is God's work. It's free! All you need to do is believe it. But still the crowd persists – in good Jewish fashion they look back to Moses and remind Jesus that God signified his approval of Moses by sending manna to the people in the desert. Can Jesus top that? Jesus then makes the most outrageous claim of all, "I am the bread of life; whoever comes to me will never hunger, and whoever believes in me will never thirst." The reading ends here, but the dialogue continues as we'll hear in the next few weeks, with Jesus unveiling the wondrous mystery of the Eucharist to his followers.

On a Kairos weekend, a similar progression occurs. On the first night, the inmates are there for the cookies, for a chance to simply get out of their cells, and the retreat team understands this. There is very little talk of God or his blessings; the evening is more of a "getting to know you" time. But the next morning, the true retreat begins – the men are gently challenged to open their minds and hearts to God, and although the cookies are still important, it is the camaraderie and friendship offered to them that begins to make the real difference. The team treats these men known by serial numbers as individual souls, as people worth saving, as valued creatures despite their crimes. That evening they come back for the cookies *and* the friendship, and you can see the glimmer of hope in their eyes. Then the retreat team begins to share with the inmates letters and cards from outside the prison, from everyday Christians who are praying for them, from churches and parishes all over the county, the nation, and the world. It dawns on the inmates that it is possible to be loved, to be forgiven, and to in turn love and forgive, even in the dark hole that is prison.

By Sunday afternoon, due to the grace of God and the power of the Holy Spirit, these men could care less about cookies. They have come to understand that Jesus is the bread of life, and they need never hunger nor thirst again. What started as a sweet tooth has transformed into a heart filled with joy. Now don't get me wrong – their lives as Christians in such an environment is no picnic – and some fall again. But many do not and go on to work on the "inside team" in future Kairos weekends. When a man who has been to Kairos has been released from prison, he is three times less likely to return.

So what do we take from these readings today? In a very simple way, Jesus gives us a plan for evangelization. It is not about going around knocking on people's doors and talking them into anything. That simply doesn't bring much pay off. What does work is taking care of their simple needs, of showing people kindness and compassion, of feeding them in a basic human way. This is why our Catholic church is so strong on the issues of social justice, of seeing each and every person as uniquely valuable, of having dignity solely because they're human. Treat the lost as human beings first, treat them with love and attention, without cost, without payback expected, and then they'll listen, they'll see, they'll want some more.

Who are you evangelizing right now? A son or daughter? A neighbor or co-worker? No one in particular? Stop for a moment and pick someone in your mind. OK, got a candidate? Think about your strategy, your approach, and start by inviting this person to something simple, something non-religious. Become a friend to them. Bring them some cookies. Show them what a life in Christian community looks like. Invite them to a parish event. Follow the prompting of the Holy Spirit and surprise yourself – you're really a lot more like Jesus than you thought. And remember, it's not about you doing the work – you're simply preparing the soil, dropping in some seeds, and letting God do the rest. It's really a lot of fun – and endlessly fascinating, to be God's instrument. Give it a try…

Oh, and by the way, the next Kairos weekend is this coming October. I'm going to need some cookies…

Cookies Save Lives!

Scripture Referenced: Mk 13:24-32

> *Amen, I say to you, this generation will not pass away until all these things have taken place.*
>
> *Heaven and earth will pass away, but my words will not pass away.*
>
> *But of that day or hour, no one knows, neither the angels in heaven, nor the Son, but only the Father.*

As our liturgical year of Mark winds down, our readings feature images of the end times, images that seem to emphasize darkness and fear on the one hand, and the saving power and glory of God on the other. We're caught in the middle, aren't we? Should we be fearful or hopeful? Three weeks ago, when we asked 36 inmates at Donovan State Prison what they were expecting as we started the Kairos retreat, this exact same mixture of fear and hope was expressed. Due in no small measure to their own actions and decisions, their worlds had collapsed around them – their sun was darkened, the moon gave no light, and depression and remorse ruled their days. As one inmate said, "God must be lonely at night – he keeps waking me up!" But they had curiosity and hope as well – many had heard of this Kairos program and were ready to try it out. What did they have to lose? Plus, they had heard about these cookies...

A month ago, when the Kairos team asked me how many dozen cookies I could commit from St. James, I took a big gulp and said 100 dozen. Then Katie went out and bought a couple dozen eggs, just in case we needed to whip up a few batches if we ran short. On Kairos cookie weekend, the 5 PM Mass brought in about 60 dozen cookies. Impressive. 7:30 brought in another 50 dozen, the 9 brought in 60 dozen more, the 11:30 another 40 dozen, and the 6 PM about 30 dozen. (I think the teenagers ate as many as they baked). In the final total, St. James came up with 240 dozen cookies! The vast majority were chocolate chip, but we had peanut butter, oatmeal, snicker doodles, Halloween cookies with icing and a batch of gluten free cookies for special needs inmates. All homemade, all made with love, and all gratefully accepted. That night, Katie and I ate scrambled eggs for dinner.

On the first night of the retreat, we typically give the inmates a dozen cookies each to take home with them. Instead we gave them two dozen. You should have seen their faces. They came back on Friday. We split the inmates among six tables, and each table also featured three outside guys. At my table were six inmates, the oldest was 61 years old, the youngest 25. Two white men, three black men, and a Samoan. The prisons are very segregated places generally. This is a matter of both self-selection and intention. Prisons are places of fear, and when men are fearful, they seek their own kind first, an almost instinctual response. At Kairos, we very deliberately break this unspoken rule, and mix the races from the first moment. We outside guys also learn their first names quickly – it is so important for each of them to gain some individuality back, to be addressed as Tom or Steve, rather than Smith, 5B112 Lower, which is their last name and building bunk location.

So what's the point of a Kairos weekend? What are we trying to do? In short, the weekend is about forgiveness, about the forgiveness of God, the forgiveness of others, and most importantly, the forgiveness of ourselves. Despite the Hollywood images of hardened convicts, and the scare tactics of politicians, most inmates are sad and broken men. They carry their crimes as heavy burdens, and they miss their families desperately, if they even have families. Once an inmate has been in prison for more than 5 years, outside contact from families drops to zero. They are forgotten. We are there to give them a new family, a family of Christian believers, a family composed of the very brothers that surround them, a family of love that will sustain them for the long haul. The talks we give, the homilies preached, the cookies we share, all make a difference. But what really makes a difference is the witness of the men come to serve them, the friendliness, the expressions of dignity, the life offered in the name of Jesus Christ. This "hidden agenda" sinks in slowly but steadily over the course of the three days until it dawns on each of them that we speak the truth – no one is lost in the eyes of God, no one. Like the fig tree that sprouts leaves in the spring, these men sprout tendrils of hope and reach out to each other. By Sunday, these men, all races, are hugging each other in delight, and there is a hope and strength in their eyes that was notably absent Thursday night.

Kairos is Christian, of course, but we don't restrict attendees to those who are Christian. There were two Muslims on the weekend, as well as two men who followed American Indian spiritual walks. Sunday afternoon, at the end of the Kairos weekend, we have a little graduation ceremony and invite people from the outside, our wives and friends, to be a witness. Trusting in the Holy Spirit, we open the mike and ask any of the inmates what the weekend meant to them. One by one, as the Spirit moves them, they come up to speak. One of the Muslim men expressed his appreciation for the love shown to him, and remarked how we are all brothers under the same God. Another man, only 19 years old, already four years in prison, shared his loneliness and depression leading into the weekend and poignantly asked if any of the other men would be willing to be a father to him. Immediately, five other inmates came forward and wrapped him in a hug, for the call is to fatherhood as well as brotherhood. One large black man went to the mike and remarked that God shows up in many surprising ways, and looking at me, he said, "even skinny little white preachers!" I wear that label with pride.

Yes, the end times can be frightening to ponder, but even more frightening to ponder is the misplaced certainty that for any person, their end time is already at hand, even though they're only 20 years old, or 30, or 40 or any age. Last Tuesday night, I went back to the prison for a Kairos reunion and sat down with a black man, his beard speckled with gray, to share stories of God's working in our lives. He has been in prison for 35 years, had gone in when he was 20, and in a moment of shock, I realized that he and I were the same age. What different paths our lives had taken! Then a second shock came to me. This man was the picture of peace, completely accepting his fate, completely devoted to God and the "words that will not pass away". He is living the life of a Christian that would be the envy of any monk in any monastery. Could I claim to be any happier than he is? Could I claim to be in God's favor any more than he could? When the final days do indeed come around, it wouldn't surprise me if he were ahead of me in line at the pearly gates.

Never give up. Never give up on anyone in your family or your friends who seem lost, who seem far from God. The word *Kairos* is a Greek word that means *time*, but not clock time. In Greek the word for clock time is *chronos*. Kairos means the right time, the opportune time, God's time. When Kairos weekends are coming up in the prison, so many men sign up that they hold a lottery to pick the attendees. Who gets picked? Kairos – God chooses. Grace. Thank you for your prayers and your cookies over the Kairos weekend. You helped save some lives.

Chapter 12 – Mary and the Church

Mary is an example, perhaps the best example, of a disciple of Jesus. Beyond any of the twelve apostles, beyond Peter or Paul, beyond any saint, Mary is the one to emulate. Her life is a yes to God, a yes to whatever was coming. Mary may have been born without sin, but it doesn't mean that she was immune from suffering, from ignorance, from confusion. She knew that Jesus was special, but she did not know how the story would play out, what would happen when, what the outcome would be. But Mary was full of grace, full of trust, full of love, full of hope. She was always yes.

Why bother with Church? What's the point? The short answer is the best answer – we need each other. The Christ in me recognizes the Christ in you, and we are both humbled by the knowledge that neither of us have all of the answers. We each have a *taste*, and by sharing the taste that each of us has experienced, we grow in understanding, we grow in wisdom, we come to appreciate the contents of our faith just a bit more each day we meet. The structure, the container, the hierarchy, is all here to serve *you*! We learn together, dine together, experience Christ in the Word, in the Eucharist, in the priest, in the people. We are all in the ark together.

Where's Your Yes?

Scripture Referenced: Lk 1:26-38

> *Mary said, "Behold, I am the handmaid of the Lord. May it be done to me according to your word."*

As many of you know, I have been involved with the Christian Initiation of Adults for many years. Most of the teachings of the Church are straightforward and relatively easy to explain, but among all Church teachings, the Immaculate Conception is a difficult one for most aspiring Christians to grasp. First of all, it has nothing *overtly* to do with Jesus. The feast is all about Mary, basically stating that Mary was born without the stain of original sin. Secondly, there is only the barest hint of a biblical source for this feast, and it takes a lot of squinting to get the connection. Thirdly, this feast is very recent, which begs the question why did it take 1854 years to come to this doctrine?

The observation that Mary must have born without sin can be traced back to writings in the Middle Ages. There was a very simple logical formulation that brought forth this idea. Jesus, of course, is God and man, the Incarnation. We know Mary to be the mother of Jesus, and since Mary is the *Theotokos*, the Greek word for "God-bearer", it is only right and fitting that the womb that bears Christ be a pure and undefiled vessel -- the first tabernacle, if you will. So logically, Mary must have been pure and undefiled from the beginning – free from sin, particularly Original Sin. This logical inference slowly gained credence over the centuries until finally being declared Church dogma by Pope Pius X in 1854.

So does the Feast of the "Logical Inference" have a certain ring to it? No, I suppose not, but it does indicate why many aspiring Catholics struggle with the feast of the Immaculate Conception. It feels like it was formed by a committee. The challenge is to look beyond the theological machinery, beyond the Churchy language and ask the question: is there a lesson here for us, an invitation to change? What does it ask of us? What does it tell us? What are we called to do?

For reasons that are as much cultural as theological, many people have the unfortunate tendency to put Mary on an exalted pedestal. Yes, she is our most revered saint, but I don't want her way up there, far distant from us struggling souls. I want her down here with us, walking our path, praying with us, showing us the way to her Son. I think that's what she wants as well. St. Francis would tell his followers that Jesus is the sun, the source of light and warmth, and Mary is the moon who reflects the sun. She is not the source of the light, but she shows us that the light exists even when we are in the dark of night. She reflects the hidden light and gives testimony that the sun still exists and the dawn will come. Mary always points to her Son.

Mary is an example, perhaps the best example of a disciple of Jesus. Beyond any of the twelve apostles, beyond Peter or Paul, beyond any saint, Mary is the one to emulate. Her life is a yes to God, a yes to whatever was coming. Mary may have been born without sin, but it doesn't mean that she was immune from suffering, from ignorance, from confusion. She knew that Jesus was special, but she did not know how the story would play out, what would happen when, what the outcome would be. But Mary was full of grace, full of trust, full of love, full of hope. She was always yes.

Are you always yes? Do you accept whatever comes your way? Peace, sorrow, happiness, grief, joy, pain, life, shock, laughter, death? By Mary's example, we are challenged to radically open ourselves to God's request to enter our lives, to let Him take charge. How does this look in real life? I would ask you to stop a moment and look inside yourself. Is there something nagging at you, something that you are being challenged to accept, to move with, something that will pull you out of your comfort zone, something that may cause you pain to do? Is this something that will make you a better person, something that will help you to better reflect the light of Christ? Ask Mary for some help here. She can show you how to do this, how to make it happen.

I first thought about becoming a deacon in 1989. That thought flitted in and out of my consciousness for seven years. I was first asked about becoming a deacon in 1996. That thought nagged me for five years before I said yes. It was five more years from then before I was ordained. You could say that it took me 17 years to get the point. I don't tell you this to make you think better of me. I tell you this to show you what kind of yes God seeks. He's very persistent. Mary, thankfully, didn't take 17 years to say yes to the angel's request. She took about 1.7

237

seconds. That's what grace will do. That's what being born without sin allows. But we all have access to grace. And we all have an invitation sitting on our heart right now. Maybe not so dramatic, but there just the same.

The Feast of the Immaculate Conception is about saying yes. It's about asking Mary to help us discern the yes, to show us the Christ shining as she always does. Do you feel the pull to the light? Where's your yes?

Content Vs. Container

Scripture Referenced: Acts 13:43-52

> *On the following Sabbath almost the whole city gathered to hear the word of the Lord. When the Jews saw the crowds, they were filled with jealousy and with violent abuse contradicted what Paul said.*
>
> *Both Paul and Barnabas spoke out boldly and said, "It was necessary that the word of God be spoken to you first, but since you reject it and condemn yourselves as unworthy of eternal life, we now turn to the Gentiles.*

You've probably noticed that during the Easter season, the first reading is taken from the Acts of the Apostles rather than the usual Old Testament accounts. The Church does this to emphasize the new life that has blossomed forth from the Resurrection moment, the unstoppable outrushing of the Holy Spirit that begins to take over the world. The Acts of the Apostles starts in Jerusalem and features Peter and John preaching fearlessly, healing the sick and forming the community that would become known as Christian. Today we leap ahead to the other stars of the book, namely Paul and Barnabas, and find them in Antioch, which is in modern day Turkey. As was typical for Paul and Barnabas in their earlier journeys, they are preaching in the local synagogue, attempting to convince the Jews that Jesus is the promised Messiah.

At first they seem to make some progress, but then the backlash occurs, and the Jewish leaders abusively contradict them and eventually drive them out of the city. In dramatic tones, we hear Paul and Barnabas proclaim that they will now turn to the Gentiles, since the Jews have condemned themselves as unworthy of eternal life. If you then pair this reading with John's gospel, we hear Jesus telling us that his sheep hear his voice and will have eternal life. This combination is a little dangerous because it seems to indicate two things: one, that the Jews have blown it big time ("condemned themselves") by missing the Messiah-ship of Jesus, and two, the Gentiles are now the chosen people, the ones destined for eternal life. Please, please resist this anti-Semitic, adolescent interpretation of today's readings. We can go a little deeper...

Remember that Paul and Barnabas are Jews, very intensely religious men, who sincerely believe that their mission is to reform Judaism. There is nothing in Jesus' words that contradicts Judaism; in fact, Jesus attempts to show his followers that his message completes the Law and the prophets. Paul and Barnabas, filled with the Holy Spirit, are preaching this reality. What stymies them, however, are people who are closed to the truth, who refuse to listen, who are so locked into the trappings and phraseology of Judaism that they have stopped evolving spiritually. They have grabbed onto the structure, the framework of Judaism and completely ignored its meaning and revelation. They go through the motions and think that they are doing it right. When Paul and Barnabas arrive and call them to re-examine the content of their faith, they are taken aback and react how? Note the word used – they were filled with *jealousy*. Their thinking? "Oh my God, we're going to lose membership because of this! We've got to put up the barriers and drive these two out."

Brothers and sisters, that same trap faces us today! I'm sure you've seen the emails circulating around, concerned about the growing Islamic population in the world, concerned about losing Catholics to other denominations, concerned about the pope's reputation, the latest attack or defense coming from some Vatican official. There was a letter to the editor a couple of weeks back – you may have seen it. A Catholic woman wrote to say that she was no longer going to attend Catholic services because of the clerical abuse scandals. I was saddened, because, using Richard Rohr's terms, she is mixing up the container with the contents. The only person she is hurting by her stand is herself! The institutional Church, the hierarchy, the magisterium, the diocese, even parish leadership -- this is all the *container* – it is made by people, ruled by people, messed up by people. Don't spend a lot of time fretting about containers. When you're distracted by the container and over-identify with it, you are almost certainly missing the contents.

Here's the key question – why do you follow Jesus? Habit? Baptized as a baby? Mom is watching? Do you *hear* the voice of Jesus? What have you heard recently? In the last three weeks, we've heard "Peace be with you. Do you love me? Feed my sheep. Follow me." Note that nowhere does Jesus say, "worship me", or "build me a big church" or "let's start a new religion". Instead he says, "My sheep hear my voice; I know them, and they follow me." Note how personal this is, how intimate. This is a gut-level connection, an invitation to a relationship that transcends everything else, that is so powerful and so transformational that is goes beyond our lives here on earth. It is eternal. This is the *contents* – everything else is container!

You may ask, then why do we need the container? Why bother with Church? What's the point? The short answer is the best answer – we need each other. The Christ in me recognizes the Christ in you, and we are both humbled by the knowledge that neither of us have all of the answers. We each have a *taste*, and by sharing the taste that each of us has experienced, we grow in understanding, we grow in wisdom, we come to appreciate the contents of our faith just a bit more each day we meet. The structure, the container, the hierarchy, is all here to serve *you*! We learn together, dine together, experience Christ in the Word, in the Eucharist, in the priest, in the people. We are all in the ark together.

As we grow spiritually, it seems necessary, perhaps imperative, to examine the container of our faith, to question it, to test it. This is good if done constructively, recognizing the limitations of human beings even when prompted, pushed, and pestered by the Holy Spirit. It seems that all revelation is marked by two steps forward, one step back. You can focus on the steps forward or the steps back – it's up to you. Church history is a fascinating subject. If you think we have problems today, take a spin back to the middle ages. In the past 50 years we've had the amazing content boost that is Vatican II and the horror of sexual abuse that has shaken us all. What does Jesus say? Follow me. The Father and I are one.

The Catholic Church is a great container for me – perhaps that is obvious! But it took a long time to realize this. I struggled with some Church teachings. I was bored with poorly conducted liturgical events. I was saddened by hypocritical leaders. However, as I looked into the wisdom teachings of the saints, the great spiritual writers, the compiled wisdom of two thousand years of reflection and inspiration, I came to realize that this container called the Catholic Church had an amazing and nearly endless supply of content that was there to help me on the journey. All I had to do was tap into it. So I did. My walk with Jesus was enhanced because I came to know who I was, what questions to ask, how to move the dialogue along, and most importantly, how to hear the call of the Good Shepherd amidst the noise of the world. You can too – remember the two "X's" – experience Jesus and explore your faith!

Hypocrisy

Scripture Referenced: Dt 4:1-2,6-8; Mk 7:1-8,14-15,21-23

> *He summoned the crowd again and said to them, "Hear me, all of you, and understand.*
>
> *Nothing that enters one from outside can defile that person; but the things that come out from within are what defile."*

In the last few weeks we've been hearing from John's gospel on the aptly named "bread of life" discourses. We now return to Mark's gospel and pick up with Chapter 7. The scene is somewhat odd, at least to us, in that the Pharisees are complaining to Jesus that his disciples haven't washed their hands before eating. You Moms out there can certainly relate, and I know that before I got any dinner as a child, my hands had to pass inspection. They rarely passed. But this gospel isn't about cleanliness – it's about ritual, about religious practice.

Let's take a quick look at the first reading from Deuteronomy. Moses has just given the people the law, the way of life that would both protect them and brand them as people of the covenant. Moses says something important in the middle of the reading, "In your observance of the commandments of the Lord, your God, which I enjoin upon you, you shall not *add* to what I command you nor *subtract* from it."

But over the many years from Moses to Jesus, people would naturally ask questions about the law and appeal to experts for a ruling. These experts of the law, called scribes, would debate an issue and eventually produce a ruling that would clarify the law. These rulings added up to hundreds of little laws that eventually governed everything the people did. One need only take a peek at our legalistic society today to get a flavor of this same tendency.

Let's take an example. In Jewish law, before eating a meal, a good Jew must wash his hands. But what is meant by "wash your hands?" Does a quick splash in a stream count? How about a damp wash cloth? Does the water have to be clean?

We smile at these apparently silly questions, but since this is a religious law, it is taken very seriously. So the scribes over many years evolved an elaborate process. Clean water from a special jug was poured over your hands with the fingers held up, after which you'd scrub your palms with your fists, and then water was poured over your hands with your fingers held down to wash off the bad water. If you did this, you had washed your hands. The disciples weren't doing this – and therefore they were ritually impure. They weren't so much dirty as "unclean", a religious term meaning *profane*, or unworthy to be in God's presence.

Jesus scolds the scribes not because they're being silly, but because they have taken religious practice and made it the whole of their relationship to God and neighbor. Basically, the scribes and Pharisees had carefully constructed a world in which every contingency is covered, so if they followed the Law in all its little details, they were right with God. Jesus says no, it is not what's on the outside that counts, but what's on the inside! They were being hypocrites, and even more dismaying, they didn't even realize it.

One of the nice things about being a deacon is that everyone in the Parish knows who you are. It also means that I am recognized without necessarily knowing who is recognizing me. This struck home to me recently when I was in a restaurant eating dinner with my wife and some friends. During the meal, my wife pointed out some parishioners in a different part of the restaurant, people who I did not know. But it suddenly occurred to me that I should forego that second glass of wine. What would a parishioner think if I was seen to be a bit tipsy? I was afraid of hypocrisy! As people of faith, as people of religion, we do need to pay attention, because we can become hypocrites without realizing it too! How?

When religion is an *end* in itself, and not a *means* to an end, hypocrisy is inescapable. We are sinners, and our sin will always show itself to the world, despite our best efforts. If we wear our religion as a label, if we define ourselves by our religious identification only, our sin and our religion are linked in people's eyes, and we are rightfully seen as hypocrites. If, however, we use religion as a means, a vehicle, to invest our lives with purpose, and attend to the damaged world around us, we can never be accused of hypocrisy.

The second reading from James' letter states this with perfect clarity: "Religion that is pure and undefiled before God and the Father is this: to care for orphans and widows in their affliction…"

Look at the example of the great saints. Mother Theresa is not known for the number of rosaries she said, or the Masses she attended, or the habit she wore. No, she is known for her willingness to sit in the gutter and hold the head of a dying, filthy, starving beggar. Over and over and over again. Her sinfulness, whatever it was, paled in the brilliant light of her loving actions. Don't get me wrong – there is great benefit in rosaries and Masses and prayer, but it can't be all there is. Rosaries and Masses and prayer infuse our hearts, give us context, and reveal God's love to us – so we *can* act.

The Church is not an end in itself. It is a vehicle, a container, wonderfully described by Vatican II as an *ark*, which carries us and holds us. But the world out there is stained, afflicted, and full of widows and orphans, the Biblical term for the dispossessed, those on the edge of society. Jesus' love for us pushes us to seek out others who share the same love, so that we can grow in this love and learn with others how to be Christ's love to the world. The Church is on a mission, and the mission is not simply what the priests and deacons and religious orders do. It's about what *you do*, and not what you *say*. It's about being authentic, and not a hypocrite. There's a wonderful verse in a song by Catholic composer Tom Booth that says it all.

Be holy, the Lord be glorified. Be holy, cry the Gospel with your life!

There's Something About Mary

Scripture Referenced: Lk 1:39-56

When Elizabeth heard Mary's greeting, the infant leaped in her womb, and Elizabeth, filled with the holy Spirit, cried out in a loud voice and said, "Most blessed are you among women, and blessed is the fruit of your womb.

And how does this happen to me, that the mother of my Lord should come to me?

Okay, here's a test for you. How many feast days worldwide are devoted to Mary? 5? 10? 25? Would you believe 400? How many of these are recognized on the Roman Catholic Church liturgical calendar? 5, 10? Actually, 23 are recognized "officially" by the church and celebrated worldwide. Okay, last question, of these 23, how many are holy days of obligation? Exactly three – January 1st, the Solemnity of Mary, Mother of God; Dec 8th, the feast of the Immaculate Conception, and of course, today, Aug 15th, the feast of the Assumption. So, what is it about Mary? Why all of these feasts, these celebrations of a person who is not even mentioned by name in the Gospels of Mark and John?

To quote Hollywood, there's something about Mary!

Much of Marian devotion is intensely cultural at its base. Many of the 400 feasts of Mary I mention are very specific to a particular country or region of the world, everyplace from Ireland to Africa to Mexico to Southeast Asia. The themes are quite similar across the spectrum – usually an unanticipated appearance of Mary in a place that is very poor, usually to people who are particularly undeserving – peasants or children – and almost always accompanied by miracles, healings, and immediate devotion by the local population. Some of these are quite famous – Fatima, Lourdes, Knock, Guadalupe, and so on – but many are obscure and relatively unknown outside of a small region.

Most people fall into one of two camps when it comes to Mary. The first group, the *Marianists*, enthusiastically celebrate all things Mary, from the rosary to the feast days to the novenas to the apparition sites. The second camp, the Marian skeptics, are vaguely embarrassed by all of the Mary attention and tend to agree with our Protestant brethren that Mary should be seen simply as the mother of Jesus, an important apostle of the early Church, and that's about it. To this group, most of the feasts are seen as borderline idolatry or mere emotionalism.

Is it possible to be someplace in between? Is it possible to honor Mary and keep her as a human being? Is it possible to visit Lourdes and see the wonder of God in action through Mary's intervention? Can you pray the rosary in a spirit of humility and openness to God, and not as a means of getting God to do something for you? The answer to all of these questions is yes, but it means developing a mature faith perspective about Mary, a perspective that quite frankly is well summed up in our Marian feast today.

Let's review briefly what the Church actually teaches us about Mary. It's surprisingly brief. First of all, Mary was real, a human being just like you and me. But she was also special, unlike you and me. Mary was given a gift by God from the outset, the gift of pure, untouched innocence, a person who did not, like the rest of us, have a God-sized hole in her heart. Mary had a knowledge of God that was unique, a knowledge that is summed up in the profound phrase, "full of grace". This gift of God to Mary is celebrated in our feast of the Immaculate Conception – two 50-cent words that could easily by distilled into the three simple words, "full of grace".

But, lest you misunderstand, being full of grace does not mean being full of knowledge, or somehow a slave to God. No, not at all. Mary had free will, and it was her choice ultimately to accept God's invitation to bear a child. She could have said no! But she thankfully did not. So the second key Church teaching is simple – Mary is the mother of Jesus, the human mother of the Man-God, the perfect receptacle, the first tabernacle. Jesus carries the genes of Mary, probably looks a bit like Mary, maybe has her eyes or her hands – we don't know for sure of course. But we will know someday. In any event, the Church celebrates this Marian reality on January 1st, the Solemnity of Mary, the Mother of God.

The third Church teaching about Mary is the one we celebrate today, the Assumption. Simply put, when Mary died, her body was not allowed to decay in a grave somewhere in Asia Minor. The Church teaches that Mary was "assumed" into heaven, body and soul. At first hearing, one is tempted to say, so what? Why is this important? For years, that was a very good question! This teaching about Mary's assumption first arose in the 5th century, but was not declared to be Church doctrine until 1950. A lot of theological reflection needed to occur, apparently, before this was settled. At one level, you can see this feast as very similar to the Immaculate Conception. Mary is given a gift from God, a gift that reflects her status as both full of grace and the mother of Jesus, the mother of our Lord. It is only right and fitting that Mary be so honored by God. But that's not the only part that's important. Mary's assumption is about us, too! Mary's assumption is a promise to us that, similar to Mary, our body and soul will be reunited in the heavenly kingdom at some future point. Mary, totally human, is totally in God's presence – and we can look forward to the same reality at the end of time.

Mary's journey is meant to be a model for us to follow. Yes, Mary is full of grace, but we've been given grace too. The key is what to do with that grace. Mary responded to the most incredible challenge given to any human being, saying yes to God's invitation without any idea of how this would happen or what would happen to her as a result. God gave her the grace to be able to deal with it, but she had to say yes. God gives us grace to handle life's challenges, each to us according to who we are and how God gifts us. Can we say yes as readily, allowing God's grace to be activated in a unique way in each of us? Mary's life was far from pain-free, and I'm sure she worried and fretted just as we do. But she stuck with her promise and saw it through, and the final promise, delivered to her, is awaiting us as well – the promise of eternal life in God's presence. Mary models what it means to follow God's path through life.

Mary gave birth to Jesus, who became the Christ. We have the opportunity to bring forth Christ to the world as well. It all begins with a yes, an openness to what God has in store, as vague and as unsettling as that may be at first glance. Invite Mary to walk the path with you, to be a companion on the journey and show you the "yes" moments. How? Join me – Hail Mary, full of grace, the Lord is with you. Blessed are you among women, and blessed is the fruit of your womb, Jesus. Holy Mary, mother of God, pray for us sinners, now, and at the hour of our death. Amen.

The Greatest Commandments

Scriptures Referenced: Mk 12:28-34

One of the scribes, when he came forward and heard them disputing and saw how well he had answered them, asked him, "Which is the first of all the commandments?"

Jesus replied, "The first is this: 'Hear, O Israel! The Lord our God is Lord alone!

You shall love the Lord your God with all your heart, with all your soul, with all your mind, and with all your strength.'

The second is this: 'You shall love your neighbor as yourself.' There is no other commandment greater than these."

This is one of the few times in the Bible when Jesus actually answers a question directly. You can forgive him for often seeming evasive, because the questioner is usually trying to trick Jesus into saying something that could be used against him – sort of like Perry Mason. But this case is different. Perhaps Jesus sensed that the expert in the law (as he is called) was sincere. It is an interesting question, especially to a Jewish audience. With over 600 laws governing every aspect of life, any reasonable person would ask the same question, "what are the greatest commandments, the ones that you should focus on above all else?"

Jesus gives as answer two laws. The first is one that every good Jew knows by heart; it is the essence of Judaism. It is called the Shema, (Shh – *mah*), and is taken from the book of Deuteronomy. "Hear O Israel, the Lord is our God, the Lord alone…" The Shema is usually written on tiny scrolls and stored in little leather boxes called phylacteries, 3 of which are tied to the body, one to each of the wrists and one to the forehead of a devout Jew in prayer. The Shema is also contained in a little cylindrical box called a mezuzah, which is placed at the door of every Jewish house (you may have seen one). On entry, the good Jew touches the mezuzah to remind himself of his connection with God. We use holy water in the same way when we enter our Church, blessing ourselves and reminding ourselves of our Baptism and the call to discipleship that entails.

So Jesus provides as the first part of his answer the Shema, and you can bet that every head was nodding at his choice. But for the second commandment, Jesus tosses them a curve. Once again he quotes the Scripture, this time Leviticus (19:18). Here's the complete verse: "You shall not take vengeance or bear any grudge against the sons of your own people, but you shall love your neighbor as yourself." Note that Jesus leaves that first part off. Why? The passage defines a neighbor as someone in your own *tribe*. Basically, the law was that you were to love your *kinsperson* as yourself. Jesus pointedly omits this narrow definition of neighbor, and expands the law to everyone, both in and out of your tribe. If you find this same passage in Luke's gospel, the questioner then asks, "and who is my neighbor?" Jesus goes on to tell the parable of the good Samaritan, emphasizing the point that your neighbor is not only outside of your tribe, but is someone that is very foreign to you, perhaps someone you have been taught to distrust.

Now lest we miss something quite important, note that the questioner in Mark's gospel goes on to agree with Jesus, and adds something even more to His words – that these two commandments "are worth more than all burnt offerings and sacrifices." Jesus gives the man great praise for his answer, "You are not far from the kingdom of God." This commendation is unique in the New Testament. Most of the time Jesus is patiently explaining for the umpteenth time His message to his un-comprehending disciples. This guy gets it. What does he get? He gets the essence of Jesus' radical message for the time. Basically, the man is saying that love of God and love of neighbor, acted out, is much more important than ritual sacrifice, than adherence to a set of laws. Hmm! Does this mean that ritual is unimportant? That we should dispense with Sunday worship?

The question is important to reflect upon -- why go to Mass on Sunday? Why are you here? Obligation? Habit? Don't feel too bad if you think yes – most of were taught at a young age that we were obliged to attend Sunday Mass. But the challenge in today's reading is clear. Jesus is saying love of God is equally as important as love of neighbor – you can't have one without the other. Our Church fathers tell us that the Sunday Liturgy is the source and summit of our lives. It is the place we come to *deliver* our sacrifice and the place we *receive* the food that builds and sustains us to do the same in the coming week.

The Liturgy at its finest brings both of the great commandments together, love of God and love of neighbor. However, we have a tendency to over-emphasize the first commandment and minimize the second in our worship. At its worst, this is the height of hypocrisy. If our lives during the week are sinful and selfish, knocking down our neighbor every chance we get, and then we come to Mass on Sunday to worship God, can you see the problem? At best, we only get half the picture – and it's bound to be unsatisfying and leave us feeling like we've simply satisfied an obligation.

Think of the best Liturgy you ever attended. Perhaps it was your marriage. Perhaps it was your child's baptism or first communion. Maybe it was a funeral? Or perhaps a Mass at a small retreat or among immediate family. I'll bet that if you search your memory, you will find that it was the people who were there with you that made that Liturgy powerful. You were celebrating both love of God and love of others at the same time. This is the essence of good worship.

Is it possible to have that kind of Mass all of the time? Perhaps not, but you can come close. I've been working in the RCIA process here at St. James for over 15 years. Virtually every Mass, I see someone who I have walked with in the initiation process. That connection gives the Liturgy that much more meaning to me. Many other parishioners are active in care for the sick, the dying, and the needy in our midst. As we care for others in and outside the parish - all of this adds to our worship each week.

So if Mass seems a little stale to you, ask yourself which of the great commandments is out of balance in your life. Do you need to walk humbly with your God for a while and appreciate the love he shows to you? Or is our neighbor getting minimal attention in our busy lives? To the extent we respond to both challenges, integrating the love we have for God with the active love we have for our neighbor, we too will hear the words of Jesus, "you are not far from the kingdom of God."

Scripture Referenced

CPSIA information can be obtained at www.ICGtesting.com
Printed in the USA
BVOW03s1338020414

349481BV00004B/22/P